Girl Reporter

Gender, Journalism, and the Movies

Howard Good

The Scarecrow Press, Inc.
Lanham, Md., & London
1998

SCARECROW PRESS, INC.

Published in the United States of America
by Scarecrow Press, Inc.
4720 Boston Way
Lanham, Maryland 20706

4 Pleydell Gardens
Kent CT20 2DN, England

British Library Cataloguing in Publication Information Available

Library of Congress Cataloging-in-Publication Data

Good, Howard, 1951–
Girl reporter : gender, journalism, and the movies / Howard Good.
p. cm.
"Filmography of Torchy Blane series": p.
Includes bibliographical references and index.
ISBN 0-8108-3398-0 (cloth)
1. Women journalists in motion pictures. 2. Torchy Blane (Fictitious character) I. Title.
PN1995.9.J6G59 1998
791.43′652097—dc21 97-43284
CIP

ISBN 0-8108-3398-0 (cloth : alk. paper)

™ The paper used in this publication meets the minimum requirements of American National Standard for Information Sciences—Permanance of Paper for Printed Library Materials, ANSI Z39.48–1984. Manufactured in the United States of America.

To my daughters,
Brittany and Darla,
and yours

Contents

Acknowledgments

If it weren't for some very nice people, I never would have completed this book. I would like to thank Madeline Matz of the Motion Picture, Broadcasting and Recorded Sound Division of the Library of Congress for going all-out to get viewing copies of the Torchy Blane films for me; the Museum of Modern Arts Film Stills Archive for the use of the photographs in this book; Barbara Petruzzelli of the Sojourner Truth Library of the State University of New York at New Paltz for handling my many and complicated requests for interlibrary loans as if they were her own; my sons, Gabriel and Graham, and my daughters, Brittany and Darla, for sort of keeping it down while I was writing; and my wife, Barbara, for everything else.

Introduction

or, Close Cover before Striking

This book is about Torchy Blane. And who, you may ask, is Torchy Blane? She is the lead character, a reporter, in a series of nine Warner Brothers films released from 1937 to 1939. In the first four films, as well as in films six through eight, Torchy was played by Glenda Farrell, a vivacious comedienne who specialized in tough-blonde-with-heart-of-gold roles. Lola Lane played Torchy in the fifth film—Farrell had quit Warners to freelance—and Jane Wyman (later Mrs. Ronald Reagan) played her in the ninth.

The Torchy Blane series is the only series of feature films ever produced by Hollywood about a journalist (not counting Superman or, rather, his dreary alter ego, Clark Kent). That the journalist is a woman increases the claim of the films upon our attention. Women journalists were common on the screen in the 1930s, but rare in newsrooms. The contradiction offers a glimpse forward into the unreality of our own image-ridden age.

If the subject of this book seems odd to you, its structure may seem even more so. The book consists of 25 chapters, many of them no longer than a few pages and some of them no longer than a few paragraphs. I.C. Jarvie, in *Movies and Society*, lamented the "difficulties of talking about a complex and mysterious creation of the human spirit"—film—"in a clumsy, verbal language," and went on to prove his point by writing 394 pages of turgid prose.[1] Through my use of short chapters, I hoped to generate, or at least suggest, something of the manic energy of film, with its jump cuts and zooms and freeze frames.

Then, too, I wanted to get in the sort of stuff that usually gets left out of scholarly works. Academic writing, as most often practiced, has all the charm of unwaxed dental floss. It is reason rather than intuition, football rather than baseball, Veterans Day rather than Mardi Gras. In such a bare, brutally functional style, there is little room for surprise or serendipity and no encouragement for just poking about. Yet poking about—being curious and inclusive when collecting information, and slow and careful when sifting it—is an ideal way to study culture. Anthropologist Clifford Geertz reached a similar conclusion. As he explained in his memoir, *After the Fact*, he realized early in his distinguished career that "a conception of culture as a massive causal force shaping belief and behavior to an abstractable pattern . . . was not very useful. . . . Something a good deal less muscular is needed, something a good deal more reactive; quizzical, watchful, better attuned to hints, uncertainties, contingencies and incompletions."[2]

I have tried to conduct my analysis accordingly. Instead of maintaining a single perspective on the Torchy Blane films, I have juxtaposed conflicting views, introduced obstacles, left gaps—have created the possibility for what postmodernist critics call "plural readings" and everyone else calls confusion. My chapters resemble the little multicolored tiles in a mosaic, the overall design of which readers must decipher for themselves.

When I was a doctoral student in American Culture at the University of Michigan in the 1970s, the American culture we studied was generally old and pale and literary—much like our professors. It is hard to believe now that a program so tepid ever could have seemed cutting-edge. We went to endless classes on Emerson and Thoreau and Hawthorne and Melville and the rest of those long-dead white guys. Meanwhile, we remained quite unaware that John Berger and Laura Mulvey were laying the groundwork for feminist film theory, that Louis Althusser was writing about "Ideological State Apparatuses," or that Theodor W. Adorno was raising hell in a new English translation of his 1967 essay, "Culture Industry Reconsidered." A warning in the essay could have been directed specifically at us: "The culture industry is important as a moment of the spirit which dominates today. Whoever ignores its influence out of skepticism for what it stuffs into people would be naive."[3]

I quote Berger, Mulvey, Althusser, Adorno, and other theorists in the following pages. But I cite less intellectual sources as well—comic strips, fan magazines, pulp fiction—primarily to recapture the image environment in which Torchy Blane existed. Torchy can't be understood apart from the trends and values of the 1930s. In fact, she might never have existed at all if it weren't for the advent, in the mid-thirties, of the "double bill" (the practice of showing two feature films for the price of one), itself a response to the Depression's devastating impact on film attendance.

Although the Torchy Blane series ended with the release of *Torchy Plays with Dynamite* in August 1939, the spirit of Torchy still burns. Her fiery light can be seen in comic-strip character Brenda Starr, who first appeared on the funny pages in 1940. The current illustrator of the strip, Ramona Fradon, has described Brenda in terms that recall Torchy: "Brenda is a cynical female reporter. She's cynical about men and editors. She's also very attracted to men, but has trouble in her relationships."[4] Another character in the Torchy mold is Murphy Brown of the TV comedy series of the same name. Murphy, played by Candice Bergen, is a top reporter with sexy blonde hair and a tough, masculine manner.

Figuring out the cultural implications of Torchy Blane is the central project of this book. I used to think, like most people, that popular culture is escapist—you get drawn into a novel or film and temporarily forget who and where you are. Now I'm not so sure. Maybe there is no escape from time and self and geography, none, not even in the dark.

Chapter 1

Why Are There Newspaper Films?

Because, said Alex Barris, convention had it that newspapermen were fast and witty conversationalists, and with the advent of the "talkies," they came to be considered ideal characters.[1]

Because, said Ezra Goodman, "many ex-newspapermen are Hollywood producers, writers, and executives."[2]

Because, said Deac Rossell, "it was recognized that the newspaper film allowed a range of story possibilities much more vigorous and flexible than any other genre."[3]

Because, said Thomas H. Zynda, "the press is . . . clothed with an aura of importance and some mystery that lends it well to the dramatic requirements of popular art."[4]

Because, said Sam Fuller, "Page One and the Screen are bedmates. . . . A headline has the impact of a headshot, pulp and rawstock fight lineage and footage, a news lead is the opening of a film."[5]

Because, said Chip Rowe, "moviegoers have always had a fascination with the hardened city reporter, the crusty editor, the visionary newspaper boss, the debonair foreign correspondent."[6]

Because . . .

Chapter 2

Girl Reporter

Depression-era films featured an unprecedented number and variety of working women—detectives, spies, con artists, secretaries, stenographers, chorus girls, and especially reporters.[1] Film historians attribute the eruption at least as much to the Production Code of 1934 as to the influence of harsh economic conditions. The code set standards of proper decorum on the screen. As Molly Haskell put it, "Women were no longer able to languish in satin on a chaise lounge and subsist on passion; they were forced to do something, and a whole generation of working women came into being."[2]

But especially reporters. Nick Roddick, in his history of Warner Brothers, a studio that specialized in newspaper films, asserted that the "girl reporter" was "the most successful embodiment of the non-passive female professional."[3] Deac Rossell agreed, noting in "The Fourth Estate and the Seventh Art" that "the newspaper film genre was the only place where an actress could portray a role that stood on equal footing with men. Reduced to a symbol of power in the gangster film cycle, and to a symbol of civilization in the schoolteachers and reformers of the western genre, in the newspaper film a woman could take the lead, be an accomplisher, catch the crooks, save the day, scheme for power, find success."[4]

By far the busiest girl reporter of the 1930s was Torchy Blane, who appeared in a series of nine low-budget films produced by Warners. Although barely remembered today, the films were "surprisingly popular" when released. Torchy herself, as played by Glenda Farrell, "won a tremendous following."[5] Farrell told the *New York Times* in a 1937 interview that people "did nice things for Torchy the star sob-sister that they wouldn't do for just an ordinary Hollywood star."[6]

What little scholarship has been published on the Torchy films in recent years tends to treat her as a somewhat exceptional figure—exceptionally attractive, exceptionally energetic, exceptionally tough. David Zinman, for example, wrote, "Until Torchy Blane appeared on the screen, most movies portrayed women reporters as gushy, homely old maids or sour, masculine-looking feminists."[7] Elizabeth Dalton and William K. Everson also emphasized Torchy's refreshing brashness, with Everson describing her as "a wisecracking, fast-talking blonde, a newspaper reporter bundle of energy."[8]

The truth, however, is that Torchy was less exceptional than her modern fans have claimed. By the time Warners introduced her, the newspaper film was a well-established genre, and the brassy girl reporter a familiar character within it. This is apparent from the reviews that greeted the first film in the Torchy series, *Smart Blonde* (1937). "I seem to remember having seen the story in pictures before; strange that the same mistake should be made again," Frank S. Nugent of the *New York Times* said.[9] A reviewer for *Variety* added that Farrell "plays the kind of a sob sister who does all that newspaper girls never do. Her act is to prove how useless cops are and she succeeds. That makes the newspaper angle not unlike the general run."[10]

There was another way in which Torchy resembled the general run of girl reporters: she sooner or later submitted to male authority and control, represented in her case by her boyfriend, police Lt. Steve McBride. Her frenetic energy, rapid-fire repartee, and man-tailored suits may have suggested that she was the equal of any man, but the image was misleading. Torchy didn't challenge the old notion of woman as the weaker sex; she just reproduced it in a more contemporary—and insidious—form.

Of Man Born

The Torchy Blane films were based on characters created by Frederick Nebel (1903–67), who wrote for *Black Mask* and other pulp magazines before graduating to the better-paying "slicks." The characters appeared in 37 stories published in *Black Mask* from the late 1920s to the mid-1930s. They included the team of police Capt. Steve MacBride and reporter Kennedy of the *Richmond City*

Free Press, as well as Gahagan, MacBride's lead-footed driver, and Bettdecken, an absentminded desk sergeant.[11]

MacBride was an honest cop who acted with "swift, hard precision," though it was usually the bibulous, wisecracking Kennedy who solved the mystery at hand.[12] Nebel described the reporter in the 1934 story "Take It and Like It" as "a slight, frail figure in an unpressed gray suit and a gray fedora whose brim was pulled down all around. He had about him an air of languid, washed-out decadence."[13] Essentially, the MacBride-Kennedy partnership was a union of opposites, with MacBride supplying the muscle, and Kennedy the comedy and smarts.

Nebel's stories somewhat resemble those of two more famous *Black Mask* writers, Dashiell Hammett and Raymond Chandler. All created hard-boiled heroes who pride themselves on their ability to "take it"—that is, to endure the repercussions when their sense of duty brings them into conflict with a corrupt society.[14]

The last story in the MacBride-Kennedy series was published in the August 1936 issue of *Black Mask*. A year later, Nebel's characters made it to the screen in *Smart Blonde*, but with a number of curious alterations. Capt. MacBride got demoted to lieutenant and lost the "a" from his "Mac," while Kennedy underwent a sex change and emerged as Torchy Blane—in Elizabeth Dalton's opinion, "one of the toughest, wittiest, hardest-driving sob sisters that ever appeared on the screen."[15]

Why would Warners turn Kennedy into a newspaper gal? To provide a conventional love interest for MacBride—excuse me, McBride—is certainly one possibility. Journalism was already "a popular vocation for female secondary characters in pulp series."[16] Christine Stewart was both reporter and love interest in the "Candid Camera Kid" series, as were Diane Elliot in *Operator 5*, Betty Dale in *Secret Agent X*, Doro Kelly in *Captain Zero*, and Winnie Bligh in *Masked Detective*.

On the other hand, female leading characters were rare. Harry Steeger, who published *Dime Detective*, recalled, "The pulp editors did not do much to regulate the appearance of women characters. Quite frequently, they did ask an author to put female characters in a story, but generally speaking, the habit of having only male characters was too ingrained in the writing habits of authors to make them change their accustomed ways."[17] Even in those few instances when women were elevated from sidekick to detective-reporter—

Katie Blayne in a series in *Detective Fiction Weekly* by Whitman Chambers or Sally Holmes Lane in the 1937 story "Solo Job" by Paul Gallico—they inevitably proved themselves inadequate as women or detectives or both.

To be hard-boiled, then, was to be a man. Torchy Blane sprang from Kennedy because American culture had "generated no precedent for a tough-talking, worldly-wise woman who . . . also possessed the indispensable heroic qualities of physical attractiveness and virtue."[18] But if Torchy's emergence represented cultural progress, it was progress of a very limited sort. "Replacing male heroes with female protagonists," as Kathleen Gregory Klein has pointed out, "does not transform men's stories into women's."[19]

Men's Stories

These are some of the stories men tell: stories of men at war with the world and of women at home with the children . . . of men following a stern personal code and of women following their emotions . . . of men who are active and accomplished and of women who are silent, passive, almost invisible . . . of men as women's rescuers and of women as soft and delicate and in need of rescue . . . stories with happy endings that justify and subtly enforce subjugation to prevailing sex roles.

Chapter 3

B Is for. . .

"B" movies, "uncomplicated little entertainments, with simple plots readily understood by a mass audience."[1] The period from the mid-1930s to the late 1940s has been called the "golden age" of the Bs.[2] But the Bs owe their very existence to the decline in film attendance during the early years of the Depression. Between 1930 and 1933, weekly attendance figures plummeted from 110 million to 60 million. To lure patrons back, the double bill was introduced. "Where previously audiences had paid to see a single feature supplemented with shorts and cartoons," Robin Cross explained in *The Big Book of B Movies*, "they were now treated to two features, one of which was a low-budget supporting film"—the inglorious B.[3]

By the end of 1935, 85 percent of the theaters in the country were presenting double bills. The box-office take on top-half, or "A," features was split between the exhibitor and the producer/distributor on a percentage basis—a bookkeeping exercise in the case of the major Hollywood studios since they owned the theaters in which their films were shown. Bottom-half features, on the other hand, played for a fixed rental fee. About the most a studio might hope to make on a B picture was $15,000, and even this small profit was achievable only through vigorous budget-cutting techniques.[4] The Bs generally looked cheap because they were cheap.

Each of the five major studios—Warner Brothers, MGM, Paramount, Twentieth Century-Fox, and RKO—maintained a B-picture unit. Warners was headed by Bryan Foy, son of Eddie Foy, Sr., and one of the Seven Little Foys of vaudeville fame. The unit produced 25 to 30 films a year, about half of Warners' output. Scripts often were recycled from already successful films, including many silent productions.[5]

At all the major studios, the B unit provided an excellent means of keeping facilities and personnel operating at full capacity.[6] Second-rank contract players became accustomed to shuttling between supporting roles in A films and lead roles in the Bs. Glenda Farrell, who starred with Barton MacLane in Warners Torchy Blane series, appeared in 38 films in her first five years with the studio.

Compared with other B units, Warners produced few series, principally the nine films featuring Torchy Blane and four featuring the teenage detective Nancy Drew.[7] Contemporary reviewers didn't rate the Torchy Blane films too highly. "Latest Torchy Blane exploit," "Hobe" wrote in *Variety*-ese of *Torchy Runs for Mayor* (1939), "is about average for the series—crammed with hoke action and skillfully concocted for lower-deck dual fodder. Like a newspaper comic strip, it's without a pretense of intellectual maturity or plausibility. . . ."[8] Despite supposedly having a longer view, film historians have dismissed the series in the same curt manner. Don Miller, in his *"B" Movies*, observed, "As with the typical Warner low-budget product, the Torchy Blanes never excited the imagination or the intellect, but they started, continued, and ended swiftly, and relatively painlessly."[9]

Given the assembly-line, factory-based system of B-picture production, it was almost inevitable that the Torchy Blane films would be short, unpretentious, formulaic affairs. Each was made as cheaply and quickly as possible—usually in a mere month—by men with little or no artistic ambition. The films were designed simply to fulfill a need for low-budget programming and turn a modest profit. This they did, though it wasn't all they did. They also embodied the most conventional notions about women, journalism, the law, and a hundred other things, partly because more imagination and effort went into holding down the costs of the films than went into the films themselves.[10]

Chapter 4

What's in a Name?

The name "Torchy" is highly suggestive. But suggestive of what exactly? Someone or something fiery, brash, vibrant—a hotshot, a hot story, a hot blonde.

Then again, the dictionary defines "torchy" as "pertaining to or characteristic of a torch song or a torch singer." It defines "torch song" as "a popular song concerned with unhappiness or failure in love," usually sung by a woman. *The New Oxford Companion to Music* adds that the term was used in the late 1920s and the 1930s, and was "probably simply a slang abbreviation of 'carrying the torch' with its implication of suffering."[1]

So Torchy's very name recapitulates the conflict between work and love underlying her film series. On the one hand, the name suggests her brilliance as a detective-reporter. On the other, it suggests that loneliness and heartache wait for any woman who dares to stray beyond the conventional boundaries of marriage, home, and family.

Ashes, that's what's in a name.

Poster Girl

The few film journal articles about Torchy Blane describe her as a progressive figure, a kind of proto-feminist.[2] But that wasn't necessarily how Warner Brothers advertised the character to audiences of the late 1930s. Indeed, studio-created posters for the Torchy films often featured romantic or sexually suggestive images, confining Torchy within traditional notions of a woman's role.

Consider the poster for *Torchy Plays with Dynamite* (1939), the last film in the series and the only one starring Jane Wyman as

Torchy and Allen Jenkins as police Lt. Steve McBride. The poster is dominated by a photographic image of a sultry-looking blonde—Wyman with bleached hair—wearing an oversized robe that has drooped open to reveal a white shoulder, a hint of breast, a long, shapely leg. She leans seductively toward the spectator, a pouty expression on her face. Behind her shoulder, meanwhile, is a drawing of a large signpost with the warning "DANGER!" in capital letters. Although further text refers to the danger from "bullets and bandits" that Torchy braves in the film, the word "DANGER!" itself is visually linked with the blonde, heightening her eroticism.

"Women," art critic John Berger once said, "are depicted in a quite different way from men—not because the feminine is different from the masculine—but because the 'ideal' spectator is always assumed to be male and the image of woman is designed to flatter him." He added that this "unequal relationship is so deeply embedded in our culture that it still structures the consciousness of many women. They do to themselves what men do to them. They survey, like men, their own femininity."[3]

Berger was discussing the European tradition of nude oil painting. It was Laura Mulvey who first applied the concept of "to-be-looked-at-ness" to women in mainstream film. In her groundbreaking 1975 essay, "Visual Pleasure and Narrative Cinema," she wrote that "pleasure in looking has been split between active/male and passive/female. The determining male gaze projects its fantasy onto the female figure, which is styled accordingly."[4]

Looking at the poster for *Torchy Plays with Dynamite*, we see woman reduced to a sex object. We see the burden imposed on woman by a male-dominated society. We see the false image of femininity that woman has interiorized. We see why blonde, beautiful Torchy has reason to pout.

Notes Toward an Investigation

So just how does the ideology of the ruling class become the ruling ideology? Feminist critic Michele Barrett has identified four processes by which the ideology of the dominant patriarchal order is reproduced, particularly in the mass media: stereotyping, compensation, collusion, and recuperation.

Stereotyping refers to how gender difference is rigidly represented. *Compensation* refers to the presentation of images and ideas tending to romanticize femininity, thus "compensating" for the systematic denial of opportunities for women. *Collusion* refers to attempts to manipulate women's consent to their own subordination and objectification. *Recuperation* refers to efforts to negate and defuse challenges to male hegemony.[5]

The Torchy films were sites of these ideological processes. As we have just seen, even posters for the films paraded and exploited gender stereotypes. Audiences of the late 1930s seemed to be taking only innocent pleasure in the popular series, but they were always at the same time inserted into ideology.[6]

Louis Althusser, the influential Marxist theorist, observed that there is usually no need in Western societies to call upon the repressive state apparatus—the army, the police, the prisons—in support of the ruling class.[7] What is taught in school, preached in church, published in the newspaper, and imaged in film is taught, preached, published, and imaged in forms ensuring social control. "This concert," as Althusser metaphorically put it, "is dominated by a single score"—the established ideology.[8] And the band plays on.

Chapter 5

One Discourse among Many and All the Same

The girl reporter was a popular character in more than Hollywood films. She also frequently appeared in comic strips, short stories, and novels from the late 1920s through the 1930s. As Michael Renov noted, "The cinema has never existed in a representational vacuum," but is situated in a network of mutually reinforcing cultural practices, an image context that conditions audience expectations.[1] Examining the portrayal of the girl reporter in the funny papers or pulp fiction thus provides a better sense of what meanings audiences found in the Torchy Blane films and why.

Before Torchy, there was Connie.[2] Created in 1927 by illustrator Frank Godwin, Connie was the eponymous heroine of a comic strip published in newspapers around the country. She was just one of a host of female title characters—others included Tillie the Toiler, Winnie Winkle, and Blondie—who invaded the comics in the twenties. Such characters, according to *The World Encyclopedia of Comics*, were aimed at "the growing number of working girls," presenting them with "a flattering self-picture of independence, attractiveness (even glamour) and poise. . . ."[3]

In the early years of the strip, Connie was a debutante living with her parents and attending picnics and masquerade parties escorted by upper-crust suitors. During the Depression, however, she went to work, first as a reporter, then as a private detective. Later still, she became an interplanetary traveler, a kind of female Buck Rogers. Maurice Horn was referring to this long and varied pursuit of adventure—the strip ran until 1944—when he dubbed Connie "the ultimate pioneer of women's liberation in the funny papers."[4]

But was she really? The feminist claim made for Connie sounds suspiciously like that made for Torchy and seems just as overstated. In both cases, critics emphasized the spunkiness of the girl reporter at the expense of other elements tending to contradict or undercut her feminism.

For example, while Connie demonstrated the kind of initiative usually associated with male protagonists, her appearance was quite feminine. She was slim, leggy, and, of course, blonde—the embodiment of the period's standards of female beauty. Whatever else she might have been, Connie was primarily an image "coded for strong visual and erotic impact."[5]

Godwin's strip played a subtle game of duplicity. Story lines presented Connie as an autonomous individual—catching crooks, piloting a plane, even thwarting a revolution in the mythical republic of Anchovy—but the iconography contradicted this. Drawn with fashionably bobbed hair, bow-shaped lips, and a lean, elegant body, she became just one more sign "functioning in a circuit of signs the values of which were determined by and for men."[6]

Connie, in effect, conformed to the "traditional exhibitionist role" of women under patriarchy.[7] "*Men act* and *women appear*," John Berger explained in an oft-quoted passage from his book, *Ways of Seeing*. "Men look at women. Women watch themselves being looked at. This determines not only most relations between men and women, but also the relation of women to themselves. The surveyor of women in herself is male: the surveyed female. Thus she turns herself into an object—and most particularly an object of vision: a sight."[8] If working girls of the late 1920s and the 1930s, the target audience for Godwin's strip, actually did identify with Connie, then they identified with the male view of women. They colluded in their own objectification.

As for men who read the strip—and research indicates that the majority of readers of the funny papers are male—Connie played to their sexual fantasies. There is indirect proof of this in the fact that Tillie the Toiler, Winnie Winkler, and Blondie, among other female characters, showed up in so-called "eight pagers," pornographic comic books sold under the counter at drugstores and newsstands.[9]

Even in narrative terms, Connie was something less than a progressive figure. She was routinely kidnapped by male villains, who imprisoned her in a cave or secret room and kept her bound to a chair or bed. The sadistic overtones of these episodes suggest that the strip provided male readers with vicarious revenge on the independent modern woman. At the same time, the episodes may have served as a subliminal warning to female readers against carrying challenges to gender stereotypes too far.

Connie promoted traditional male interests in yet another way—by working on the side of the law. When still a cub reporter for the *Daily Buzz*, she solved crimes that baffled the police, as represented by the aptly named Sergeant Bluster. "By golly! She's a smart one," he declared after she published the solution to "The Gold Cup Case." "She ought to be on the force instead of wasting her time as a reporter."[10] Overt praise for Connie's abilities obscured an important fact, however: she was employing those abilities in support of a system of entrenched male power and privilege.

The law has historically been gender biased. In the United States in the 1800s, married women weren't allowed to testify in court, hold title to property, or establish businesses. Despite passage of the Nineteenth Amendment in 1920, giving women the vote, some 1,000 state laws continued to discriminate against their sex. As late as 1940, 11 states prohibited a wife from holding her own earnings without her husband's consent; 16 states denied married women the right to make contracts; 7 states granted the father superior guardianship rights; and over 20 states prohibited women from serving on juries.[11]

"Ideology," Louis Althusser wrote, "represents the imaginary relationship of individuals to their real conditions of existence."[12] Connie was part of the cultural apparatus through which the real conditions of existence for women in a male-dominated society were refracted, blurred, and disguised. By assisting the police, she sanctioned or even sanctified the workings of the law. She made it appear that the law operated equally for all, not in the interests of a particular class. Someone should have told her that, as a woman, she was a member of an outgroup and more logically allied with lawbreakers than with lawmen.

Dead Babies

The undercutting of strong female characters isn't limited to just comic strips. It has been almost routine across a wide range of popular art forms. Kathleen Gregory Klein, in a study of the female detective in English and American novels, referred to the process by which the undercutting occurs as "double voiced discourse," a term borrowed from Russian literary theorist M.M. Bakhtin.[13] At the outset of the novels, the detection plot is foregrounded and seems to suggest a liberal attitude about women's rights and abilities, but this gradually gives way to a subplot—what Klein called "the woman script"—that returns the female detective to the world of traditional sex roles.[14]

Magazine fiction of the 1930s featured a number of female detective-reporters. Loren Ghiglione and others have taken the simple existence of these characters to mean that career women had attained new heights of social acceptability.[15] A little probing, however, reveals that most of the fiction employed double voiced discourse. One particularly slippery example is "Solo Job," a short story by Paul Gallico that originally appeared in *Cosmopolitan* magazine in December 1937 and was later included in Ellery Queen's 1946 anthology, *The Great Women Detectives and Criminals*.

Gallico introduces his protagonist, Sally ("Sherlock") Holmes Lane, as "the best girl reporter on the *Standard*, and probably the best man, too." This sounds like authorial praise or approval, but is actually an early indication that Sally has confused the distinct roles of men and women, falling into an in-between category. Her indeterminate status is reflected in her very appearance, which is at once mannish and kittenish. "She was," Gallico writes, "small, wiry, with a grave, thin face topped by a shaggy mop of silky platinum-colored hair. . . . She rarely used make-up."[16]

Sally has only recently—and, for a hard-boiled dame, somewhat incongruously—become engaged to Ira Clarke, the "big, ugly night editor." The city editor, a figure of paternal wisdom and authority named "Pop" Durant, doubts whether the engagement will work out. "He claimed that Sally hadn't been halter-broke—love or no love. She was a reporter first." Sally herself confirms as much. When Ira begs her to stop going out on stories alone because "You're just a girl, Sally, after all," she replies, "No, Ira, I'm not. I'm a reporter," and adds: "I won't let what we are to each other change what we are to ourselves."[17]

By the end of "Solo Job," Sally has recanted—been, in Pop's deceptively folksy phrase, "halter-broke." There is an underlying connection between the mystery element in the story and her transformation. Sally has a hunch that some awful crime is being concealed at the farm of John Polonok and his wife, Bertha, where two boys have just been legally shot for trespassing. Posing as Mary Donovan, an unwed pregnant girl who has run away from home, Sally seeks shelter with the creepy couple one stormy night. The Polonoks are suspicious of her act, but agree to let her stay until she gives birth. Sally becomes a prisoner in the farmhouse: watched, threatened, even drugged.

Sally's ordeal may be understood as a rite of passage that prepares her to accept the limited roles culturally prescribed for women. In Bertha Polonok, she confronts the alternative, and it is truly nightmarish stuff. "From [Mrs. Polonok] came a fetid odor that made Sally sick. The woman's face was foul, with a pronounced moustache and vagrant black hairs. She had coarse, greasy black hair and a small mouth like a polyp. Her nose was flat, and her eyes were like shoe buttons sunk in swollen masses of flesh. Her frame was enormous."[18] Mrs. Polonok represents a horribly deformed version of femininity—something, the story implies, Sally risks becoming, too, if she persists in her independent ways.

The point is reinforced by the nature of the Polonoks' crime: infanticide. Young unwed mothers, it seems, have paid the Polonoks to find homes for their babies. Instead, Mrs. Polonok has strangled the babies and, with the help of her husband, buried them about the farm. That Sally impersonates a "girl in trouble" is ultimately to her discredit. In fact, "Mary Donovan" is less an impersonation than an expression of Sally's inner turmoil. Mary is the monstrous side of Sally, the warped side that wants a career and personal freedom—"I can stand on my own feet, Ira"[19]—over marriage and motherhood.

Ira rescues Sally in two senses. First, he physically rescues her, bursting into the farmhouse at the exact moment when Mrs. Polonok realizes Sally isn't who she says she is. Second, and perhaps more important, he ideologically rescues her, restoring her to woman's traditional status as man's property. Ira is in full control of their relationship at the end of the story. "I'll always watch over you as long as I live," he declares. "It's what I'm here for." To which Sally "meekly"—the adverb is Gallico's—responds: "Never change. Never stop. Always watch over me. Oh, my darling, my darling!"[20] This is a kind of self-betrayal, except the world calls it love.

Chapter 6

The Yellow-Haired Peril

Frank Godwin's Connie was a blonde. Paul Gallico's Sally ("Sherlock") Holmes Lane was a blonde. Warner Brothers' Torchy Blane was a blonde. Three of the first four Torchy Blane films contained the word "blonde" or "blondes" in their titles. *Smart Blonde* was followed by *Fly-Away Baby*, but then *Torchy Blane, the Adventurous Blonde* and *Blondes at Work*.

Promotional campaigns, particularly for the early films in the series, played up the theme of blondness. "Meet Torchy Blane—the Yellow-Haired Peril," Warners trumpeted on the release of *Smart Blonde* in January 1937.[1] Later that year, the studio recommended to theater owners that they create audience interest in *Torchy Blane, the Adventurous Blonde* with hair-related stunts and contests:

> Conduct a poll in your theatre week before picture's run on the universally famed question: "Do Gentlemen Prefer Blondes?" Best gag answers in 50 words win prizes, winners' answers read on stage.
>
> Run a fashion show in the lobby using blondes only for models. Tie up with dress shoppes in town to exhibit their styles for blondes. Feature sports clothes and invite high school girls to take part.
>
> Dress a gal in a blonde wig and hoity-toity outfit and have her chase a couple of young fellows through the town's streets. Copy on her back: " 'Just an Adventurous Blonde' come to town, staying at Strand Theatre."
>
> Embellish the familiar "are blondes smarter than brunettes" question by having patrons write their answers. These are to be

> enhanced by calling on the famous blondes of history, Helen of Troy, Lady Godiva, etc. Add fact that question is big one confronting Hollywood today.
>
> Have an open car filled with a bevy of blondes driven through town with a plug for picture on banner: "We are Adventurous Blondes on our way to see Torchy Blane at the Strand." Take advantage of crowd at local football game by taking gals to the game.
>
> Contact the school paper's editorial departments to have their girl reporters come to the theatre as your guests. Find the prettiest blonde in the group and as a special prize, give her free tickets, The Torchy Blane Award, etc.
>
> Present the first ten blondes in line to see the first showing of your picture with a pair of ducats. A flock of adventurous blondes around your box-office should be good for newspaper breaks. Be sure to have photographer handy.[2]

Blonde is obviously more than just a hair color. Blonde means youth; it means soft and pure; it means sexually attractive.[3] Marjorie Rosen claimed in her 1973 book, *Popcorn Venus*, that the transition from silent to sound films transformed the blonde from "virginal heroine" to "temptress."[4] Actually, blonde hair has had sexual overtones since ancient times. In the early Roman Empire, prostitutes were required to either bleach their hair blonde or wear blonde wigs.[5]

But sound did add an important human element to the image of the blonde in film. While such blonde stars of the 1930s as Jean Harlow and Mae West may have looked like goddesses, they sounded more like waitresses. They spoke fast and often crudely, with hoarse, everyday kind of voices that made their glamorous appearance seem attainable by other women (and their attentions more obtainable for men). Only a generation earlier, beauty advisor Isabel Mallon had noted, "It almost goes without saying that a well-bred woman does not dye her hair."[6] Now nationwide sales of peroxide skyrocketed.[7]

Women's magazines encouraged Hollywood's influence in matters of beauty and fashion. In 1936 Ruth Murrin suggested in *Good Housekeeping* that readers copy the hairstyles of film stars. "For example," she wrote, "Ginger Rogers sometimes arranges her red-gold locks in a fluffy long bob that almost touches her shoulders, a style which is not practical for you or me. . . . But you might start with the basic idea of this arrangement. . . . If your face is thin, try the center part so attractive in the natural, unstudied coiffures of Eleanor Powell and Gladys Swarthout."[8]

British researcher Jackie Stacey asked women to write to her about their favorite stars of the 1940s and 1950s. She found that "copying" was "the most common form of identificatory practice" among respondents. Moreover, the most often copied attribute of the stars was hairstyle. "Perhaps this is not surprising," Stacey commented, "given the centrality of physical appearance to femininity in general . . . , and to female Hollywood stars in particular."[9]

Nor is it surprising, perhaps, given the centrality of consumption to the capitalist economy. Product endorsements by film stars became a feature of American advertising as far back as the 1920s.[10] Female stars were usually associated in ads with beauty products. During the late 1930s and early 1940s, Lana Turner endorsed Woodbury Complete Beauty Cream, Merle Oberon and Ginger Rogers endorsed Max Factor Pan-Cake Make-Up, and a host of actresses—Rita Hayworth, Loretta Young, Veronica Lake, Judy Garland, Rosalind Russell—endorsed Lux Toilet Soap.[11] Such ads established a sense of connection between the distant world of the stars and the lives of ordinary women, promising that the purchase of this cold cream or that face powder would confer Hollywood-like glamor and romance on the purchaser.

The most popular role models in America in the 1930s weren't scientists, soldiers, businessmen, or politicians, but female film stars.[12] And how not when film viewing and product consumption reinforced each other? Film displayed the stars as the ultimate embodiments of feminine beauty. Women's magazines encouraged readers to copy their appearance. Ads offered all kinds of potions with which to work the wondrous transformation. Thus what began with women gazing worshipfully at the screen often ended with those same women gazing discontentedly in the mirror.

Chapter 7

Star Light, Star Bright

Our knowledge of film stars is constructed of many things, not just the roles they play onscreen, but also representations of their selves offscreen. We see stars trading familiarities and quips with the hosts of TV talk shows. We read accounts of their home life in women's magazines. We come across their names in bold-faced type in newspaper gossip columns. All of this media exposure contributes to stars' public function.

Glenda Farrell, who played the lead in seven of the nine Torchy Blane films, was never one of the bigger stars in Hollywood or even on the Warner Brothers lot. She was a big enough star, however, to merit interviews and profiles in fan magazines throughout the 1930s. These articles had two major themes: that her private self contradicted her screen image as a fast-talking, gum-chewing, hard-boiled blonde, and that her fame and wealth were largely attributable to her adherence to the good old-fashioned values of the Protestant work ethic.

Film scholar Richard Dyer has noted that "stars are supremely figures of identification."[1] Inspired by the studio publicity department, articles about Farrell were designed to make her appear at least somewhat similar to the average woman. "Believe it or not, after seeing me on the screen, but I've never been a gold-digger!" she said in an interview published in October 1933. "I never owned a diamond, and no one has ever even offered me one!"[2] Four years later, Dorothy Spensley wrote in the magazine *Motion Picture*, "It seems practically unbelievable that witty, wise-cracking Glenda should ever be completely done in by disappointment. But she is. . . . She is not so brightly lacquered, so well fortified against below-the-belt blows, in real life, as she is on the screen."[3]

Thus for almost every set of details representing Farrell as privileged, there was a counter set representing her as ordinary. On the one hand, she was a divorcee in an era when divorce was considered sensational; on the other, she still believed in the institution of marriage, saying, "I often think how swell it would be to marry again . . . to have a husband to depend on, someone to take over all the bother of money and such."[4] On the one hand, she was "Twenty-nine, blonde, vivacious"; on the other, she was "a whole lot of mother to her eight-year-old son, Tommy."[5] On the one hand, her clothes came from Paris; on the other, she claimed that she was "too short to wear clothes well."[6]

Obviously, the little homey touches in the articles allowed female readers to identify better with Farrell. Less obviously, perhaps, such touches limited—or, in the terminology of feminist criticism, "recuperated"—the more radical implications of her screen persona. Journalists emphasized that Farrell didn't actually resemble the hard-bitten, sarcastic characters she played. "Yes," Polly Birchard reported, "Glenda is afraid of the dark. She plays gangsters' molls. She gets thoroughly tough before the camera . . . but when she goes home at night, she locks and bolts the front door and the back door, and locks and bolts the door to her bedroom before she feels safe. . . ."[7] Readers got the sense that Farrell was just about ready to renounce in her own life the strength and independence she possessed on film. "You know, I'm sort of sick of being so darned competent," she told Birchard. "I'm getting to the point where I want to be cherished. I want to be taken care of. I want to be helpless for a change."[8] It wasn't Farrell in the role of ambitious chorus girl or energetic sob sister who was held up as a model for other women; rather, it was Farrell in the conventional female roles of wife, mother, and decorative object.

Nor was that the only ideological function Farrell served in fan magazines. She also represented the American ideal of success. At the very bottom of the Great Depression, 1933–37, she was used to reaffirm the possibility of rising in the world through pluck and perseverance.

All the articles told basically the same story of Farrell's life. Born in Enid, Oklahoma, in 1904, she was "part-Irish, part-German, and wholly Thespian."[9] She made her debut at age seven as Little Eva in an *Uncle Tom's Cabin* troupe, "going to Heaven nightly, via the pulley."[10] After receiving some formal education—it was never clear from the articles how far she went in school—she joined a series of stock companies on the West Coast. In the mid-1920s, she left for New York, becoming, in her own words, "just another girl trying to get a foothold."[11] Her first big break came when she played a gangster's moll in the Broadway hit "On the Spot," which propelled her to the role of Olga, Douglas Fairbanks Jr.'s sweetheart and dance partner in *Little Caesar*. Other films quickly followed, including *Life Begins*, *I Am a Fugitive From a Chain Gang*, *The Match King*, *The Mystery of the Wax Museum*, *Grand Slam*, and *Blue Moon Murder Case*. By the early 1930s, she was a full-fledged Hollywood star.

And a Hollywood star was expected to spend lavishly even when times were tough for the rest of humanity. "She may have some sense of economics," Terrence Costello wrote of Farrell in 1933, "but, if so, she carefully hides it. Characteristically, she lives in one of Hollywood's most expensive apartment houses. Her one ambition is for protracted stays in Paris and London, and her single grief is that her salary goes so fast she cannot afford a chauffeur."[12] Writing in 1936 in *Silver Screen*, Maude Cheatham noted that Farrell and her friend and frequent costar Joan Blondell were called the "Magnin Kiddies." "Whenever they can inveigle the director to give them a couple of hours off," Cheatham explained, "they dash for their favorite shops and the studio can always locate them by paging either Bullock's Wilshire or Magnin's."[13] The next year, Dorothy Spensley reported that Farrell was "living a very comfortable life" in her new Spanish-style house "on an acre of ground (with fruit and nut trees) in San Fernando Valley."[14]

What kept Farrell from seeming ostentatious was the fact that journalists attributed her stardom more to her inner strength than to her luck or looks. Polly Birchard listed for the readers of *Movie Classics* magazine all that Farrell had endured to get where she was: "the years of poverty, the months of illness that robbed her temporarily of confidence and beauty before her child was born, the anguish that she proudly faced alone when she realized that her marriage was doomed to failure, the death of her mother, her responsibility for the future of her son."[15] How could you resent someone who had struggled unaided against overwhelming odds to the top of her profession? How could you not admire someone who had achieved that which others only dream about?

As presented in the fan magazines, Farrell's career was a version of "America's favorite folk tale," the story of rags to riches.[16] Of humble origins—"Glenda's cradle was the open drawer of a theatrical trunk," Maude Cheatham wrote—she had fought her way into the ranks of the very successful.[17] But success wasn't defined simply in material terms. Fame and wealth were rewards for showing moral character, and nothing brought out moral character like sacrifice and suffering. "Glenda," Dorothy Spensley observed, "has a warmth and generosity that come most often from having rubbed shoulders with actual need; from having shared her small portion with others who had less. She boasts today, in one of her expansive Irish moods, that she has lived on fifty dollars a month and would do it again."[18]

This portrait of a plucky Farrell suggested what Depression-era audiences desperately wanted to believe: all setbacks were temporary; hard work and perseverance would someday pay off; and America, despite evictions and bread lines and bankruptcies, was still the land of opportunity. Farrell's rise to stardom served as an example of the continued vitality of American free enterprise. If she could succeed, so could anyone—though, of course, it never hurt to be well built and blonde.

Chapter 8

At the Wax Museum

Glenda Farrell appeared in a total of 122 films, mostly during the 1930s and usually as a gold digger, gangster's moll, or chorus girl. "She invented and developed that made-tough, uncompromising, knowing, wise-cracking, undefeatable blonde," screenwriter Garson Kanin said on Farrell's death in 1971 at the age of 66.[1] Her role in the Torchy Blane series of the late 1930s conformed to the hard-boiled image she had created—or, more accurately, that Warner Brothers had created for her. In an interview published about the time of her appearance in both *Smart Blonde*, the first Torchy film, and *Gold Diggers of 1937*, Farrell even complained of being type-cast: "Sometimes, of late, I am a little sorry that I am so proficient in gold-digging parts. That, too, gets monotonous and producers forget, when they are casting, that you have done tragedy, and softer roles."[2]

The role for which producers remembered Farrell when they cast her as Torchy was that of the fast-talking girl reporter in *The Mystery of the Wax Museum*.[3] This 1933 film was Warners' boldest foray yet into the horror genre, which Universal Pictures had almost single-handedly revived in 1931 with the release of three monster films: *Dracula*, *Frankenstein*, and *Dr. Jekyll and Mr. Hyde*. Directed by Michael Curtiz, who would later direct *Casablanca*, *Wax Museum* was filmed in an innovative early Technicolor process that rendered its horrors more horrible.[4]

There is no need to go into great detail about the Gothic plot of *Wax Museum*; it concerns a murderous sculptor (Lionel Atwill) who embalms his victims in wax. What is of interest is how Farrell's character, Florence Dempsey, overshadows the nominal heroine—played by "Queen of Scream" Fay Wray—and foreshadows Torchy Blane.

Farrell received more mention in reviews than did Wray, though not all the mention was favorable, or even coherent. "Like most newspaper stuff," *Variety* said, "the flippant, cynical and hardboiled manifestations in the role essayed by Miss Farrell rarely convince. The studious cynicism of the character creates a theatrical artificiality that harks back to the Richard Harding Davis and Jesse Lynch Williams newspaper stuff fiction. This time it's in sobbie form."[5] Mordaunt Hall of the *New York Times*, on the other hand, found Farrell the best thing in *Wax Museum*, a film he termed "too ghastly for comfort." "As an antidote to the abhorrent scenes," he wrote, "there is some good comedy afforded by Glenda Farrell, as a girl reporter, and by Frank McHugh, as a newspaper editor. . . . It is a relief to hear Miss Farrell wise-cracking to Mr. McHugh, and she gives a vivacious and clever performance."[6]

Years later, Elizabeth Dalton, a student of women's roles in Depression films, would claim that Farrell gave "the definitive sob-sister performance" in *Wax Museum*.[7] A look at the film reveals that Farrell, at the very least, reenergized the stereotype of the hard-boiled girl reporter. The stereotype had existed since the late nineteenth century, when yellow journals added young women to their reporting staffs as a kind of circulation stunt. One such addition was Elizabeth G. Jordan, who turned her experiences on the *New York World* into a collection of short stories, *Tales of the City Room*, published in 1898. Her characters included Miss Masters, an early example of the girl reporter with gold hair and brass balls.[8]

Jordan, in what may have been an apologetic gesture to readers for her own unconventional lifestyle, noted with disapproval that Miss Masters wears "dyed blonde hair," "smokes and drinks, and is regarded as 'a good fellow' by the boys."[9] Despite its quaint title, *Wax Museum* isn't so Victorian. "You raise the kiddies," Florence cheerfully tells her roommate, Charlotte Duncan (Wray), "I'll raise the roof."

Throughout the film, Florence "cracks wise" about men, love, and marriage. She takes particular aim at Charlotte's boyfriend, Ralph (Allen Vincent), deriding and undercutting his courtly manner. Forced to break a lunch date, he says to Charlotte, "I'm sorry I'm going to have to disappoint you." "Don't worry," Florence interjects, "she'll get used to it." Later, Ralph comments, "Gee, that's a pretty dress. Have I seen it before?" "Yes, I think so," Charlotte replies. To which Florence sardonically adds, "Thank goodness that's settled."

Florence has more important things on her mind than romance—such as holding onto her job. "There is no room on this rag for the purely ornamental," her editor (McHugh) warns early in the film. "You're fired unless you bring back a story for the next edition, even if it's only a new recipe for spaghetti." The story she brings back—of madness and murder at the wax museum—initially meets with skepticism. "Work that up into a comic strip," the editor says, "and we'll syndicate it." But she perseveres, vowing to the editor, "I'm going to make you eat dirt, you soap bubble!" With the help of her friends on the police force, she exposes the sculptor and scoops every reporter in town.

As often happens to strong female characters, Florence is rewarded for her efforts by having her freedom curtailed. Suddenly, in the final seconds of the film, the editor who has bossed and threatened and razzed her turns romantic. "Cut out this crazy business, act like a lady, and marry me," he says. And she does.

Farrell told David Zinman, author of *Saturday Afternoon at the Bijou*, that newspaperwomen were generally misrepresented in 1930s films. "So before I undertook to do the first Torchy," she recalled, "I determined to create a real human being—and not an exaggerated comedy type."[10] But Torchy wasn't real; Torchy was Florence again. The same brassy blonde hair. The same rapid speech. The same unerring news sense. The same last-minute crucifixion.

Chapter 9

Sisters

Scholars and critics have recognized for some time that genre films address in symbolic fashion problems too painful or subtle for society to address directly. They also have recognized that each genre, through its particular subject matter, plot formulas, characterizations, and iconography, deals with a particular set of oppositions or cultural conflicts.[1] Thus the Western deals with questions of law and order, the gangster film with the dark underside of the American Dream, the musical with the search for a compatible partner, and the horror film with the turmoil of teenage sexuality.

While journalism films constitute a genre that has endured since at least the early 1930s, no article or book has even tried to identify the thematic concerns distinguishing this genre from others.[2] Instead, the writings tend to focus on how well journalists are portrayed; that is, whether they are seen in a positive or negative light.[3] Such obsession with the public image of the press ignores the deeper and more serious cultural role performed by journalism films. As Vivian Sobchack reminds us in her essay, "Genre Film: Myth, Ritual, and Sociodrama," "What is of interest . . . is . . . what relationships and conflicts between the individual and society are played out, what culturally real and irreconcilable contradictions are narratively reconciled within each genre model."[4]

Journalism films, then, aren't simply about journalism. In the films, journalism functions as a vehicle for exploring certain gender-based conflicts—career versus marriage, workplace versus home, co-workers versus family, freedom of the night versus middle-class domesticity. Significantly, these conflicts pervade *The Front Page*, the 1931 film generally regarded as the archetype of the genre.

Adapted from Ben Hecht and Charles MacArthur's 1928 play

of the same name, *The Front Page* was directed by Lewis Milestone, and starred Pat O'Brien as reporter Hildy Johnson and Adolphe Menjou as his editor, Walter Burns.[5] Milestone was nominated for the Academy Award for best director, and Menjou for the award for best actor. The film itself was nominated for the best picture award.[6] It has been remade three times—as *His Girl Friday* in 1940, again as *The Front Page* in 1974, and as *Switching Channels* in 1987.

Most students of the genre agree with *New York Times* critic Jane Gross that the original *Front Page* "set the standard for all the cynical journalism movies that followed."[7] Chip Rowe called it "the blueprint for press films," while Jeffrey Brown Martin said it "crystallized a set of newspaper stereotypes that journalists, both fictional and actual, would be measured against for decades."[8] Brooks Robards added that " 'Front Page' clones appeared on the stage and in the movies as fast as writers could crank them out."[9]

But the film did more than launch the image of journalists as hard-boiled, irreverent lowlifes who are willing to do anything—lie, cheat, bribe, steal—for a story. It also helped establish gender relationships as a central preoccupation of the genre. This is demonstrated by the very first shot of the film, a close-up of a sack inscribed with the legend,

SUNSHINE FLOUR
Ensures Domestic Bliss

Suddenly, there is a clatter, and the sack, attached at the top to a rope, falls through the trapdoor of a gallows.

The rope is being tested in preparation for the hanging of anarchist Earl Williams, an event the city government is using to win votes and the newspapers are using to entertain readers. While waiting in the press room for the 5 A.M. execution, reporters play cards, trade wisecracks and insults, and mislead their respective city desks. In the midst of all this, Hildy drops in to say good-bye to the boys. He is resigning from the *Post* to marry his sweetheart, Peggy, and move to New York, where he has a job lined up with an advertising agency. "You'll be a fire horse tied to a milk wagon," one of the reporters observes drolly.

And he is right. The idea of settling down appeals to Hildy in the abstract; actually doing it is something else again. Hildy visibly sags when Walter, trying to keep him on the job, describes in excruciating detail the routine of married life: "The 5:15 out to some quiet suburb. A home-cooked dinner every night at exactly 7 and by 10 in bed, unless, after the tapioca, the wife has a few friends in for a neighborly chat."

By comparison, tabloid journalism is glamorous and exciting, though only by comparison. No one has to tell Hildy, a veteran reporter, that the business has its drawbacks. "Journalists!" he declares in what is probably the best-known speech from the film,

> Peeking through keyholes! Running after fire engines! Waking people up in the middle of the night to ask them what they think of Mussolini. Stealing pictures off old ladies after their daughters get attacked in Grove Park. A lot of lousy, daffy buttinskis swelling around with holes in their pants, borrowing nickels from office boys! And for what? So a million hired girls and motormen's wives will know what's going on.

Somehow Hildy is still attracted to "this idiotic jumping around at all hours." Journalism is everything marriage isn't: wild, unconventional, free—and all-male. When Williams escapes, Hildy automatically reverts to form and gets on the story, even using money meant for the trip to New York to buy information about the jail break.

The rest of the film follows the battle between Walter and Peggy for control of Hildy, with ultra-cynical Walter maintaining the edge for most of it. Walter likes women, but deeply distrusts them and explains to Hildy why he should deeply distrust them, too.

> **Walter:** Listen, Hildy. Let me tell you something. I was in love once with my—with my—with my third wife. I treated her white—let her have a maid and everything! I was sweet to her!
>
> **Hildy:** Never mind!
>
> **Walter:** I trusted her. Then I let her meet a certain party on the *Tribune* and what happened? One night I came home unexpectedly—I let myself in through the bathroom window, and there they were!
>
> **Hildy:** I don't want to hear about it.
>
> **Walter:** The very next morning, what do I find in the *Tribune*, all over the front page? My traction story, I'd been saving for two months!

Hildy: You know a lot about women! You and your stable of tarts! You never met a decent woman! You wouldn't know what to do with a pure girl!

Walter: Oh, yes I would!

Hildy: You take that back!

Walter: Say, Hildy, listen! What do you think women are? Flowers? Take that dame that shot the dentist! And Mrs. Vermilya! Husband comes home all worn out, hungry, takes a spoonful of soup and falls dead! Arsenic! And Mrs. Petras! Burning her husband up in a furnace! When you've been in this business as long as I have, you'll know what women are.

Women, including Peggy, are a threat to man. They take away his fun, his friends, his freedom—take away, in short, his manliness. On the other hand, Hildy knows there isn't any future in sticking with journalism. As he warns the boys in the press room, "You'll all end up on the copy desk, gray-haired, humpbacked slobs dodging debt collectors when you're 90." The choice he faces between Walter and Peggy is in a sense a choice between one kind of living death and another.

Produced during the dark early days of the Depression, *The Front Page* reflects a prevailing loss of faith in society. Medical science, as represented in the film by Dr. Englehoffer, is incompetent; government, as represented by the mayor and Sheriff Hartman, is corrupt; and the press, as represented by Walter, Hildy, and their colleagues, is irresponsible. But if newspapermen are no less devious or self-serving than the rest, at least they are witty and unhypocritical about it.

That is what vaguely qualifies them as heroes, and makes Hildy's falling in love with Peggy seem so out of character. In a world where everyone preys on everyone else, love, or anything that smacks of idealism, violates the group's unwritten code of cynical detachment. Love is for newspaper readers and other saps, not for tough-talking newspapermen on the inside track of all the crazy shenanigans that go down.

Thomas Schatz, author of *Hollywood Genres*, has pointed out the capacity of genre films to "'play it both ways,' to both criticize and reinforce the values, beliefs, and ideals of our culture within the same narrative context."[10] *The Front Page* doesn't so much resolve the conflict between masculinity and domesticity as camouflage or submerge it. Hildy's ambivalence about leaving Walter and journalism for Peggy and married life lasts right through to the end, with the film celebrating two contradictory outcomes. Love triumphs when Hildy and Peggy finally board the train for New York, but then male virtues triumph as well when Walter arranges to have Hildy arrested at the first stop and brought back.

I can think of several possible reasons why journalism, and not some other profession, is at the center of a genre that deals with the tensions between work and home. For one thing, reporters and editors have historically worked "late hours, long hours."[11] When E.O. Chamberlin, managing editor of the *New York Evening World*, died in 1887 at 38, the trade magazine *Fourth Estate* took occasion to decry the pressures an editor operated under:

> Midnight often finds the man who began his day's toil at 8 A.M. still jogging away at his desk. He gets his meals at irregular hours. His night's sleep is often disturbed by the impatient ringing of the telephone bell at the head of his bed by some one of his assistants, who finds it necessary to consult with him upon some vital question that has arisen since he left the office. His time is never his own. His wife may find fault with him for his apparent neglect of her and the children, but he cannot help it. He is working for a master that is merciless.[12]

The reporter's lot was just as difficult. Recalling his first job in journalism, Samuel Blythe said, "I soon discovered that all the ideas I had about the ease and dignity of the work of a reporter on a daily paper in a small city were entirely erroneous." Blythe worked six days a week, from 1 in the afternoon to 1 or 1:30 in the morning. "I frequently had fourteen or fifteen assignments in a day," he noted, "not big ones, but fourteen or fifteen places that had to be visited, whether they produced copy or not."[13] The long shifts and furious pace left little time or energy for anything else, including family.

The sort of sensational stuff that typically makes news added to the tensions between journalism and middle-class existence. Reporters chased around after criminals, politicians, businessmen, and other liars and creeps, and acquired in this way a secret fund of cynical knowledge. Their cynicism darkened them, roughened them, and potentially made them unfit for normal living. They knew too much—and some of them drank too much to relieve what they knew—to be able to settle down without a struggle.

A final possible reason that journalism films are concerned with issues of masculinity, femininity, and domesticity is that the American press has been, for most of its two-century run, "distinctively a masculine institution, offering women only the frills and fringes of journalistic work."[14] In 1889 Allan Forman, editor of the trade magazine *The Journalist*, devoted an entire issue to women journalists. "I want to disabuse thousands of case-hardened old fogies of the idea that a newspaper woman in any way interferes with the men," he explained, "or that she is any less a woman because she earns her living by wielding a 'Dixon' [pen] instead of sewing on buttons for the 'lords of creation.' "[15] Forman failed of his goal—miserably. Almost 60 years later, Stanley Frank and Paul Sann, in an essay with the sexist title "Paper Dolls," were writing that most editors "will take a dumb man of erratic social habits over a smart gal every time."[16] Successful or visible women journalists remained the exception until the 1970s, when the modern feminist movement kicked in.[17] "Among all professions," historian Lois Banner said, "that of journalism offers perhaps the most impressive example of women's intrepid persistence in the face of professional hostility."[18]

Given this background, it isn't terribly surprising that journalism would be portrayed in classic Hollywood films as a masculine stronghold, or that the films would address gender-based conflicts, or that in those films where the journalist was a woman, the conflicts would take on an even sharper edge.

Big News

Scoop artist Torchy Blane had many celluloid sisters—too many for me to examine them all. And so I will examine five from journalism films produced between the late twenties and early forties, and trust that they typify the rest. The films, in chronological order, are *Big News* with Carole Lombard and Robert Armstrong, *Dance, Fools, Dance* with Joan Crawford and Clark Gable, *Mr. Deeds Goes to Town* with Jean Arthur and Gary Cooper, *His Girl Friday* with Rosalind Russell and Cary Grant, and *Woman of the Year* with Katharine Hepburn and Spencer Tracy.

Big News (1929) was directed by Gregory La Cava, who worked in the early teens as a cartoonist for the American Press Association, the *New York Evening World*, and the *Sunday New York*

Herald.[19] La Cava was an alcoholic, and at least one scholar has noted that drunkenness "plays a very large role in the lives of most of La Cava's characters."[20] Steve Banks (Armstrong), the reporter hero of *Big News*, is an example. When the films opens, he is sleeping off his latest binge in the editor's chair.

Yet the drunken or hung-over reporter is a cultural stereotype that predates narrative films. Jesse Lynch Williams's short story "The Old Reporter" (1899), a seminal work in the minor genre of newspaper fiction, concerns a star reporter destroyed by drink.[21] There was apparently a basis in fact for this kind of story. "Between 1899 and 1904," H.L. Mencken recalled with his usual levity, "there was only one reporter south of the Mason & Dixon Line who did not drink at all, and he was considered insane. In New York, so far as I could make out, there was not even one."[22] Samuel Blythe, a contemporary of Mencken's, acknowledged in more somber tones that newspaper life "has a tendency to invite the forming of ruinous habits," and that "young men become old in it quickly and that old men become useless."[23]

Two main theories have arisen to explain the heavy drinking of reporters and editors, one focusing on the personality of journalists, the other on the nature of journalism. Charles J. Rosebault, a reporter on the *New York Sun* in the 1880s, was among those who expressed the first theory. His colleagues, he said, were often "strays in the social sense, for whom the irregular habits imposed by their calling were not its least attraction. Not a few had drifted into journalism from other vocations for the very reason that they could not tolerate the conventional life."[24]

The second theory holds that something about journalism itself drives most journalists to drink. According to this theory, journalists witness too much raw reality—people bleeding, crying, fighting, lying—not to get drunk and want to stay that way. In the words of novelist and ex-newspaperman Richard Hoyt, "It doesn't take a reporter long, not long at all, to know the awful, unbearable truth. And so across the land they sit in the bar next door hunkered down under the weight of their burden and swap callous, barbarous, outrageous stories of life in the city. These are men who know that God is, in fact, dead."[25]

Steve Banks gives the initial impression in *Big News* of being one of these cynical, godforsaken men. He drinks hard, talks tough, and dares the business manager to fire him for his drunkenness and insubordination. There is, however, a Mrs. Banks (Lombard), a sob sister on a rival paper, and her role in the film isn't so much to compete with her husband for scoops as to reform him, domesticate him, bring him back to the self-disciplinary virtues of the Protestant work ethic. Mrs. Banks, or Marge, may look like a modern liberated woman—she strongly resembles the flapperish reporter Connie from the contemporary comic strip of the same name—but she nags and moralizes like a stereotypical middle-class housewife. Her very first speech, delivered after Steve has stayed out all night with a drinking buddy, sets the tone for her entire characterization:

> For two years, I have been trying to make a home for us, and last night he was coming home to his favorite dinner, liver and onions, and his faithful little wife sits there like a dumbbell until 11 o'clock, entertaining herself with a plate of cold liver. If this were the first time, I wouldn't say anything, but it's been going on for two years, and I'm through this time. If I'm going to be a widow, I might as well make it official. . . . You're always blaming something besides yourself, you're always making excuses, and I'm always forgiving you. Well, last night I thought it all over and said to myself, What's the use?

Big News places Steve at odds not only with his Mrs., but also with Reno, a speakeasy owner and drug runner. Reno bumps off Steve's editor and frames the nosy reporter for the killing. After various complications, Steve exposes Reno with the aid of the office Dictaphone (in today's films, it would be a computer). His solution of the crime stands in for a solution to his existential despair, allowing him to return to his wife and a "normal" daily routine. "Man is protected by the secure and limited alternatives his society offers him," philosopher Ernest Becker once said, "and if he doesn't look up from his path he can live out his life with a certain dull security."[26] Steve embraces the standards of a middle class that lives with its head down.

In a rave review of *Big News*, *Variety* noted that Lombard "steps before the camera [as Marge] just often enough to provide the necessary touch of romantic interest and not spoil a good job."[27] The review didn't even bother to mention the other woman journalist in the film, Vera (Cupid Ainsworth), a colleague of Steve's who writes the advice-to-the-lovelorn column. Vera is a fat, gross, Felliniesque freak; Steve calls her "Big Girl" and "Tubby," and cracks,

"If you begin to waste away, save me the slow-motion movie rights." She serves as a visual counterpoint to Marge and a validation of male prejudices against the working woman. Where Marge is slender, Vera is blimpish; where Marge is blonde and fair-skinned, Vera is dark and oily; where Marge is sexually attractive, Vera is repulsive; where Marge dresses femininely, Vera has short, masculine hair and wears a tie. Whatever ideological advantage comes from the beautiful Marge being a journalist is undercut by the monstrous Vera being one, too.

Many of those involved in *Big News* went on to still bigger things in the thirties. La Cava would direct *My Man Godfrey* and *Stage Door*, both classics of their respective genres. Armstrong would star in *King Kong* and Lombard in a number of celebrated screwball comedies, including *Twentieth Century* and the newspaper film *Nothing Sacred*. Finally, Tom Kennedy, who played a patrolman named Ryan in *Big News*, would become the only actor to appear in all nine Torchy Blane films. He would play—no surprise here—a dumb Irish cop.

Dance, Fools, Dance

Film historians see in *Dance, Fools, Dance*, a 1931 production starring Joan Crawford and Clark Gable, references to the St. Valentine's Day Massacre and the gangland-style killing of *Chicago Tribune* reporter Jake Lingle.[28] Yet that wasn't what contemporary reviewers saw. What they saw when they looked at the film was Crawford in "a sweet series of shots doing a high kick and tap, in brief costume."[29] The film may feature gangsters and speakeasies and one-way rides, but its raison d'etre was then, and remains today, sex: the half-naked female form. The home video of the film, distributed by MGM/UA, comes in a box prominently labeled "Forbidden Hollywood."

Variety claimed in its review that few films have "emerged from studios with a more mixed up story" than *Dance, Fools, Dance*. The review nonetheless predicted that the film would "rock the b.o.," mainly because of Crawford's "s.a.," or sex appeal. "Metro," it said, "has tried here to have Joan Crawford show everything she had. She does."[30]

Crawford plays socialite Bonnie Jordan. After her father is

wiped out in the stock market crash, she and her brother, Rodney (William Bakewell), must find work. Rodney suggests that she open a tea shop or try modeling, but she refuses to do anything "stupid and conventional." "I'm going out to get myself a man-sized job," she says and becomes a reporter for the *Star*. A veteran on the staff named Bert Scranton (Cliff Edwards) gives her a quick course in news writing. "Clearness, condensation. Where, what, when, and why. That's the idea," he tells her. Within a scene or two, she has been promoted from the home-and-garden section to the crime beat.

Meanwhile, Rodney has gotten tangled up in the rackets and wars of gang chieftain Jake Luva (Gable). When Bert is gunned down for knowing too much, it is Rodney who is the triggerman. Bonnie goes undercover to catch Bert's killer, never suspecting that it will turn out to be her own brother. Posing as Mary Smith, a tough moll from Missouri, she is hired by Luva to sing and dance at his nightclub. This allows her to do the "hot" number *Variety* so admired.

Rodney eventually expiates his crime by shooting it out with Luva and one of Luva's goons. All three die, Rodney in Bonnie's arms. She then phones in the story to the city desk, which might seem callous if she weren't crying copiously. The film ends with her giving up journalism to marry a rich snob who had blown her off earlier when her family fortune evaporated. "I love you," he declares. "I've always loved you. I know that now." And despite her superior intelligence, she believes him.

Bonnie enacts several contradictory versions or aspects of femininity in the film. For part of it, she is a young woman forced to fend for herself. As such, she displays traditionally masculine traits—strength, courage, adaptability. "Miss Jordan, how's your nerves?" the city editor asks at one point. "Haven't any," she replies.

But Bonnie is undeniably also an erotic spectacle. Made in the liberal, pre-Production Code era, *Dance, Fools, Dance* is replete with shots of her in lace-trimmed undies, satin nighties, and revealing evening gowns. Moreover, she is very much aware of herself as a sex object, a body on exhibit. When early in the film her father says with annoyance, "Must you smoke before breakfast?" she snaps back, "I must if I want to stay thin."

Her ultimate identity, however, is that of homemaker. There were occasional early hints that this would be so. For example, after a long day in the newsroom, she ties on an apron and cheerfully begins fixing dinner for her spoiled, alcoholic brother. Although smart and sassy, she is in training to be some dullard's wife. What a waste.

Mr. Deeds Goes to Town

Mr. Deeds Goes to Town (1936) was written by Robert Riskin and directed by Frank Capra, who had collaborated on *It Happened One Night* (1934), the only film to ever sweep all the major Academy Awards. *Deeds* became another big hit for them, opening to outstanding reviews—Graham Greene called it "a comedy quite unmatched on the screen"—and brisk ticket sales.[31] It was "one of those pictures," said a theater owner in Eminence, Kentucky, "that people tell their friends about."[32] Although it lost the Academy Award for best film of the year to *The Great Ziegfeld*, *Deeds* was voted best picture by the New York Film Critics and the National Board of Review, and won Capra the second of his three Academy Awards for direction.[33]

In adapting *Deeds* from a *Saturday Evening Post* serial, *Opera Hat*, by Clarence Budington Kelland, Riskin and Capra invested the original story with a poignant social vision, a kind of Christian humanism. The film was the first and purest expression of a theme Capra would continue to explore in *You Can't Take It With You* (1938), *Mr. Smith Goes to Washington* (1939), *Meet John Doe* (1941), and *It's a Wonderful Life* (1946)—the theme, in Greene's words, of "goodness and simplicity manhandled in a deeply selfish and brutal world."[34]

Goodness and simplicity are represented here by Longfellow Deeds (Gary Cooper in an Academy Award-nominated performance) from Mandrake Falls, Vermont. Deeds is a charming screwball—at least one scholar has asserted that this film launched the genre of screwball comedy—who plays the tuba in the town band and composes poems for greeting cards.[35] No sooner does the film begin than his peaceful life is disrupted. He unexpectedly inherits $20 million from an uncle and must go to New York to oversee the estate.

There follows a series of sad, disillusioning encounters between the country bumpkin and various big-city cynics and moochers.

Among these predators is Babe Bennett (Jean Arthur), a smart-aleck reporter assigned to make front-page fun out of Deeds. Babe impersonates an unemployed stenographer to gain his trust, then writes stories deriding him as the "Cinderella Man." But when he goes into rapture while visiting Grant's Tomb ("I see a small Ohio farm boy becoming a great soldier . . . being inaugurated as president"), she begins to reconsider her cynicism. "That guy's either the dumbest, stupidest, most imbecilic idiot in the world," she tells her roommate, "or he's the grandest thing alive."

Babe gradually decides that Deeds *is* "the grandest thing alive," a decision made possible by the fact that she herself hails from a small town and shares his ideals and values, though she had forgotten it for a time. She now so regrets chronicling his exploits—which included chasing fire engines and feeding donuts to a horse—that she quits journalism. Not even winning the Pulitzer Prize for her coverage of the McKay love triangle can keep her in the newsroom.

When corrupt lawyers try to have Deeds put away for wanting to use his millions to help poor farmers, Babe gets a chance at redemption. She rallies the press and public to his side, then takes the stand at his sanity hearing and declares her love for him. The final shot of the film, accompanied by the strains of "For He's a Jolly Good Fellow," shows Babe in Deeds' arms. As Charles Maland pointed out, the hero has won not only the legal wrangle, but also, presumably, a wife.[36]

Capra recalled in his 1971 autobiography, *The Name Above the Title*, that he made *Deeds* to suggest how "a simple honest man can, if he will, reach deep down into his God-given resources and come up with necessary handfuls of courage, wit, and love to triumph over his environment."[37] This is a beautiful and noble vision, but there is little room in it for the working woman. The working woman in Capra's Depression films—usually a reporter or secretary, played by either Jean Arthur or Barbara Stanwyck—has one overriding function: to give up her career and freedom for the man and shine on darkly.

His Girl Friday

In *His Girl Friday*, the 1940 remake of Hecht and MacArthur's *The Front Page*, Hildy Johnson is a woman. Rosalind Russell plays the star reporter, while Cary Grant plays Walter Burns, who now isn't only Hildy's editor, but also her ex-husband. Both Russell and Grant loved to ad lib. "So in *His Girl Friday*," Russell recalled in her memoirs, "we went wild, overlapped our dialogue, waited for no man. And [director Howard] Hawks got a big kick out of it."[38] Ironically, Russell hadn't been Hawks's first choice for the film. He had tried to get Ginger Rogers, Irene Dunne, and Jean Arthur to do it.[39]

Charles Lederer wrote the screenplay for *His Girl Friday* with an uncredited assist from Hecht. Years later, though, Hawks told an interviewer that it was his idea to change Hildebrand into Hildegarde. The idea supposedly came to him at an after-dinner play-reading session.[40] "I was going to prove to somebody that *The Front Page* had the finest modern dialogue that had been written," he explained, "and I asked a girl to read Hildy's part and I read the editor, and I stopped and I said, 'Hell, it's better between a girl and a man than between two men.'"[41]

The Front Page, as Molly Haskell and several other critics have noted, is really a male love story.[42] Toward the end of the play, Hildy responds to Walter's giving him a going-away present, a watch, by saying, "Aw, Jesus, no, Walter! You make me feel like a fairy or something." (In the first film version, he says, "You make me feel like I'm the bride.") Making Hildy a woman in *His Girl Friday*, whether or not it was the happy creative accident Hawks claimed, brought out sexual tensions that were already visible—but just barely—in the play, as well as in the 1931 film.

It also brought the main couple in line with the contemporary vogue for madcap romantic comedy, a point *Variety* underscored in its review. "With more of the feminine-romance angle injected than was in the original," the review said, "this new edition becomes more the modern-style sophisticated comedy than the hard, biting picture of newspapermen that Hecht and MacArthur had painted in their stage play."[43] Not that there still wasn't plenty of newspaper atmosphere left after Hildy turned female. The sob sister was, by 1940, a stock newspaper-film character. Russell had even previously played one in *Four's a Crowd* (1938). And, of course, Torchy Blane, herself based on a newspaperman, Frank Nebel's Kennedy, had popularized the good-looking, fast-talking girl reporter in her recently ended series of films.[44]

His Girl Friday was different from *The Front Page* in other ways than Hildy's gender. "In the process of adaptation," Jeffery Brown Martin pointed out in his book, *Ben Hecht, Hollywood Screenwriter*, "everyone has become nicer."[45] Earl Williams is no longer an anarchist, but a "poor little dope," and Walter and Hildy have acquired a streak of idealism. They don't want the story for its own sake anymore; they want to save Williams from the gallows because he is crazy.

Martin further noted that the "last vestiges of ethnic or sexual humor" have disappeared—the effect, he said, of greater censorship.[46] Molly Malloy, the whore with the heart of gold who befriends Williams in the original, is now just some woman, while Pincus, the Jewish messenger from the governor's office, has been changed into a nondescript American, Joe Pettibone.

Yet, for all these changes, the basic conflict remains the same: domesticity versus work. Hildy decides she wants to "be respectable and lead a halfway normal life," renouncing the rush and strain of daily journalism. "I'm going to be a woman, and not a news-getting machine," she tells the boys in the press room. "I'm going to have babies and take care of them and give them cod liver oil and watch their teeth grow, and if I ever see them look at a newspaper, I'm going to brain them." She plans on sharing this unadventurous, baby-filled future with Bruce Baldwin (Ralph Bellamy), an insurance salesman from Albany and the male counterpart of *The Front Page*'s Peggy.

At the opposite extreme is Walter, whom Hildy describes as "wonderful in a loathsome sort of way." We can see for ourselves in the following exchange with Duffy, his much put-upon city editor, that Walter doesn't feel bound by the rules of conventional behavior.

Walter: Get the governor on the phone.
Duffy: And tell him what?
Hildy: Quiet, Duffy, he's thinking.
Walter: Tell him if he'll reprieve Earl Williams, we'll support him for senator.
Duffy: What?
Walter: Tell him the *Morning Post* will be behind him hook, line, and sinker.
Duffy: But you can't do that.
Walter: Why not?
Duffy: Because we've been a Democratic paper for over 20 years.

Walter: All right, after we get the reprieve, we'll be Democratic again.

As the above scene perhaps indicates, the dialog in *His Girl Friday* moves at a frenetic pace. Practically every critic who has written about the film has emphasized this aspect.[47] Donald C. Willis, for example, said, "Hawks puts two, three, four, or ten people into the frame and has them cram as many words as possible into very small spaces of time. Actors overlap each other's speeches, match each other in vehemence and volume, toss in words offhandedly, mangle them (Abner Biberman: 'She ain't no albino. She was born right here in this country.')."[48] The result is a lightning-fast comedy that, to quote Manny Farber, "champions the sardonic and quick-witted over the plodding, sober citizens."[49]

Of all the characters, Walter is the quickest, with Hildy a very close second. Their near equal talent for rapid-fire repartee proves they are well matched sexually and professionally, despite her protests to the contrary. Her fiancé, Bruce, is just not in their league, as his inability to detect sarcasm or accurately judge Walter shows.

Bruce: You know, Hildy, he's not such a bad fellow.
Hildy: No, he should make some girl real happy.
Bruce: Uh-huh.
Hildy (to herself): Slap happy.
Bruce: He's not the man for you. I can see that. But I sort of like him. He's got a lot of charm.
Hildy: Well, he comes by it naturally. His grandfather was a snake.

A lot of the humor in *His Girl Friday* is based on word stunts of this sort, or what Farber called "topping," defined as "outmaneuvering the other person with wit, cynicism, and verbal bravado."[50] Late in the film, Walter and Hildy are handcuffed together, facing possible charges for having hid Earl Williams in a desk. Things look pretty bad for them, but they achieve a kind of moral victory when the inept sheriff must stop and grope for retorts to their wisecracks. "Make up your mind!" Walter even barks at him.

The Front Page ends with Hildy yielding to Peggy's wishes and leaving the newspaper game. In *His Girl Friday*, Hildy stays in the game, thus curtailing her dream of a traditional, middle-class home-

and-babies existence. Robin Wood, author of *Howard Hawks*, found her choice unacceptable and a big flaw in the film. "Given the alternatives the film offers," Wood wrote, "the only morally acceptable ending would be to have Hildy walk out on *both* men; or to present her capitulation to Walter as tragic."[51] But it isn't tragic. It is touching. Hildy gets what any grown-up would want—enjoyable work and a compatible mate.

Woman of the Year

Woman of the Year (1942) was the first of nine films that Spencer Tracy and Katharine Hepburn would make together over the next 25 years. It was written by Ring Lardner, Jr., and Michael Kanin, who received the almost unprecedented sum of $100,000 from MGM, and directed by George Stevens.[52] Although the film would win an Oscar for best screenplay, *Variety* initially wasn't too impressed, noting, "Tracy and Miss Hepburn go a long way toward pulling the chestnut out of the fire. A man with a pair of shears could do a lot more."[53]

Tracy plays Sam Craig, a down-to-earth sports columnist for the *New York Chronicle*, and Hepburn plays Tess Harding, a brilliant and peripatetic columnist on world affairs for the same paper. The film opens with Sam in a bar listening to the radio program "Information Please." When the show's guest, Tess, suggests that baseball be suspended for the duration of the war, Sam becomes enraged. Ignoring the fact that she is a colleague, he attacks her in his column as "the Calamity Jane of the fast international set." Tess responds in her own column, calling Sam "an ostrich with amnesia."

The rest of the plot is rather predictable. Sam and Tess fall in love, feud, get married, feud, and finally reconcile. At least a couple of scenes, though, stand out as classic examples of "recuperation," Michele Barrett's term for the effort to defuse challenges to male authority and control.[54]

One such scene takes place at New York's Yankee Stadium. Sam has brought Tess to a game in order to change her mind about baseball being "a frightful waste of energy." Tess wears a white straw hat with an oversized brim that blocks the view of the working-class man sitting behind her and marks her as a jerk, even if she does speak a half-dozen languages and go to state dinners. When the fellow taps her on the shoulder and says in an annoyed voice, "Da hat," she is self-centered enough to think he is paying her a compliment and replies, "Thank you."

Yet, by the end of the scene, she has fallen under the spell of the national pastime. The woman who earlier had to ask "Which one's the pitcher?" is now a baseball fan, eating peanuts from a brown paper bag and rooting for the home team. She has doffed her big, aggressive-looking hat, a sign that she has let go—for the moment, anyway—of her masculine tendencies, as well as of her un-American sophistication. Her conversion to baseball foreshadows her later and greater conversion to a more wifely role.

Most of the second half of the film is taken up with showing just how good a journalist, and how bad a wife, Tess is. She is so busy meeting with diplomats, writing her column, making speeches, and receiving an award for "Outstanding Woman of the Year" that she has little time for the usual amenities of marriage. Sam finally grows tired of her celebrity behavior and walks out.

Tess awakens to the error of her ways while attending the marriage of her widower father to an old family friend, Ellen Whitcomb (Fay Bainter). Unlike her own wedding ceremony—a two-minute rush job—Tess listens intently to theirs, realizing for the first time what marriage means. The scene is another classic example of recuperation. Ellen explicity says: "You can't live alone in this world, Tess. It's no good. Success is no fun unless you share it with someone." Coming from an older, professionally accomplished woman whom Tess had grown up admiring, this advice carries extra punch—not only for Tess, but also for the film audience.

Thus inspired, Tess goes after Sam, determined to prove herself as a real wife. She tries making him breakfast in bed, but instead makes a shambles out of the kitchen. The waffle iron explodes. The coffeepot bubbles over. The toaster flings slices of toast through the air. Although presented as hilarious, the scene has a decidedly sadistic edge, ending with Tess crying, "I can't do it. I tried. Make them stop," and diving for cover in Sam's arms.

The surprise is that having broken and humiliated Tess, the film then restores most of her original identity. Earlier there was a scene in which Tess's maid had called her Mrs. Harding, as if she were only slightly or tentatively married. Now Sam suggests a married name for Tess that will bring her public and private selves, her professional and domestic responsibilities, into better balance. "I don't want to be married to Tess Harding," he says, "any more than I want you to be Mrs. Sam Craig. Why can't you just be Tess Harding Craig?" "I think it's a wonderful name," she agrees, and something in us does, too.

It was probably because the war unsettled traditional gender roles that, of all the newspaper films discussed thus far, the two made in the early 1940s, *His Girl Friday* and *Woman of the Year*, are the most progressive. The relationship of the main couple in each film is characterized by humor, physical attraction, camaraderie, and mutual respect. True, the woman compromises more than the man does when conflict arises, but her right to her own identity and career is never in question. Whether one prefers Sam and Tess or Walter and Hildy as romantic icons, both couples represent marriage without chains. Each spouse gives the other the best of who he or she is and gives it freely and is still full.

Chapter 10

Dream Job

Watching films from the 1930s—*Dance, Fools, Dance*, *The Mystery of the Wax Museum*, *Front Page Woman*, the Torchy Blane series—it is possible to get the impression that women reporters were numerous and hyperactive back then. That was hardly the case, however. The average big-city newspaper with a staff of 30 to 50 men employed two or three women, usually tucked away in the feature departments.[1] Although she herself was a first-string news reporter, Ishbel Ross noted that there were just as few women on front-page assignments in the thirties as there had been at the turn of the century.[2] The *New York Times* didn't allow a woman reporter in the city room until 1934.[3]

When the Depression hit, the already tenuous status of women workers in male-dominated fields deteriorated further. In 1930 women editors, feature writers, and reporters numbered almost 15,000, but during the next decade, only 1,000 more women would enter journalism. Many others would be laid off as jobs and wages dwindled and men received preference in hiring.[4]

The women who did somehow break into journalism still faced rampant discrimination. Women were banned from the National Press Club and its annual Gridiron dinner.[5] They often were fired when they became pregnant. Elsie Carper of the *Washington Post* recalled that the day a woman even mentioned she was getting married was the day she was, in effect, resigning from newspaper work.[6]

Ross wrote in 1936—the year the Torchy Blane series went into production—that if "the front-page girls were all to disappear tomorrow, no searching party would go out looking for more."[7] Never thoroughly welcome in the city room, women felt continual pressure to prove they belonged there. Edith Evans Asbury, who began her journalism career in Ohio in 1929 and retired from the *New York Times* in 1981, commented that "women have to be twice as good as men to hold their own. We took it for granted."[8]

The relationship of such women reporters to their film counterparts has been interpreted in either one of two ways. Some scholars cite the film portrayals as evidence that the prestige of women reporters was rising in the 1930s, boosted largely by First Lady Eleanor Roosevelt, who insisted that only women cover her Monday morning press conferences.[9] Others acknowledge that high-profile newspaperwomen were rare, but add that the character of the wisecracking gal reporter was "too richly suited to the talkies to bypass on the grounds of accuracy."[10]

I see a third possibility—that film portrayals served as camouflage of, and compensation for, the lack of economic justice for women. The passage of the Nineteenth Amendment in 1920 (which granted women the right to vote) failed to usher in the revolution in women's work that feminists had predicted. Instead, aspiring career women were still limited to a handful of occupations. Among professional women in New York at the end of the 1920s, there were 63,637 teachers and 21,915 nurses, but only 11 engineers and 7 inventors.[11]

As the country entered the depths of the Depression, record numbers of women sought work, driven by the need to supplement meager family incomes. Most of the available jobs, however, were part-time and marginal. The proportion of women in the professions fell in the 1930s from 14.2 to 12.3 percent.[12] "If the word 'emancipation,' " historian William H. Chafe said, "is taken to mean the ability of women to function in the world outside the home on a basis of autonomy and equal access to job opportunities, then women workers remained almost as unemancipated in 1940 as in 1920."[13]

Except maybe on the screen. There, as Marjorie Rosen pointed out, "a curious conglomeration" of women worked by their wits during the Depression.[14] The vast majority were chorus girls and girl reporters, but shopgirls, manicurists, waitresses, taxi dancers, secretaries, and stenographers also were featured. "The films of the 1930s," Molly Haskell even claimed, "supply invaluable information . . . about working women and jobs—salaries, what goes on in offices," etc.[15]

Both Rosen and Haskell were rather vague as to the effects of all this. The best Rosen could do was to observe that "giving the heroine an assertive job and a telling retort livened up celluloid proceedings."[16] Haskell was almost as vacuous, writing that "women in the movies reflected, perpetuated and in some respects offered innovations on the roles of women in society. Shopgirls copied them, housewives escaped through them."[17]

Escaped to what? To where? More than 60 years since they first appeared in the city room, women remain a kind of journalistic underclass today. A University of Florida study published in 1995 found that about 40 percent of the 227 women reporters, editors, photographers, and graphic artists surveyed have been discriminated against by male co-workers and consider sexual harassment a problem on the job. In addition, 42.7 percent believe they earn less money than similarly qualified men.[18] Working-woman films were once a glittering apology for these injustices—glittering and insincere.

Stunt Girls and Sob Sisters

Film reviews and scholarly articles sometimes refer to Torchy Blane as a "sob sister." The term dates from the 1907 trial of Harry K. Thaw, heir to a steel-industry fortune who was accused of fatally shooting his wife's lover, architect Stanford White. Among the reporters covering the trial were four women—Ada Patterson, Dorothy Dix, Winifred Black, and Nixola Greeley-Smith. They were there to write with sympathy about Evelyn Nesbit Thaw, the enchantress in the case. A male wit, looking at the four seated around the press table, dubbed them the "sob sisters," and the name stuck.[19]

Most women reporters resented this label because it reinforced the stereotype of women as big-hearted but soft-minded, emotionally generous but intellectually sloppy. Mary Margaret McBride, who toiled for the *New York Evening Mail* in the 1920s, said she "loathed the title [sob sister] and fumed inwardly every time one of the men used it, which they did far too often."[20] Agness Underwood also felt herself limited and degraded by it. "I never sobbed a story in my life," she protested in her 1949 autobiography, *Newspaperwoman*. "I'm a reporter."[21]

Strictly speaking, Torchy wasn't a sob sister either. If she resembled any actual journalistic type, it was the so-called "stunt girl." This figure originated on the yellow journals of the 1880s and 1890s. As the title suggests, a stunt girl was required to do the bizarre or sensational—drive a locomotive, stay overnight in a haunted house, pose as a lunatic, witness a hanging—and then write about it from a feminine perspective. The most famous stunt girl was Nellie Bly of Pulitzer's *New York World*. She became a national celebrity in 1889 by breaking the travel record of Phineas T. Fogg, hero of the Jules Verne novel *Around the World in 80 Days*.[22]

Stunt-girl reporting enjoyed a resurgence during the formative years of tabloid journalism, a period that roughly coincided with Prohibition, 1920–33. "The tabloids," Ishbel Ross explained, "could not compete with the established papers on their own ground. They had to astonish, bemuse, dazzle or horrify the reader. Their editors did handsprings to startle the town. Their reporters had to follow suit. A group of clever girls adopted the new [sic] technique with success."[23] One of the cleverest was Dorothy Kilgallen, who, in the mid-thirties, emulated Nellie Bly by participating in an around-the-world air race against two male reporters. The stunt would be the basis for *Fly-Away Baby* (1937), the second film in the Torchy Blane series.

Ironically, the very characteristics that qualified women for stunt-girl or sob-sister reporting disqualified them from more serious journalism. Sob-sister reporting was founded upon the idea—no doubt male in origin—that women were highly emotional creatures, just as stunt-girl reporting was founded upon the related idea that strong, independent women were amusing oddities, freaks. In the eyes of most of the world, women journalists were women first, and journalists second, and suspect always.

Chapter 11

Black Bart

Barton MacLane, who played police Lt. Steve McBride in the seven Torchy Blane films with Glenda Farrell, was usually on the other side of the law. With his croaky voice, hooded eyes, and dark jowls, MacLane specialized in bad-guy roles for Warner Brothers from the mid- to late 1930s. In *Black Fury* (1935), with Paul Muni, he played a company thug who roughed up striking coal miners. In *G-Men* (1935), with James Cagney, he played a gangster modeled after John Dillinger. In *The Prince and the Pauper* (1937), with Errol Flynn, he played a sort of Fagin who exploited small children and topped off his villainies by throwing his grandmother in the fireplace. "I've never liked playing heavies," MacLane once said. "In fact, I've hated 'em. But that's what they wanted. And that's what they got."[1]

Born on Christmas 1902 in Columbia, South Carolina, MacLane was the son of the superintendent of a mental hospital. He attended Wesleyan University in Connecticut, majoring in English and football. In his senior year, he returned a kickoff 100 yards in a game against Massachusetts State. "It was good for quite a bit of publicity," he recalled. "Anyway, Richard Dix was making a football picture called 'Quarterback' and . . ."[2] MacLane's film career was launched.

Thirty-five years later, in 1961, MacLane estimated that he had appeared in nearly 300 films.[3] Actually, he had appeared in about half that number by the time of his death on January 1, 1969.[4] Film historian William K. Everson summed up MacLane's screen persona by observing, "He never spoke when shouting would do."[5] Where does his role as McBride, boyfriend and foil to reporter Torchy Blane, fit in his corpus?

Contemporary reviewers thought it a welcome change from his portrayals of gangsters and convicts. A review in *Variety* of *Fly-Away Baby* (June 1937), the second film in the Torchy Blane series, noted that MacLane was "cast for once in a sympathetic role."[6] More recent writings have echoed this. James Robert Parish, in his 1978 book, *Hollywood Character Actors*, mentioned that MacLane "occasionally broke away from the [bad-guy] mold, as Detective Lieutenant Steve McBride."[7]

What Parish and others have overlooked somehow is McBride's essential brutishness. Despite his badge, he talked and acted pretty much like the thugs MacLane usually played. He said "moidah" instead of murder, was quick to use his gun and fists, and pushed Torchy around—literally. In *Smart Blonde* (January 1937), the first film in the series, he snarled at her, "You wait here" ("here" being the lobby of a nightclub), punctuating each word with a shove. "Ain't he masterful?" sighed the hat-check girl as he strode off. "Yeah," muttered Torchy, "all he needs is a leopard skin."

Critics have been closer to the mark in describing McBride as "a slow talker, and an even slower thinker," exactly the way Elizabeth Dalton described him in her 1972 article, "Meet Torchy Blane."[8] Similar sarcasms beset McBride from the time of his first appearance in *Smart Blonde*. Frank S. Nugent, reviewing the film in the *New York Times*, called it "a static and listless little piece" in which "Glenda Farrell imitates a reporter and Barton MacLane libels the homicide squad."[9] Police departments of the period were, in fact, irritated by the way policemen were portrayed on the screen. When *Torchy Blane, the Adventurous Blonde*, the third film in the series, was released in November 1937, the *Motion Picture Herald* said, "All the picture does is what the police quite evidently don't want pictures to do"—make cops look stupid.[10]

But if McBride wasn't a smart blonde, he wasn't a complete cluck either. While Torchy often beat him to clues, he also helped her out of plenty of tight jams. For example, in *Blondes at Work* (February 1938), the fourth film in the series, he gave her paper a scoop when she couldn't because she was in jail for contempt of court. (Her offense? Eavesdropping through the wall of a supply closet on jury deliberations.) They were a team, each balancing or playing off the traits of the other: she was verbal, he was physical; she was intuitive, he was plodding; she was unorthodox, he was authoritarian; she was beauty, he was beast.

TV series, with their fast shooting schedules, formulaic stories, and core of continuing characters, now occupy a niche once filled by film series, including the Torchy Blanes.[11] Indeed, as Robin Cross pointed out in *The Big Book of B Movies*, the heroes of many film series—Hopalong Cassidy, Tarzan, Dr. Kildare, The Saint, Charlie Chan, Ellery Queen—eventually moved over to TV.[12] Although Torchy herself didn't make the move, MacLane did.[13] In the early 1960s, he starred as Marshal Frank Caine in the NBC series "The Outlaws," and later was featured as Gen. Martin Peterson in another NBC series, "I Dream of Jeannie." "TV," he told *TV Guide*, "is giving me something I have seldom had before—a chance to play the fine fellow. It's a good feeling."[14]

A Touch of the Poet

The only actor to repeat his role in all nine of the Torchy films was Tom Kennedy, who played Gahagan, Lt. McBride's comic chauffeur. Born in 1885, Kennedy came to film in 1915 after a career as a heavyweight boxer. He appeared in dozens of comedy shorts and over 175 features, usually playing a dumb Irish cop, a role for which his big, battered face and punch-drunk voice ideally suited him. His last film was *It's a Mad, Mad, Mad, Mad World* (1963) in which he made a cameo appearance as a traffic cop. He died in 1965.[15]

Gahagan may have been the most appealing character in the Torchy series. Critics have called him "brainless," "dim-witted," a "cluck," and he was.[16] But he was also sweetly innocent, growing excited and happy whenever he was allowed to use the siren. These scenes, occurring at least once per film, followed a fixed pattern. "Siren and all?" Gahagan would ask McBride as he started up the police car. "Yes, siren and all," McBride would say. "Boy, oh boy," Gahagan would gush.

Behind the rough exterior of a palooka, then, lay a capacity for simple childlike pleasure—and, more surprising still, for poetry. Gahagan was largely indifferent to the detective work that absorbed McBride and Torchy. His mind, so called, was on higher things. While they searched rooms, interviewed witnesses and suspects, and dodged bullets, he waited on the sidewalk, composing silly rhymes, such as "The amount of gas we use is a pity/I'm glad this car belongs to the city." Or, "When your head is all a muddle/And your noives are all ajar/And you got no one to cuddle/You'll get joy in a cigar."

There were other recurrent characters in the Torchy Blane films: the forgetful desk sergeant, usually played by George Guhl; Torchy's harried editor, Maxie, played by both Joe Cunningham and B Western star Raymond Hatton; and Capt. McTavish, played by Frank Shannon, more famous as Dr. Zarkov in the *Flash Gordan* serials. None of these characters, however, approached the originality—or absurdity—of Gahagan. He followed a loopy logic that nicely set off Torchy's straight-ahead style.

Of course, like any creative artist, Gahagan had moments of doubt and depression. "Gahagan," Torchy greeted him in *Blondes at Work*, "you're still writing poetry?" "Yeah," he replied gloomily, "but I'm trying to stop. I can't find a word that rhymes with orange."

Chapter 12

As the World Turns (to Crap)

When *Smart Blonde*, the first film in the Torchy Blane series, was released in January 1937, Madrid was under siege by the rebel army of Generalissimo Francisco Franco, in league with German and Italian troops. The United Auto Workers Union (UAW) had called sit-down strikes at seven General Motors plants in Detroit. Exiled Russian leader Leon Trotsky had traveled incognito to Mexico, where Stalinists had been ordered to shoot him on sight. A jury in federal court had awarded $7,500 to a 25-year-old man who had suffered a fractured skull and other injuries in a melee at Yankee Stadium following his attempt to grab a foul ball.[1]

When *Fly-Away Baby*, the second film in the series, was released in June 1937, Navy planes and ships continued to sweep the Phoenix Island area for missing aviator Amelia Earhart. A heat wave blistered most of the states east of the Rockies, causing more than 100 deaths. President Roosevelt threw out the first ball in the fifth annual All-Star Game, which the American League won, 8–3.[2]

When *Torchy Blane, the Adventurous Blonde*, the third film in the series, was released in November 1937, bestselling novels were *Citadel* by A.J. Cronin, *The Rains Came* by Louis Bromfeld, *The Turning Wheels* by Stuart Cloethe, and, in Atlanta, *Gone with the Wind* by Margaret Mitchell. Japanese forces captured Nanking, former capital of China, massacred civilians and prisoners of war, and looted nearly all the buildings in the city. The Chorus Equity Association, affiliated with the American Federation of Labor, announced plans to organize chorus girls.[3]

When *Blondes at Work*, the fourth film in the series, was released in February 1938, Spanish government troops were in full flight before Franco's army. Adolph Hitler, in an aggressive speech in Vienna, declared the annexation of his native Austria to the German Third Reich. The Moscow Show Trials ended, and 18 confessed conspirators against Soviet Russia were executed, including Nikolai I. Bukharin, chronicler of the Russian Revolution. General Motors advertised Buick with the slogan, "It's A Big Honey / For Mighty Little Money."[4]

When *Torchy Blane in Panama*, the fifth film in the series, was released in May 1938, Franco's forces had conquered two-thirds of Spain and were closing in on Catalonia. The Nazi press in Czecheslovakia had scornfully rejected the Easter peace plea of President Benes. Pitcher Jerome "Dizzy" Dean was traded from the St. Louis Cardinals to the pennant-conscious Chicago Cubs for three players and $150,000.[5]

When *Torchy Gets Her Man*, the sixth film in the series, was released in November 1938, German authorities had just issued orders banning Jews from all high schools and universities. The Congress of International Organizations was threatening a boycott of Ford products if the company persisted in its refusal to bargain with the UAW. "Telemobile units," or television trucks, made their first transmission from the New York World's Fair, showing pictures of the arrival of 1 million tulips from Holland.[6]

When *Torchy Blane in Chinatown*, the seventh film in the series, was released in February 1939, worldwide attention was focused on President Roosevelt's statement that in case of a European war the frontier of the United States would be in France. The Spanish government admitted its troops lacked arms and ammunition, and asked Britain to negotiate peace with Franco. The Brooklyn Dodgers hired Walter "Red" Barber, Cincinnati sports commentator, as chief announcer for radio broadcasts of the club's games at Ebbets Field for the coming season.[7]

When *Torchy Runs for Mayor*, the eighth film in the series, was released in May 1939, Britain was promoting British Guiana over Palestine as a permanent settlement for Jewish refugees from Nazism. Japanese planes heavily bombed the Chinese seaport of Chuanchow, with casualties estimated in the thousands. Speakers at a dinner of the National Economy League at the Hotel Astor warned that continued deficit spending and failure to balance the federal budget would bring financial disaster to every American wage-earner. The Florida Legislature passed a bill setting up a municipal primary in Miami for whites only.[8]

When *Torchy Plays with Dynamite*, the last film in the series, was released in August 1939, Germany and Russia were dismembering Poland. The Navy decided to shift "a pretty fair-sized" force of vessels to Pearl Harbor, a move seen as connected with the European war and international tension in the Far East. Rep. Martin Dies of Texas, chairman of the House Committee on Un-American Activities, said the Roosevelt administration had asked the Justice Department to begin purging 2,850 known Communists holding key government posts. And Joe DiMaggio still led the majors in batting, despite a recent slump.[9]

Chapter 13

Not-So-Great Expectations

Meaning, according to reception studies, is in the interpretive act, rather than immanent within the text, though the text may assume certain responses on the part of the "ideal" reader or viewer.[1] Numerous extratextual factors affect how real viewers will interpret a film. Such factors include age, race, class, and gender of a viewer; mood of the historical moment; and—our special interest here—what Judith Mayne has called the "institutionalized network of film reviewing."[2]

Film reviews create "horizons of expectation"—that is, they position viewers to interpet films in particular ways.[3] The ways usually don't challenge the social order, but disguise it. Patricia Zimmerman, in an analysis of Steven Spielberg's *Raiders of the Lost Ark*, pointed out that reviews in the mainstream press treat films as "pure entertainment, free of ideology, and simultaneously erase [filmmaking] as a social practice imbedded within and referring to a current social and historical context."[4]

The Torchy Blane films were only spottily reviewed in their own time and have been largely overlooked since. When, for example, Deac Rossell published an annotated filmography of American films featuring journalists, 1903–69, he omitted the Torchy Blanes from the year-by-year listings. Instead, he put them in an appendix with the porno flicks.[5]

Why all this critical contempt? Some is due to the long-standing categorization of these films as budget productions. Reviewing *Smart Blonde*, the first film in the series, Frank S. Nugent of the *New York Times* wrote, "Although the Warners deny making Class B pictures—the brothers label their product AA and A—'Smart Blonde,' the postscript to Shirley Temple's 'Stowaway' on the Palace's double bill, is pretty far down the alphabet."[6] *Variety*, the *Hollywood Reporter*, and other trade journals, though less prone to smirk than the *Times*, still emphasized in reviews that the Torchy Blanes were inexpensive supporting films. Thus *Variety* described *Smart Blonde* as "an okay dualer"; *Fly-Away Baby* as "a palatable programmer . . . constructed obviously for dualers"; *Blondes at Work* as "the not too light half of twinners"; *Torchy Blane in Panama* as a "B dualer"; *Torchy Gets Her Man* as "a mildly entertaining programmer that fits acceptably into the B groove"; and *Torchy Runs for Mayor* as "fully concocted for lower-deck dual fodder."[7]

Students of the old Hollywood studio system have claimed that B pictures sometimes managed to transcend their low budgets. Wheeler W. Dixon, author of *The "B" Directors*, said Bs offered "a much more realistic glimpse of American life in the 1930s and 1940s" than As would allow. "With millions of dollars in an 'A' budget," he explained, "the major studios would usually stick to safe escapist entertainment, [but] those B directors who wished to do so could tackle subjects like juvenile delinquency . . . or social inequities."[8] Even routine Bs—Westerns, whodunits, etc.—could be surprisingly revealing. As Brian Taves remarked in his 1993 article, "The B Film: Hollywood's Other Half," "While As concentrated on the lives of the wealthy, lower-budget films provided a contrast. With their less ornate costumes and sets, and secondary stars, B's centered more on day-to-day living, and their themes arguably constituted a better cultural and political reflection of the time."[9]

That wasn't how contemporary reviewers saw it, though. Whether writing for the general public or the film trade, they approached B films with an attitude of, at best, polite skepticism. So far as they were concerned, these films had a very specific purpose—to fill the bottom half of double bills as cheaply as possible. And this, in their eyes, automatically disqualified Bs from serious attention.

Of all the reviews of the Torchy films, those in the *New York Times* were consistently the harshest, written from an elitist, literary perspective and with arrogant authority. *Times*man Nugent, in his review of *Smart Blonde*, quoted "George Bernard Shaw's recent contemptuous description of the movies as a medium devoted to the depiction of people walking upstairs and downstairs, entering and leaving rooms, standing inside and outside doorways and doing practically nothing all the while," then dryly added: "In 'Smart

Blonde,' in which Glenda Farrell imitates a reporter and Barton MacLane libels the homicide squad, we have a murder mystery solved by an endless succession of door-openings and shuttings, taxi-hailings, jumping in and out of automobiles, and riding up and down in elevators. Mr. Shaw's pet antipathies are present, too, as well as one shot of Miss Farrell swinging aboard a moving train."[10]

Reviews in the *Times* of later films in the series continued derisive. *Fly-Away Baby*, according to a review signed "T.M.P," "might just as easily have been called 'The New Adventures of Torchy Blane,' since it is, after all, merely another chapter, and not a very exciting one, in the career of that demon reporter and her police lieutenant boy friend."[11] A few months later, B.R.C. observed of *Torchy Blane, the Adventurous Blonde*: "The story is about an absurd murder hoax perpetrated by Torchy's rivals in journalism, which turns with equal absurdity into the real thing. There is reason to believe that Miss Farrell, a competent performer in other contexts, was troubled in mind and conscience about this one. Whatever misgivings she might have had, incidentally, were justified."[12]

The *Times* didn't even bother to review the fourth Torchy Blane, *Blondes at Work*, but the fifth, *Torchy Blane in Panama*, was taken up by still another set of initials, B.C. This was Bosley Crowther, who joined the *Times* as a reporter in 1928, was promoted to film critic in 1937, and held the job until 1967, when he was named critic-emeritus.[13] Crowther found that *Torchy Blane in Panama* followed the "old familiar pattern," despite Lola Lane replacing Farrell as Torchy and Paul Kelly replacing MacLane as McBride. "To expect any more—or less—from Miss Lane and Mr. Kelly than their predecessors were able to give," he wrote, "is assuming a reasonable basis for comparison. But with material as trite and obvious as that which goes into the Torchy Blane series, the best any actor could do is 'appear at a disadvantage.' Miss Lane and Mr. Kelly are no exceptions."[14]

Torchy Gets Her Man and *Torchy Blane in Chinatown*, the sixth and seventh films in the nine-film series and the last that the *Times* condescended to review, received the usual rough treatment. For example, Crowther said of *Torchy Blane in Chinatown*, whose plot revolved around the theft of priceless jade tablets, "A reasonably wakeful customer should be able to spot the responsible party within ten minutes or so, thereby getting a jump of about fifty minutes on Torchy and her boy friend. And even a loyal Torchy fan might find that stretch too long for human endurance."[15]

Perhaps the most striking aspect of the *Times* reviews is how much they themselves were performances. The reviews weren't really calculated to recreate or analyze the Torchy films, but rather to amuse in their own right, particularly through the display of malicious wit. A lot of the malice was aimed directly at Torchy, with the reviews repeatedly referring to her in sarcastic terms. She is "that demon reporter" who "can scent a murderer without the customary aid of the heliotrope or fingerprints"; "the demon sob-sister"; "the thoroughly incredible sob-sister whose middle name is 'Scoop'"; "the superlative sob sister"; and "the demon girl reporter."[16] The whole notion of woman as star reporter was thus mocked and discredited by the reviews. Torchy's ability was made to seem the crowning improbability in a film series already swarming with improbabilities.

Trade papers were kinder than the *Times* was to the Torchy films, though never so kind as to rate any of them A-caliber. *Daily Variety*, in a generally upbeat review of *Torchy Runs for Mayor*, conceded that the production "still falls short of what it takes to lift a feature out of the strictly filler division."[17] Because the Torchy films got stuck with the "filler," or B, label, their actual workings were obscured, invisible. The trade press betrayed no recognition—and no desire to recognize—that these shabby little films might be ideologically charged and fulfilling a cultural function beyond lowbrow entertainment.

In judging the films, the trades focused on matters of technique, noting the originality of the screenplay, the naturalness of the acting, and the speed of the editing and direction—or, more often, the lack thereof. Space was devoted as well to summarizing the plots, which usually sounded pretty idiotic in the retelling. But even when the plots weren't idiotic, there was always something in the films that was. Under the headline "WB 'Smart Blonde' Routine Wisecracked Mystery Yarn," a review in the *Hollywood Reporter* commented, "The Frederick Nobel [sic] story is brightened up for laughs here and there without interfering with the guessing game, which is interrupted just once—to allow Winifred Shaw, in the indispensable night club scene, to sing, 'Why Do I Have to Sing a Torch Song?' There were those in the preview audience who were inclined to echo the question."[18]

The trades had plenty of praise for the verve and personality of the three actresses—Farrell, Lane, and Jane Wyman—who played

Torchy. What the publications didn't have was much respect for Torchy herself. Just like the *New York Times*, they referred to the character in distinctly ironic tones. She was "the irrepressible newspaper gal"; "the newspaperwoman who not only keeps a jump ahead of her rivals on other sheets, but also the police department, including the part of it she expects to marry"; "the infallible newshoundress"; "the reporter whose uncanny ability to solve murder mysteries knows no bounds"; "the demon femme reporter"; and "the juvenile conception of a star femme reporter."[19]

Reviewers found Torchy, in a word, incredible. And yet her cartoonlike quality wasn't deemed an obstacle to audience acceptance. In the midst of a longish, lukewarm review of *Blondes at Work*, *Daily Variety* declared, "[Torchy's] amazing reportorial skill will make working newspapermen writhe but will make no diff at the b.o. [box office] to the non-enlightened public."[20] Later, the *Hollywood Reporter* would say of *Torchy Blane in Panama*, "Its treatment of newspaper and police work is so preposterous that it is more to be pitied than censored. Because it has one or two exciting moments and because it is well played, audiences which are sufficiently gullible may not mind it so much."[21]

There were progessive elements in the Torchy films, only the reviewers didn't perceive them, nor did they prepare audiences to perceive them. All that the reviewers ever perceived was a "wisecracking, Goldwyn-styled girl reporter" romping through a series of routine whodunits.[22] That Torchy might have been something more—a luminous figure of female strength, pride, and courage—remained unsaid, perhaps even unsayable. She became whatever audiences expected her to be, and audiences were told to expect her to be resoundingly insignificant.

Faces in the Dark

There is very little hard information available today about who saw Torchy Blane films in the 1930s and why and how they reacted. We know that the films were classified as "general audience." We know that the films were intended for neighborhood theaters, or what *Variety* called the "nabes." We know that the films were fairly popular, since Warner Brothers cranked out nine of them. And that is about all we know.

Is it any wonder, then, that the reviews of Torchy films in the *Motion Picture Herald*, a trade publication addressed to theater owners and operators, seem especially intriguing? *Herald* reviewers recorded not only their own reactions to new releases, but also those of the audiences of plain folks with whom they sometimes watched. Sixty years later, scanning reviews of *Torchy Blane, the Adventurous Blonde*, *Torchy Blane in Panama*, and a few others, we can catch ghostly glimpses of the faces in the dark.

A reviewer writing under the initials G.M. explained in the *Herald* of September 11, 1937, that *Adventurous Blonde* was "previewed in the Warner theatre, Huntington Park [California], a neighborhood house which is typical of the types of theatres in which the picture was made to play." The audience, incidentally, "wasn't lured to the theatre so much by the promise of a preview as it was by the fact that a bathing beauty contest was being staged." This primary focus on female flesh quite possibly prevented the audience from interpreting the film in profeminist terms, even though Torchy, as G.M. commented, "outdoes all the real sleuths of factual history and visionary imagination in solving a complicated crime." "We don't know whether the audience had seen any of the previous numbers in the 'Torchy' series," G.M. added, "but it gave evidence by its attention to the film and applause upon its finale that 'The Adventurous Blonde' amused it."[23]

P.C.M. found the opposite response when taking in *Torchy Blane in Panama* at the Strand Theater in New York. "A small afternoon audience," he reported in the *Herald* of April 30, 1938, "viewed the picture silently."[24] Contributing to their silence may have been the fact that Lola Lane had succeeded Glenda Farrell as Torchy and Paul Kelly had succeeded Barton MacLane as her police-officer boyfriend. With the return of Farrell and MacLane to the roles in *Torchy Gets Her Man*, the next film in the series, audience interest would perk up.

Torchy Gets Her Man had Torchy and Lt. Steve McBride running down a gang of counterfeiters with the help of a police dog. G.M. saw the film at the Warner Hollywood Theatre. "The Saturday night preview audience," he said in the *Herald* of October 15, 1938, "seemed to derive considerable enjoyment from the show. While appreciative of the players' work, the crowd appeared to be of the opinion that the animal came close to stealing the show."[25]

The seventh film in the series, *Torchy Blane in Chinatown*, was the last to be written up in the *Herald*. P.C.M., Jr., began his review with an anecdote: "The series vogue has a way of perpetuating its characters so that they seem like old friends. Two boys in their teens, shopping for film fare although it was a Friday morning and the schools were in session, happened along at the Palace theatre as this reviewer arrived. The Palace bill won out because one of the boys had seen previous 'Torchy Blane' films."[26] *Variety* had dismissed *Torchy in Chinatown* as "lightweight," and the *Hollywood Reporter* had derided it as an "infantile whodunit."[27] P.C.M., Jr., admitted that "the story borders on the weak side," but noted that the afternoon audience with whom he saw it in New York "appeared to be enjoying 'Torchy's' latest adventures."[28]

Although few and brief, the reviews of Torchy films in the *Herald* are highly suggestive. And what they suggest, among other things, is that the public had degraded taste even before corrosive mass exposure to television.

Chapter 14

The Man-Tailored Woman

In her award-winning 1994 book, *Sex and Suits*, Anne Hollander claimed that "no matter how similar the clothes of men and women may appear, or how different, the arrangements of each are always being made with respect to the other. Male and female clothing, taken together, illustrates what people wish the relation between men and women to be."[1] If Hollander is right, and she probably is, then it makes sense to compare the clothing of girl reporter Torchy Blane with that of her cop boyfriend, Steve McBride.[2] How they dress should tell us something about how they relate, their comparative roles. Their clothing may even tell us something about how men and women in general related just before World War II.

Emancipated women of the 1930s achieved a modern look by imitating male fashions.[3] Actress Marlene Dietrich made international headlines in 1933 when she appeared offscreen in male attire, including a tight-fitting jacket that came from a boy's clothing store and emphasized her curves. Warned by the Paris chief of police that she would be asked to leave town if she continued to wear pants, she changed into a skirt, but retained a man's hat and tie.[4] "Such gestures," Hollander noted, "do not aim for real masculine effect, the look of active power; they show a desire to look erotically imaginative without looking too feminine—to mimic male sexual freedom, instead of exaggerating female compliance."[5] Fashion historian Ruth P. Rubinstein recalled that prostitutes in Venice in the late sixteenth century adopted elements of male dress to increase their sexual allure.[6]

The lead couple in the Torchy Blane films had a kind of equality of dress. McBride usually wore a dark, three-piece suit, white shirt, and conservative tie, but no one was ever going to mistake him for a banker. Maybe it was his size, or maybe the dead cigar jammed in the corner of his mouth, or maybe the gray fedora with the brim pulled down low. At any rate, he looked tough, cynical, and menacing, like the nights and city he inhabited.

When she was on the job, which was most of the time, Torchy wore a feminine version of her boyfriend's clothes. Her basic outfit consisted of a tailored jacket and a skirt of matching fabric, sometimes with a blouse under the jacket, sometimes just an artfully arranged scarf. She topped this off with an immense variety of hats—berets, cloches, turbans, hats with curled-up brims, hats with demi-veils, big, round hats that resembled pizza pans, tall, conical clown hats, and more.

Historically, hats have been phallic symbols. Hollander referred to them as "those great male emblems dating from the remote past."[7] Another fashion expert, James Laver, observed that periods of male dominance have coincided with high hats for men, among them the tall-crowned hat of the Puritans and the top hat of the Victorians.[8] Thus the fact that Torchy wore provocatively shaped hats may have reflected not only thirties' fashion, but also her manlike assertiveness.[9]

Torchy competed with distinction against the so-called "gentlemen of the press," though they complained that her closeness to McBride gave her an unfair advantage in the race for news. She and the detective were, as their somewhat similar attire suggested, special allies. "Listen, Torchy," her editor snaps in *Smart Blonde*, the first film in the series, "are you working for me or for Steve McBride?" "Ah, listen, Maxie, give me a break, will ya?" she replies. "That big palooka can't even think without me around. I got a couple angles on this case—" "Why don't you marry that guy?" the editor interrupts. "That's one of the angles," Torchy says, and breezes out the door.

But love and work weren't so easily reconciled, and certain contradictions in Torchy's appearance indicated as much. In addition to rakish hats and man-tailored suits, she wore makeup. Her Kewpie-doll looks were the result of eyebrow pencil, eye shadow, mascara, rouge, and lipstick, all deftly applied. The props and paint confirmed that Torchy well knew the traditional feminine role and was ready to play it. Even in the midst of murders, bank robberies, and scoops, she had the time—nay, the duty—to be on hand as a decorative object. And as object rather than subject, psychologist

Rita Freedman pointed out, "a woman suffers a kind of 'psychic annihilation.' "[10]

Reviewers considered McBride "perhaps the dumbest detective officer in films."[11] Torchy adored him anyway. *Smart Blonde* ended with her agreeing to marry him. The sequels ended with the marriage being unavoidably delayed. William K. Everson, in *The Detective in Film*, described Torchy and McBride as "such an ill-matched couple that audiences were hardly holding their breath awaiting the union."[12] Be that as it may, Torchy was still involved in a traditional middle-class romance. She didn't live up to her modern attire or her tough-gal image, as Editor Maxie implies in *Fly-Away Baby* when he discovers that she has gone out to buy a marriage license. "Treachery!" he exclaims. "That's what it is, treachery. . . . I made her the smartest reporter in this cock-eyed town. And how does she repay me? By running off to marry some bourgeois boob and spawn a kennel of brats. She's insane. She's cuckoo."

Adopting elements of male dress finally smacks too much of giving in to male dominance. Women who wore men's suits, hats, etc., were often just calling attention to themselves, not making a feminist statement. It took several more generations, Hollander remarked, for women to achieve "a female way to wear clothes that look both sexually interesting and ordinarily serious . . . at the same time, the way men did."[13]

The final shot of *Torchy Blane, the Adventurous Blonde*, sums up the difficult, contradictory status of women in the 1930s and beyond. Earlier in the film, Torchy filched McBride's badge in order to better investigate a murder. Now, sitting on a plane bound for Cleveland and her next assignment, she takes the badge out of her pocketbook. She holds this symbol of male power and authority to her left breast, then her right, then her left again. A puzzled expression flickers across her face, as if she suddenly realizes that although she has the badge, she will never have the ideal clothes—or chest—to pin it on.

Chapter 15

Legalese

In mid-February 1996, a fat, brown envelope arrived at my house from the Wisconsin Center for Film and Theater Research in Madison. About a month earlier, I had asked the center to reproduce from its Warner Brothers Collection material related to the Torchy Blane series. Tearing open the envelope, I found mustard-colored photocopies of contracts and other documents—and a bill for $48.33.

Was the stuff worth the money? Not at first glance. I had hoped for shooting schedules or budget breakdowns or the work journals of directors. What I got was mostly correspondence between lawyers about copyrights to titles, stories, and characters. I felt gypped.

And yet the more I studied the documents, the more I suspected there was something important buried in them, some hidden truth about the business side of filmmaking. I remembered an editorial cartoon I had seen recently, depicting art students facing a platform upon which stood a black-suited man with a briefcase. Off to one side, a woman, obviously the art instructor, was saying, "We'll begin with the most basic figure in art, the copyright attorney . . ."[1]

Some of the documents from the Wisconsin archive concerned the rights to stories by Frederick Nebel about the detective team of Capt. Steve MacBride and reporter Kennedy—stories published in the pulp magazine *Black Mask* from 1928 to 1936. A letter dated February 4, 1936, from Nebel's lawyers or literary agents, Brandt & Brandt, to Jacob Wilk of Warner Brothers confirmed that Nebel accepted Warners' offer of $1,250 cash for the "world motion picture, sound, and dialogue rights" to his story "No Hard Feelings."[2] *Smart Blonde*, the first Torchy film, was based on the story, though, as Elizabeth Dalton pointed out, "based on" might be considered an understatement.[3] The script by Don Ryan and Kenneth Gamet stuck so closely to the original that it was almost a scene-by-scene, line-by-line reiteration.

Smart Blonde opened in January 1937. The second Torchy film, *Fly-Away Baby*, opened that June, and the third, *Torchy Blane, the Adventurous Blonde*, opened in November. Neither was based on a MacBride-Kennedy story. In fact, *Fly-Away Baby* grew out of a recent around-the-world flight by Dorothy Kilgallen of the *New York Journal*.[4] Warners had been trying all the while, however, to gain access to more of Nebel's stories.[5] Finally, on December 22, 1937, a deal was signed for 25 of them, many of whose titles were the epitome of hard-boiled: "Tough Treatment," "Alley Rat," "Wise Guy," "Ten Men from Chicago," "Shake Down," "Beat the Rap," "Death for a Dago," "The Quick or the Dead," "Backwash," "Farewell to Crime," "Song and Dance," "Guns Down," "Too Young to Die," "Bad News," "Take It and Like It," "Be Your Age," "He Was a Swell Guy," "It's a Gag," "Ghost of a Chance," "That's Kennedy," "Die-Hard," "Winter Kill," "Fan Dance," "Crack Down," and "Hard to Take."[6] Nebel got only $2,000, but retained the right to "license others to produce, distribute, and exhibit photoplays based on said TORCHY BLANE stories," which was what the MacBride–Kennedy stories were now called despite having no character named Torchy Blane.[7]

Warners never made any of the 25 stories into films and Nebel never sold the film rights to the stories to anyone else. Although the sequels to *Smart Blonde* displayed the credit line, "Based on characters created by Frederick Nebel," the plots of the sequels were sometimes of strange provenance. *Torchy Blane, the Adventurous Blonde*, for example, resembled *Back in Circulation*, released a couple of months earlier. *Back in Circulation* itself was an unofficial remake of *Front Page Woman*, a 1935 film directed by Michael Curtiz and starring Bette Davis and George Brent. Moreover, several scenes in *Blondes at Work*, the fourth Torchy film, duplicated scenes in *Front Page Woman*, right down to the camera angles.

Nor was that all. *Torchy Blane in Chinatown*, the seventh film in the series, recycled the plot of the 1930 Warners film *Murder Will Out*, described in an interoffice memo as "a clever mystery satire with novel punch."[8] The early talkie starred Jack Mulhall and Lila Lee, and was based on the short story "The Purple Hieroglyph" by Will F. Jenkins.[9] More than half the documents from the Wisconsin archive dealt with "The Purple Hieroglyph" and its various spin-offs. In the spring of 1948, almost a decade after the Torchy series had ended, Warners was inquiring of lawyers about the copyright status of "The Purple Hieroglyph," as if planning yet another remake.[10]

Filmmaking in the studio era was essentially a "factory-based, assembly-line system."[11] To ensure a steady flow of product, Warners cannibalized previous films. There were no limits, evidently, on the number of times a plot could be reused. Producer Bryan Foy, known as the "Keeper of the Bs" because of his low-budget assignments, said:

> In the old days at Warner, I made one picture eleven times. It started off with a picture called *Tiger Shark*, a fishing story, in which Edward G. Robinson lost his arm. I followed the script of *Tiger Shark* scene for scene and made the same thing as *Lumberjack*, only this time the guy lost his leg. Then I made it as *Bengal Tiger*, exactly the same, only now he was a lion tamer with a circus and lost his arm. The writers protested that he had lost his arm in *Tiger Shark* too; and I told them that he may have lost his arm in *Tiger Shark* too, but he's got two arms.[12]

Newspaper films of the 1930s, populated by alcoholic star reporters, hard-boiled sob sisters, grouchy editors, and money-mad, power-hungry publishers, were just as contrived. The distortions offended members of the press, one movie-trade paper warning that "the average Horace Greeley resented the manner in which newspaper life was Hollywood handled."[13] Such criticism led the Motion Picture Association in the mid-1940s to monitor screen portrayals of journalists—with little discernible effect then or later.[14] When, for example, director Danny DeVito shot a scene at the *Detroit News* for the 1993 film *Hoffa*, he instructed editor Phil Lacura to "act like you'd been up all night drinking and screwing around."[15] The *Front Page* type of newspaperman isn't really representative of journalism, but since most of the people who write and direct films know only what they see in other films, that tradition has been perpetuated.[16] Besides, such colorful characterizations usually make money at the box office.

Money. . . . There were copies of actors' contracts mixed in with the other documents from the Wisconsin archive. Larry Williams, who played Bill Canby, a rival reporter in *Torchy Blane in Panama*, had a 26-week contract with Warners at $150 per week.[17] John Miljan, who played the more substantial role of Dr. Dolan, the villain in *Torchy Runs for Mayor*, had a 13-week contract at $750 per week, but could be laid off without pay for up to three weeks.[18] The *Hollywood Reporter*, incidentally, thought Miljan was "swell as 'the man behind the administration.' "[19]

Tom Kennedy was the only actor to appear in all nine Torchy films. In May 1938 he signed a three-picture deal with Warners—for *Torchy Gets Her Man*, *Torchy Runs for Mayor*, and *Torchy Blane in Chinatown*—guaranteeing him at least three weeks' work per picture at $500 per week.[20] His signature on the contract looked brisk and firm, nothing like his blundering character Gahagan.

Glenda Farrell and Barton MacLane also signed three-picture deals in May with a minimum guarantee of three weeks' work per picture. Both were returning to the series after a break during which Lola Lane and Paul Kelly had played Torchy and McBride in *Torchy Blane in Panama*.[21] Under their latest contracts, MacLane got $1,666.67 per week, and Farrell, $2,500.[22]

Warners has been romanticized in histories of Hollywood in the thirties as "the workingman's studio."[23] Its Depression-era films, Thomas Schatz wrote, "were fast-paced, fast-talking, and socially sensitive . . . treatments of contemporary stiffs and lowlifes, of society's losers and victims rather than heroic or well-heeled types."[24] Russell Campbell, the founding editor of the *Velvet Light Trap*, once observed that "Warners was the only studio to feature working class characters with any regularity. Shop girls, bellhops, linen girls, barbers, stenographers, taxi drivers were presented convincingly, without any condescension."[25] But how much of that treatment was sincere, how much simply exploitative? The average yearly salary in the United States in 1938 was $1,284, or $1,316 less than Farrell made—*per week*.[26] The irony of a fabulously wealthy film star playing an ink-stained wretch seems to have been lost on just about everyone.

Chapter 16

Love Is Murder

To contemporary reviewers, the first four films in the Torchy Blane series were just routine whodunits.[1] Each film begins with a murder—sportsman Tiny Torgensen's in *Smart Blonde*, jeweler Martin Devereaux's in *Fly-Away Baby*, actor Harvey Hammond's in *Torchy Blane, the Adventurous Blonde*, and department-store owner Marvin Spencer's in *Blondes at Work*—and each ends with the murderer being exposed. Still, Torchy and her boyfriend, police detective Steve McBride, do more than crack cases. Although reviewers didn't notice it, the two also restore order to male-female relationships that had been in dangerous disarray.

In all four films, Torchy and McBride are surrounded by secondary, or satellite, couples. These are invariably misaligned in some important way. For example, Fitz Mularkay, owner of the Million Club in *Smart Blonde*, is engaged to Boston socialite Marcia Friel, but belongs by class and experience with Dolly Ireland, a singer at his nightspot (who performs a musical number that asks the loaded question, "Why do I have to sing a torch song when a song of love is ringing in my heart?"). As another character says, "Dolly's crazy about Fitz, but he's going high hat with a swell dame." Actually, Marcia isn't the "swell dame" she seems. Her real name is Marcia Corson, and she is working a scam on Fitz with Louie Friel, a slickly handsome shyster posing as her brother.[2] It takes about 60 minutes—the entire length of the film—for Torchy and McBride to sift through this confusing mess and, in the process, to clarify their own relationship. "He doesn't appreciate anything I do," Torchy remarks to Fitz and Dolly in the closing scene, played, symbolically, in a cheery hospital room, a place of hope and help and healing.

McBride: All right, all right, I'll pat you on the back. You're great, you're colossal. You ought to be a detective.
Torchy: So should you.
McBride: Doesn't make any difference what I was, I'd never be able to figure out what goes on in that dizzy brain of yours.
Torchy: It'll take you the rest of your life to find out.
McBride: All right, I'll the take the job.
Torchy: Are you proposing to me?
McBride: Well, yes.
Torchy: Oh, darling.
(Fadeout on kiss.)

The preoccupation of the films with couples is traceable, at least in part, to confusion over the increased opportunities for intimacy and the erotic outside of marriage. Early in this centuy, American society began moving toward sexual liberalism. Sex became "something to be discussed and displayed, whether through popularizations of Freud, the true-confession magazines, or the romantic imagery of Hollywood films."[3] As one observer put it just before World War I, "sex o'clock" had struck in America.[4]

John D'Emilio and Estelle B. Freedman, authors of *Intimate Matters: A History of Sexuality in America*, attributed the shift in sexual behavior to economic changes. "Labor for wages," they explained, "allowed more and more men, and some women, to detach themselves from a family-based economy and strike out on their own; the anonymous social relations of the metropolis gave them the freedom to pursue their sexual yearnings." In addition, the sober work ethic that characterized nineteenth-century capitalist development was withering away, to be replaced by the values and institutions of a consumer society. "An ethic that encouraged the purchase of consumer products," D'Emilio and Freedman noted, "also fostered an acceptance of pleasure, self-gratification, and personal satisfaction."[5]

By the mid-1920s, the traditional patriarchal form of marriage—in which men were "rule makers and breadwinners," and women were "mothers and domestic managers"—was fast losing its appeal, particularly among middle-class youth.[6] Some sociologists and advice writers responded with a campaign to bring marriage into the modern era. They redefined the conjugal relationship in more egalitarian terms, arguing for so-called "companionate marriage," which stressed the emotional compatibility of husband and wife, rather than fulfillment of gender-prescribed duties and roles.[7]

The popular image of the twenties is of "a nonstop revel featuring jazz bands, risqué dances, and uninhibited sex."[8] Social historian Frederick Lewis Allen pointed out, however, that the prevailing mood of the decade "was not one of abandonment so much as of rowdiness. Witness the women's fashions, which made mature females look like short-skirted, long-waisted, flat-breasted, short-haired little girls trying to look worldy wise; witness, too, the bright vogue of dances such as the 'Charleston,' which was a lively but unseductive romp."[9] William F. Chafe, author of *The Paradox of Change: American Women in the Twentieth Century*, similarly observed that the flapper with a cigarette in her mouth and a cocktail in her hand was a feminist rebel in only the most superficial sense. Her rebellion "focused on style, not substance—on the appearance of sexual liberation, not on the radical restructuring of all relationships."[10]

With the coming of the Depression of the 1930s, sexual adventure gave way to the anxieties of hard times. Men lost their jobs. Women went to work. Widespread poverty and uncertainty created tensions in many marriages.[11] People found themselves wondering, "If the economic promises of American life could be reversed so suddenly, what was to prevent emotional promises from breaking down as well?"[12]

The Torchy Blane series began production in late 1936. Historians generally agree that by then the worst of the Depression was over, though threats to the economy would continue until the outbreak of World War II. Significantly, national movie attendance bounced back in 1936 to pre-Depression levels, reaching a healthy 88 million a week.[13]

Virginia Wright Wexman, in *Creating the Couple: Love, Marriage, and Hollywood Performance*, observed, "As a form of modern popular ritual, movies define and demonstrate socially sanctioned ways of falling in love."[14] The need for this kind of demonstration grew throughout the twenties and thirties as the very meaning of "the couple" turned chaotic, first under the impact of sexual liberalism and then under that of the Depression. Of all the many possible relationships between men and women, Hollywood most heavily promoted the "ideal of monogamous marriage to a 'suitable' partner."[15] Torchy Blane and Steve McBride are a prime example.

They may not seem such, though, in *Fly-Away Baby*, the second film in the series. It opens with their marriage being delayed when McBride is called away on a murder case and closes with their marriage being delayed yet again when Torchy is called away on a reporting assignment. In between, an excess of plot—two additional murders and an around-the-world air race—keeps Torchy and McBride jumping. As they drive from a jewelry store, scene of the first murder, to police headquarters, Torchy tries to turn the conversation to the topic of their aborted wedding, but McBride has other things on his mind.

Torchy: Well, I spent 55 cents on a taxi, 35 cents on a fresh gardenia, and I borrowed two bucks from Johnny to pay for the marriage license—that's two dollars and 90 cents. If I'd spent my money on a horse, he might've showed.
McBride: I got a hunch that Luger's a cold potato. A checkup's liable to show it wasn't even bought in this country.
Torchy: Only six months for talking to myself? Thank you, judge.

At least Torchy and McBride share car rides and clues. They work together, usually pretty amicably, on a solution to the case, which is also a solution to the immediate obstacles to their marriage. By contrast, the other couples in the film are disintegrating, seemingly beyond saving. Lucien Croy, the reporter son of the publisher of the *Star Telegram*, has been involved with self-centered and sybaritic nightclub singer Ila Sayre. After Croy departs in the air race, a jealous Sayre goes to the police and accuses him of shooting jeweler Martin Devereaux to death.

McBride: Why did you wait till now to tell me?
Sayre: Because I was engaged to Croy and he ran out on me.
McBride: So you want to get even, hey?
Sayre: Yes, I'm talking. . . . Croy's guilty and I hope he gets the chair.
McBride: You must be crazy about him.

Competing against Croy in the race are Torchy and an impish, alcoholic reporter named Hughie Sprague. Sprague is married to a rich woman on whom he cheats and about whom he continually jokes. Just before boarding the plane—it is a peculiarity of this race that all three competitors seem to be traveling on the same flight—Sprague asks the gate attendant, "Do you know my wife?"

> **Attendant:** No, I don't.
> **Sprague:** Allow me to congratulate you.

Also on the plane, incidentally, is a private detective hired by Sprague's wife to gather evidence for divorce proceedings. The detective is none other than Tom Kennedy's wacky character, Gahagan, who has now taken leave of the police force as well as his senses.

Torchy eventually wins the race, no doubt aided somewhat by the fact that Croy, her main rival, is murdered along the way. The murderer turns out to be Devereaux's business partner, Guy Allister, who dies a deservedly horrible death when his parachute fails to open during an escape try. With his demise, order is restored, particularly to male-female relationships. The triumph of love and romance over crime and violence is marked, as in Shakespearean comedy, by a celebration.[16] Here the celebration takes place in a newspaper office, where Torchy and McBride stand before the assembled staff like a bride and groom standing before family and friends. She even holds a bouquet.

> **Publisher:** My dear Torchy, you made good on everything you promised, and on behalf of the *Herald*, I'd like to present you with this little token. (He hoists a loving cup.)
> **Torchy:** Oh! (She hands the bouquet to McBride and accepts the cup.) Thank you, Colonel Higgam. (She glances inside the cup.) And a bonus check! (She extracts it.) Here, you take this. (She hands the cup to McBride, too.)
> **City Editor:** Whatever happened to Hughie Sprague? He didn't even reach town to finish the race.
> **Torchy:** Mrs. Sprague was so glad to see him that she took him straight to Florida for a second honeymoon. (General laughter.)
> **Publisher:** And more than winning the race, Torchy, you delivered an amazing story.
> **Torchy:** But an even more amazing story is about to break. Steve and I . . . are on our way to buy a marriage license.

As mentioned earlier, they never get there, but that doesn't much matter, since the award ceremony has already served as a kind of surrogate wedding. Whether formally married or not, Torchy and McBride have demonstrated the legitimacy and resilience of the modern heterosexual couple of reproductive age. Thus all is right with the world, a point driven home when Gahagan—he has returned to the force—recites his last little poem of the film: "What is so rare as a day in June/Nature in tune, nature in tune/And overhead an awesome moon."

Torchy Blane, the Adventurous Blonde and *Blondes at Work*, the next two films in the series, follow the same basic pattern as *Fly-Away Baby*. A sensational murder is committed. Torchy and McBride delay their wedding to investigate. They encounter liars, gangsters, and obstacles from their respective superiors before catching the murderer. Finally, with law and order restored, marriage occurs, though not between them.

The chronic postponement of their wedding—Torchy and McBride are still not married when the series ends—suggests a certain ambivalence about marriage itself. In 1938, the second year of the series, sociologist Ernest Groves published *The Marriage Crisis*, warning that because birth control and the growing independence of women had made sex more readily available, the institution of marriage was in danger of decay.[17] The films seem to reflect similar concerns. After department-store owner Marvin Spencer is found murdered in *Blondes at Work*, for example, police compile a list of his girlfriends. "Quite an extensive list, isn't it?" McBride says to an assistant. "Yeah," the assistant cracks. "It looks like the only dame who didn't carry a torch for Spencer was the Statue of Liberty."

Married couples in the films don't exactly inspire confidence in the holiness of matrimony, either. Actor Harvey Hammond, the murder victim in *Torchy Blane, the Adventurous Blonde*, was a compulsive philanderer. He had just broken off an affair with Theresa Gray, the wife of a newspaper publisher, and attempted to start another with Grace Brown, the ingénue in his latest show. Both women had reason to kill him—as did his own wife of 21 years and assorted boyfriends and husbands. In such a dark atmosphere of conflict and betrayal, even jokes can take on a nasty edge. When Torchy agrees at the end of the film to cover the Cleveland air races, Gahagan, wildly misunderstanding, blurts out, "But, chief, you ain't going to get married in the air, are you? It's dangerous!" "It's dangerous anywhere," McBride replies.

And yet marriage, for all its shortcomings, remains the biggest goal in these films. The marital status of characters is a frequent subject for discussion and evaluation. "Why don't you muzzle that girl—or marry her?" Capt. McTavish urges McBride in *Blondes at Work*. "I'm going to marry Hugo," Grace Brown tells McBride in *Adventurous Blonde*. "Are you a married man?" Hughie Sprague asks Gahagan in *Fly-Away Baby*. "Why don't you marry that guy?" city editor Maxie says to Torchy in *Smart Blonde*.

Although Torchy and McBride never quite get around to marrying, they expedite marriage for other couples: Fitz Mularkay and Dolly Ireland in *Smart Blonde*, Hugo Brand and Grace Brown in *Adventurous Blonde*, Maitland Greer and Louisa Revelle in *Blondes at Work*. Our protagonists root out the sources of murder and mayhem—from an adulterous spouse to a crooked business partner to an overprotective boyfriend—so that the married couple can be restored as the basic social unit, thereby enabling sexual reproduction and ensuring national survival. "Yes, indeed," Torchy exclaims in *Adventurous Blonde*, "it's going to take a wedding to make us forget all about this case," and proceeds to arrange for the magistrate, who has been waiting the whole film to marry her and McBride, to marry Hugo and Grace instead.

We may very easily overlook just how conventional Torchy is. Michel Foucault once wrote that the "success of power is proportional to its ability to hide its own mechanisms."[18] Torchy seems progressive, but actually serves traditional gender norms. Her function is camouflaged by her last-minute escapes from marriage, her masculine clothes, her brash manner. She regularly stands up to McBride and McTavish, as well as to her city editor and male reporters, and you find yourself admiring her courage and spunk. Then the irony of it hits you: all the while she has been talking like a champion of women's liberation, she has been quietly preparing another woman for the (sacrificial?) altar.

Chapter 17

The Kiss

The film often considered as the first and greatest screwball comedy, Frank Capra's *It Happened One Night* (1934), is a newspaper film.[1] Several other old newspaper films are now regarded as classic screwball comedies, among them *Mr. Deeds Goes to Town* (1936), *Nothing Sacred* (1937), and *His Girl Friday* (1940). Not surprisingly, then, the screwball genre left a mark on the Torchy Blane series.

Probably the screwball influence is most readily apparent in the goofiness of key supporting characters. Besides Gahagan, the subliterate police driver spouting homebrewed poetry, there is the desk sergeant, usually played by George Guhl. Guhl's character is so absentminded that sometimes he doesn't even recognize his own boss, Lt. Steve McBride.

The screwball influence is reflected as well in the brisk pace of the dialogue. Frank McDonald, who directed the first four Torchy films, attributed the success of the series to the machinegun-style delivery of Glenda Farrell—a remarkable 390 words a minute.[2] At such speed, almost anything could have passed for clever, but some of the repartee was genuinely amusing. When, for example, a police officer blocks Torchy from entering a murder room in *Smart Blonde*, she protests, "You don't understand. I'm from the *Herald*. I'm Torchy Blane." To which the cop replies, "I don't care if you're Flaming Youth. You can't go in there."

The incongruous relationship between Torchy and McBride provides the series with its deepest connection to screwball comedy. As Wes D. Gehrig, an expert on the genre, said, "Screwball comedy turns the American courtship system on its ear: the female leads the charge while the male holds back in the manner of the stereotyped weaker sex."[3] We have already seen in the previous chapter how

Torchy, during the finale of *Fly-Away Baby*, reverses traditional gender roles, handing McBride the bridal bouquet, but keeping the bonus check herself.

Like just about every other screwball couple, Torchy and McBride carry on a combative love affair, for the most part battling over a woman's place—which McBride believes to be at home with the children.[4] His position is often made to seem unreasonable, if not plain ridiculous. He can tell Torchy, as he does in *Blondes at Work*, "After we get married, you're gonna chuck your job on the newspaper and stay home where you belong," but that doesn't mean she must pay attention to him. In fact, she will coolly look him in the eye and say, "Listen, we've been over this a thousand times. I got ink in my blood and a nose for news that needs something besides powder."

The comedy in screwball comedy resides precisely in its subversion of male dominance, its put-down of machismo. Elizabeth Kendall, author of *The Runaway Bride: Hollywood Romantic Comedy of the 1930s*, noted that screwball comedy responded to Depression-era audiences' anger and frustration by "making a virtue of personality traits usually thought of as feminine—a moral subtlety, an unashamed belief in the validity of emotions."[5] It follows that the man of action—tough, laconic, repressed—was treated as more or less a jerk.

McBride is no exception. His attempts to exercise authority and control, particularly in the first four films of the series, are a source of raucous humor. In *Smart Blonde*, Gahagan is busy one day, so McBride decides to drive himself. Full of confidence in his ability, he gets behind the wheel while Torchy slides onto the seat beside him. The car won't start, and he soon begins to grimace and growl. "Works better," Torchy finally advises, "with the switch on."

Torchy also has a good deal of fun with McBride's dislike for public displays of affection. She coos and gurgles at him and calls him "Stevie" and other pet names just to see him wrinkle up in embarrassment. A scene from *Blondes at Work* illustrates her technique. They are sitting in a restaurant, the Press Cafe, bickering over who helps whom more on the job.

McBride: Maybe you're psychic enough to get your scoops without any tips from the inside.

Torchy: All right, and let's see if you're sleuth enough to crack cases without any leads from the outside.
McBride: Listen, from now on. . . .
Torchy: You go my way, and I go yours. Let's swing it. (She sticks out her hand, and he shakes it.)
McBride: All right, from now on when we're together, we talk about nothing except. . . .
Torchy: Love and kisses. Ahhhhh.
McBride (irritated): I wasn't going to say that!
Torchy: I know, but it's nice work if you can get it.

Joan Mellen, in *Big Bad Wolves*, her study of masculinity in American film, contended that "the most masculine man . . . has carried all along an essentially homosexual sensibility, as a person who can express his manhood fully and uninhibitedly solely through interaction with other men. Only weak men allow themselves to become entangled with women . . . heterosexual interaction feminizes, as if women and their ways were like a virus."[6] The Torchy films, or at least the first four of them, satirize this male fear and distrust of emotion. Yet the satire can go only so far before traditional patriarchal power avenges itself, with revenge taking the form—surprise!—of long, slow, wet kisses.

Although it is doubtful that sex owes its popularity to film, one might think it did from the comments of early twentieth-century observers. "For the first time in the history of the world," a New York newspaper reported in the teens, "it is possible to see what a kiss looks like. . . . Scientists say kisses are dangerous, but here everything is shown in startling directness. What the camera did not see did not exist. The real kiss is a revelation. The idea has unlimited possibilities."[7] Moral guardians warned that not only the content of films, but also the physical environment of theaters aroused sexual interest. Jane Addams found that in Chicago "the very darkness of the room . . . is an added attraction to many young people, for whom the space is filled with the glamor of love making."[8] Back rows became known as "lovers' lanes."[9]

When I was growing up in the sixties, certain films were designated as "makeout movies"—in my case, without any memorable effect. Years later, researchers are still trying to determine whether sex in films inspires imitative behavior on the part of viewers. A smaller but perhaps easier question is whether the cinematic kiss serves a special narrative function. In her book, *Creating the Couple*, Virginia Wright Wexman pointed out, "Hollywood's traditional stories of courtship and marriage have typically focused on the woman's resistance to romantic attachments; therefore, the kiss often represents a significant moment of change for her and documents her surrender to the erotic will of men. . . . Highlighted close-ups of the actress's face at such moments," Wexman added, "emphasize her pleasure and even relief in this abandonment of separation and independence."[10]

About half the Torchy films—*Smart Blonde*, *Blondes at Work*, *Torchy Blane in Panama*, and *Torchy Blane in Chinatown*—end with Torchy and McBride locked in a kiss. In *Torchy Blane in Panama* and *Torchy Blane in Chinatown*, the fifth and seventh films in the series, respectively, the kiss occurs after McBride rescues her at the last possible minute from violent death. "Oh, Skipper, you don't know how glad I am to see you," she says in *Torchy Blane in Panama* as she falls into his arms. The hard-boiled girl reporter who earlier had told him, "Why, you're so dumb that all our kids, if we had any, would probably turn out to be morons," has now softened into a believer in male authority.

But after they kiss, then what? One of their peculiarities as a couple is that they never seem terribly anxious to consummate their relationship. In the ninth and final film in the series, *Torchy Plays with Dynamite*, McBride tries to dodge all sexual contact, including even the mandatory kiss from Torchy for saving her life. "Nix, nix," he barks in his best tough-guy manner when she goes to give him a smooch.

If you compare the kisses in the Torchy films with, say, "The Kiss," the famous sculpture by Auguste Rodin, you begin to realize just how sexually immature Torchy and McBride are. Although mild by today's standards, "The Kiss" was greeted with shock in Rodin's time. Its exhibition in Brussels in 1887 provoked comments like "What! Make them naked. Who ever heard of such a thing? It's dreadful."[11] When Rodin sent "The Kiss" to the 1893 Chicago Exhibition, it was branded pornographic and placed in a private room with admission by special application only. As late as 1957, the sculpture was considered "too sexy" to appear on a poster planned for the London subway.[12]

Jacques de Caso and Patricia B. Sanders, coauthors of a critical study of Rodin, explained that in "The Kiss," Rodin's contemporaries were confronted with two nude people of their own era making love. The woman's leg slung over the man's was a traditional symbol of sexual intercourse; however, Rodin dared to use it without explicit mythological or allegorical references. For him, nudity represented untarnished, primal nature. The pretty interlacing of "The Kiss" was the prelude to "mankind's participation in the generative forces of the universe"—that is, a good fuck.[13]

Sometimes Torchy and McBride are also on the verge of screwing, but then work intervenes, apparently to their secret relief. Their evasion of marriage and procreation reflects a larger evasion of adult responsibility. Perhaps our protagonists, and American society with them, wanted to remain in a permanent state of adolescence, where sex is quick and uncomplicated—a kiss, a feel, a sudden and savage shudder down below.

Chapter 18

Criminal Behavior

When categorized by theme, the Torchy Blane films fall into two distinct groups. The films in the first group—*Smart Blonde*, *Fly-Away Baby*, and *Torchy Blane, the Adventurous Blonde*—follow with a certain relish Torchy's challenges to, and occasional triumphs over, entrenched male authority. The films in the second group—*Torchy Blane in Panama*, *Torchy Gets Her Man*, *Torchy Blane in Chinatown*, *Torchy Runs for Mayor*, and *Torchy Plays with Dynamite*—are later in the series and considerably more conservative. At times, they almost seem designed to teach Torchy lessons in feminine deportment.

The fourth Torchy film, *Blondes at Work*, can be seen in retrospect as the dividing line between the two groups. In it, Torchy flouts the Law of the Father, but instead of getting away with her bold behavior, as she had in previous films, here she is tracked down and punished. Incidentally, the title *Blondes at Work* is misleading. There is only one blonde at work in the film—Torchy.

From the very beginning of the series, her work rankled key male characters, including her boyfriend, police Lt. Steve McBride. "This rat hole is no place for a woman," he tells her in *Smart Blonde*, their first appearance together. "But I'm a newspaperwoman," she protests. "You just sit quiet," he replies crossly, "and maybe no one will notice it."

McBride has reason to be cross: Torchy's stunts and scoops keep him in constant trouble with his superiors. As early as *Torchy Blane, the Adventurous Blonde*, the third film in the series, Capt. McTavish lectures McBride on the subject of his bride-to-be.

McTavish: I hope you've induced her to give up her job.
McBride: Give up her job? Say, she'd rather give me up.

McTavish: I see. Then you won't mind if I ask her publisher to move her to the woman's page.
McBride: The woman's page? Why Maxie'd sue you. Say, what's the idea?
McTavish: Well, maybe police reporting isn't the right spot for a girl.
McBride: Torchy's done alright.
McTavish: With your help, yes. And that's the point, Steve. The other reporters are beefing.
McBride: Sure they are, 'cause Torchy's too smart for them.
McTavish: But the point is, with you married to Torchy, the boys are going to say she gets all the breaks.
McBride: Well, what do you want me to do, marry the boys?

Probably. Obsessive male friendships dot the history of American film: the cowboy and his sidekick, the gangster and his partner, the comic and his stooge. These friendships, feminist film scholar Joan Mellen said, "resemble the preadolescent bonding of young males who temporarily fear women and prefer each other's company. . . ."[1] She added that the depictions of grown men in schoolboy relationships—or in what literary critic Leslie Fiedler once called "asexual romances"—reinforce male identity.[2] But why should male identity need such frequent reinforcing?

At least one theory holds that a "crisis of gender" began with the Industrial Revolution. According to this theory, man's body as the primary tool for shaping the world has been rendered obsolete by machines, and distinctions between men, and between men and women, based on differences in physical strength have lost their significance.[3] "A 200-pound man," Arnold R. Beisser, psychiatrist and author, noted, "can easily lose a business encounter (symbolic combat) to a 130-pound man or to a 90-pound woman. Slender feminine fingers can push buttons on a computer as well as can thick, strong, male fingers, perhaps better. Machines are stronger than either men or women, and to the machine it makes no difference if its buttons are pushed hard or lightly."[4]

Each successive film in the Torchy series seems increasingly nostalgic for an era when masculinity was synonymous with dominance over women. By *Blondes at Work*, McTavish has reached the point of threatening to remove McBride as chief of the homicide squad unless he can control Torchy. "Don't have Torchy Blane headlining your hunches all over the *Star* front page . . . ," the captain orders in his dour Scottish accent. "All the sheets are squawking. Boyle of the *Express* wants to know if we're running the police department for the taxpayers or for Torchy Blane. . . . Why don't you muzzle that girl—or marry her?"

In earlier films, McBride's attempts to muzzle Torchy usually backfire. "You're a nice kid," he tells her in *Fly-Away Baby*, the second in the series, "but running down criminals is a man's job. It takes a masculine mind and years of experience to crack these cases. So why don't you just go back to your newspaper and write a nice little story about what the woman's clubs are doing to promote world peace, and I'll take you out to dinner." "OK, Skipper, you win," she says disingenuously. She is soon leading McBride on an around-the-world chase after a diabolical killer.

Blondes at Work punishes Torchy for all the previous occasions on which she has shown up men. Under pressure from McTavish, clearly representing the primal father and an older, harsher version of masculinity, McBride stops exchanging tips about police cases with her. For a while she manages to continue scooping the other reporters by sneaking looks at a diary that Gahagan, McBride's driver, keeps in his glove compartment. This further infuriates McTavish. "One of these days," he warns her, "you'll be reading the *Star* in jail!"

And he is proven correct. At the trial of Maitland Greer for murder, Torchy eavesdrops on the jury in private session, overhears their decision finding Greer guilty, and breaks the story in an extra before the verdict is announced in court. Outraged, the judge sentences her to jail for contempt. When McBride visits her a few days later in her cell, he says, "I hope this will be a lesson to you."

While addressed to Torchy, McBride's remark is intended, perhaps, for the audience as well. We have seen McBride threatened with demotion for sharing inside information with Torchy. We have seen Torchy pursued by the fury of the police for challenging male authority and control. We have seen Torchy hauled before a stern, old, patriarchal judge. We have seen Torchy sitting in jail. To me at least, the lesson is unmistakable: in a phallocentric culture, not having a penis can be a crime.

Chapter 19

Accept No Substitutes

Torchy Blane in Panama, the fifth film in the Torchy series, was the first without Glenda Farrell in the title role. She and her usual costar, Barton MacLane, had gone off to freelance at other studios after their contracts with Warners expired. Among the films in which Farrell starred during this period were two for Universal along Torchy lines.[1] In *Exposed* she played a magazine photographer named "Click" who teams up with a lawyer to fight racketeers, while in *Prison Break* she helped MacLane clear himself of a murder charge.[2]

For a time rumors flew that Anne Sheridan would replace Farrell as Torchy, but the role finally went to Lola Lane, one of the Lane sisters who were among Hollywood's top leading ladies in the thirties and forties.[3] Lane, whose real name was Dorothy Mulligan, was born in 1906 in Macy, Indiana, and grew up in Indianola, Iowa, where her guitar-playing father was a dentist. Vaudeville star and songwriter Gus Edwards discovered her singing in a flower shop in Des Moines. He changed her name to Lola Lane, and she toured the country with his production of *Ritz Carlton Nights*. A Fox talent scout later saw her in *War Song* on Broadway and gave her a screen test, leading to her first film, *Speakeasy*, in 1929.[4] This is the story of a woman reporter who falls for a boxing champ and proves his manager is crooked.

Paul Kelly took over the role of Torchy's boyfriend, police Lt. Steve McBride, from MacLane. Born in Brooklyn in 1899, Kelly began his show-business career at the age of eight, appearing on Broadway with David Warfield in *The Grand Army Man*. By the early 1920s, he was playing romantic leads on both stage and screen. Then, in 1927, scandal threw his life into disarray. He was arrested in the beating death of Ray Raymond, musical comedy star and husband of actress Dorothy McKaye. After a lurid trial in which his love affair with McKaye was exposed, Kelly was found guilty of manslaughter and sentenced to one to ten years in San Quentin. His only comment was, "I guess the jury said what they thought was right."[5]

Kelly served two years and one month before being paroled for excellent behavior. In 1933 he returned to the screen as square-dealing gangster Frank Rocci in *Broadway Thru a Keyhole*. There followed a long series of supporting roles in big budget productions and occasional leads in quickly forgotten "B" movies, including *Torchy Blane in Panama*.[6]

Contemporary reviewers accepted the cast changes in the Torchy series matter-of-factly, with *Variety*, for example, saying, "Lola Lane is more metallic than her predecessor and possibly a bit more vigorous. Between Paul Kelly and Barton MacLane there is not much choice."[7] Some seemed to even prefer the new Torchy and McBride to the old. Headlining its review, "Lane, Kelly Stand Out in Slim Story," the *Hollywood Reporter* noted, "Lola Lane injects plenty of verve and personality into the Torchy role. Paul Kelly, worthy of so much better material, takes over as the detective with skill, and the credibility he lends the part is a genuine tribute to his ability."[8]

The public had a different reaction to the replacements—shock. P.C.M., a reviewer for the *Motion Picture Herald* who saw the film at the Strand Theater in New York, reported back that a "small afternoon audience viewed the picture silently."[9] This was something of a portent. *Torchy Blane in Panama* turned out to be, in the words of Torchy scholars, a "total disappointment," a "dud."[10] Maybe the reason was the story, which the *New York Times* called "trite and obvious."[11] But more likely, Farrell and MacLane had become so identified with the roles of Torchy and McBride after four films that the public just couldn't accept anyone else as the girl reporter and her cop boyfriend.

Lane did manage a pretty good imitation of Farrell's supersonic speaking style, but she couldn't imitate Farrell's comic genius. Farrell had a way of cocking her head, widening her eyes, or jingling her voice that made every line she delivered a potential joke. Lane came off as too literal and intense to joke at all. The combative exchanges between Torchy and McBride, which had had a quality of play about them in the earlier films, now seemed downright nasty.

Consider a scene occurring midway through *Torchy Blane in Panama*. A New York bank has been robbed and a teller killed during a convention of the Loyal Order of Leopards. Torchy finds a lodge pin wedged in the teller's cage and theorizes that the robber is a member of the Los Angeles contingent, who are about to return home by boat via the Panama Canal. McBride disputes her theory—one review described him as "perhaps the dumbest detective officer in the films"—but takes the boat.[12] After Torchy catches up by parachuting into the ocean, she isn't much in the mood to banter with him.

McBride: Well, hello, Torchy. How did you get here?
Torchy: The stork brought me. I'm giving you one more chance. Start ducking. (McBride bobs and weaves around his cabin, but Torchy closes in and lands a right to his stomach.)
McBride: Umpfff! (He sits down hard on the bed, clutching his stomach and grimacing.)
Torchy: You thought you were fast enough to run away with my hypothesis.
McBride: Your what?
Torchy: Hypothesis. Hypothetically, I solved that Hayward Bank murder and holdup, and you said I was dreaming on my feet. When I tag the killer and send in my story, your name won't even be mentioned. (She storms out. McBride, still sitting on the bed holding his stomach, gulps.)

In the just-previous film in the series, *Blondes at Work*, Torchy had been sent to jail, ostensibly for contempt of court, but actually for violating cultural expectations for women. *Torchy Blane in Panama* continues this kind of "double voiced discourse."[13] Throughout the film, gender definitions are in flux, with Torchy appearing tough and aggressive, while McBride appears weak and confused. By the end, however, Torchy needs rescue—having fallen into the hands of the robber and his confederates—and McBride duly rescues her, thus restoring traditional gender roles.

How the rescue happens doesn't matter as much as that it does happen, and that similar rescues happen in the remaining Torchy films. Farrell and MacLane would return by popular demand to the next film in the series (and the next and the next), but the relationship between their characters had irrevocably shifted in *Torchy Blane in Panama*. Henceforth Torchy would be less potent. She would get herself into dangerous jams, depending on McBride's superior male strength and courage to get her out. Where once his excessive displays of machismo had been treated with tongue-in-cheek humor, they now would be presented straight. It was the idea of a strong, self-directed career woman—in 1938 a poll found that 80 percent of Americans opposed women's salaried work—that had become laughable.[14]

Chapter 20

Unequal Partners

Through nine films, reporter Torchy Blane and her boyfriend, police Lt. Steve McBride, carry on an unofficial and highly controversial detective partnership. One sign of its controversial nature is that their respective superiors are always trying to break it up. "Listen, Torchy," her city editor says in *Smart Blonde*, the first film in the series, "are you working for me or for Steve McBride?" Capt. McTavish, McBride's chief, asks him in *Blondes at Work*, the fourth film in the series, "Can't you lovebirds find something to bill and coo about besides murders and bank robberies?" When McBride replies by pointing out all the useful clues Torchy has uncovered, the Old Man seethes: "She shouldn't have to uncover anything for you. You're supposed to crack your own cases, without help from reporters or anyone else. If you can't do that, we'll put someone in charge of the squad who will."

Why so much resentment? What exactly is wrong with having a male–female detective partnership? For one thing, claimed Kathleen Gregory Klein, author of *The Woman Detective: Gender & Genre*, it isn't a partnership in the true sense. "The detective partnership story with its implied parity and cooperation," she said, "has been overwritten by the more familiar tale of female–male inequality and of male privilege and power contrasted with female limitations." She added that male–female detective partnerships are a kind of marriage, and that, as in conventional marriages, the "women relinquish their right to function separately and independently but receive little of value in return."[1]

Klein examined the woman detective in British and American fiction from, obviously, an ultrafeminist perspective. While some of what she found does apply to the Torchy films, more doesn't. To all appearances, Torchy, not McBride, is preeminent in their partnership. Contemporary reviewers often referred to his lack of detecting ability, especially as compared with her. G.M., reviewing *Fly-Away Baby* for the *Motion Picture Herald*, observed, "Two or three murders take place which McBride has a difficult time in trying to fathom and does so only when Torchy provides the leads and clues."[2] *Daily Variety* described him in the same film, the second in the series, as "a stooge who has his crimes solved for him by Torchy."[3]

McTavish seems to object to the Torchy–McBride partnership because it violates professional etiquette. "All the sheets are squawking," he tells McBride in *Blondes at Work*. "Boyle of the *Express* wants to know if we're running the police department for the taxpayers or for Torchy Blane." Despite similar statements throughout the series, McTavish actually objects to the partnership because it compromises the traditional definition of masculinity. A man isn't supposed to depend on a woman, but dominate her. As feminist film scholar Joan Mellen noted, masculinity has long been synonymous in American culture with control over others.[4]

A scene in *Smart Blonde* illustrates just how far McBride is from being a "real" man. While he stands behind his desk looking big and brawny, Torchy slouches nearby in a chair. Visually, she is in a subservient position, but the film soon undercuts McBride's apparent authority. "Ah, why don't you go home?" he asks with characteristic impatience. "There's nothing in the icebox," she answers. "And besides, I like the company." Deaf to this last, he picks up a fly swatter, takes careful aim at a fly buzzing around the room—and misses. "Nothing like a man of action," she quips.

The wisecrack reflects the precarious state of masculinity in the modern age. By the time of the first Torchy film, most American men lived in the impersonal mass society created by industrialization. "There was no longer opportunity for the bodily testing provided by rural life. . . ," historian T.J. Jackson Lears wrote. "There was only the diffuse fatigue produced by a day of office work."[5] The shift away from physical strength as a "ready affirmer of masculinity" coincided with a loss of personal control over much else.[6] Politics grew remote, escaping the influence of ordinary citizens. People's livelihoods depended increasingly on huge, bureaucratic corporations. Sprawling cities induced feelings of impotence and disorientation in their inhabitants.[7]

Viewed against this backdrop, Torchy becomes less a character in her own right and more a vehicle for resolving the identity crisis of the modern male. In *Torchy Blane in Chinatown*, the seventh film in the series, McTavish challenges McBride's masculinity by saying, "What are you, a mouse or a detective? Three days you've been on this case, and you haven't even got a suspect." The very next scene finds McBride full of masculine bravado. "I know, I know," he razzes Torchy, "you're smarter than the whole police department. You got a hunch about who killed Fitzhugh. Well, I can't use any of your hunches today. So you just run along, and if you're a nice little girl, I might give you a big story break tonight." For McBride, the mystery isn't primarily who killed Fitzhugh and why; it is how to be a man.

Masculinity was defined from the beginning of the series in conservative, or patriarchal, terms. The early reviewers who described Torchy as the lead detective overlooked the fact that McBride usually got to sum up. At the end of *Smart Blonde*—and again at the end of *Fly-Away Baby* and *Blondes at Work*—McBride delivers the official recap of who did what to whom: "Friel planned the whole thing. He wrote to Marci Corson in Boston and told her to come here and pose as his sister," etc. Torchy may solve the cases, but only McBride, as a male representative of male law, an establishment figure, is entitled to explain them.[8]

Other oddities and inconsistencies arise. Among the more intriguing is that Torchy calls McBride "Skipper" and *means it.* Sure, she competes with him for clues. Sure, she steals his badge to impersonate a cop. And sure, sometimes she even doubts his intelligence. But through it all, she continues to refer to him as "Skipper," acknowledging his superior authority, and not just in their detective partnership. She uses the term to signal submission in their personal relations, too. Listen as they ride in the back seat of a police car in *Smart Blonde*.

McBride (putting an arm around Torchy): Ah, you're aces with me, kid. . . . I ought to be hung for slamming you around the way I have.

Torchy (melting): Skipper.

McBride: Yeah, from now on the rough stuff is out as far as you're concerned. I'm going to treat you right.

Torchy (melted): Ohhhhh, Skipper. (She cuddles against his shoulder.)

The tendency to build up McBride at the expense of Torchy is particularly apparent in the last three films in the series to star Glenda Farrell: *Torchy Gets Her Man*, *Torchy Blane in Chinatown*, and *Torchy Runs for Mayor*. In *Torchy Gets Her Man*, Gilbert, a secret service agent, asks McBride's help in capturing a counterfeiter known as "Hundred Dollar Bill" Bailey. McTavish orders McBride not to breathe a word of the investigation to Torchy, and he obeys right off—in itself a change from earlier films. Gahagan, McBride's driver, is under the same ban and even composes a poem—of sorts—about it: "McTavish is a Scotsman / McBride and me are Micks / If I talk to Torchy / They'll send me to the sticks."

The hush-hush atmosphere only inflames Torchy's curiosity. One night she tails Gilbert's car, but he loses her by switching a detour sign, whereupon she drives full speed into a creek. This spectacle of humiliation never would have occurred when the series was first getting under way and Torchy was, by all estimations (including her own), the best "newspaperman" in town.

Later in the film, with the aid of Gahagan and a police dog named Blitzen, she follows Gilbert once again. This time she winds up at a remote house in the country, where she and Gahagan are taken captive. Gilbert himself turns out to be the counterfeiter Bailey. He ridicules McBride as both a man and a detective for failing to see through his ruse. "Don't misunderstand me, Miss Blane," he says. "I can understand your affection for him. But you must admit his appeal is brawn rather than brains."

The stage is now set for McBride to demonstrate his masculinity. He arrives just before a time bomb is due to go off and rescues Torchy and Gahagan. "What was that crack about brains and brawn?" Torchy taunts Bailey, whose whole gang has been rounded up. McBride then explains in tedious detail how he solved the case while Torchy clings to his arm and beams up at him. All the old questions about his competence suddenly have been erased.

Production of *Torchy Gets Her Man* ended August 16, 1938. Production of *Torchy Blane in Chinatown* began the following day. "Purpose in rushing the second picture into work," the *Hollywood Reporter* said, "is to retain the cast which worked in first pic for sequel."[9]

Not only was the cast retained, but so was the emphasis on strengthening McBride's masculine image, largely by marginalizing Torchy. Even that dodo Gahagan gets to exercise authority over her.

As the film opens, he is guarding the door to McTavish's office, with strict orders from the captain to keep Torchy out. She soon shows up and snaps, "Step aside, Gahagan, and let a lady in." "Oh, quit kidding, Torchy," he says. "You ain't no lady. You're a reporter." In similar situations in *Fly-Away Baby*, *Torchy Blane, the Adventurous Blonde* and *Blondes at Work*, she had quickly and completely outmaneuvered him. Here he can't be budged.

Torchy Blane in Chinatown was directed by William Beaudine. One of the most prolific directors in Hollywood history, Beaudine also directed *Torchy Gets Her Man*. Wheeler W. Dixon, in *The "B" Directors*, described Beaudine's directorial style as "monotonal, detached"—the camera "simply gazes at the actors in somnolent stupefaction."[10] The *Hollywood Reporter* called his direction of *Torchy Blane in Chinatown*—which, incidentally, had nothing to do with Chinatown except for some stock shots behind the opening credits—"unbelievable in its old-fashioned technique."[11]

The film nonetheless features probably the most inspired moment in the entire series. Even if Farrell was responsible for it, Beaudine at least had the grace not to interfere. McBride and Gahagan have been sent to the Adventurers Club, three members having received death threats after smuggling jade tablets into the country for Sen. Baldwin, an art collector. Torchy paces the sidewalk outside the club—back and forth, back and forth—a hungry reporter on the prowl. During her pacing, she happens to glimpse her reflection in the rear windshield of a parked car. She immediately stops and checks her hair and makeup in the glass. Although a brief, wordless, seemingly gratuitous gesture, it suggests how feminine she has become, how completely she has transformed into (and sees herself as) a decorative object, a collectible.

Her status as a sexual prize is made explicit at the end of the film. Thieves have taken the jade tablets and demand that Dick Staunton, the wealthy fiancé of Baldwin's daughter, deliver a $250,000 ransom to the last buoy in New York Harbor. Instead, McBride surprises them in a borrowed Navy submarine. "This just about makes you tops in cops, Skipper," says an adoring Torchy, who has come along for the arrests.

McBride: You mean that, Torchy?
Torchy: If you don't believe me, read the *Star*. It'll be all over the front page in an hour.

McBride: Nice work. (He goes to kiss her.)
Torchy: Ah, ah. . . . The whole crew's watching.
McBride: I don't care if the whole fleet is in. (They kiss.)
Torchy: Oh, Skipper, I'm dizzy.
McBride: That's nothing new. (He picks her up and carries her off.)[12]

Torchy Runs for Mayor was the eighth Torchy film and the last featuring Glenda Farrell.[13] Contemporary critics liked it—some quite a lot. The *Motion Picture Herald*, for example, raved, "As swift and actionful as its predecessors, or more so, this edition of the continuing adventures of the girl reporter and the plainclothes man contains just about all of the excitement that can coherently be packed into an hour of screen time."[14] Both Michael R. Pitts, author of *Famous Movie Detectives*, and Elizabeth Dalton, author of "Meet Torchy Blane," an article from 1972, were of the opinion that it "may well be the best film in the series."[15]

In actual fact, *Torchy Runs for Mayor* merely completes the masculinization of McBride and the simultaneous refeminization of Torchy that had begun three or four films earlier, with *Torchy Blane in Panama* or even *Blondes at Work*. The plot follows a by-now-familiar pattern: Torchy scents a hot story; the police and others warn her off; she persists despite their warnings; her headstrong behavior puts her life in danger; McBride comes to the rescue.

Variety said in its review that Barton MacLane, playing McBride, was "as credibly masculine as ever"—this from a publication that had once described the chief of homicide as "a soft-hearted dick who is kicked around by his newspaper sweetie."[16] But if McBride wasn't your typical action hero in past films, he finally fills the role here, defeating evil with his manly fists. And what does Torchy do while McBride pummels Dr. Dolan, the criminal mastermind who kidnapped her, murdered a crusading newspaper editor, and corrupted city government? Why, she watches the fight wide-eyed, the back of her wrist to the big, dark "O" of her mouth. She is the very image of female weakness and passivity.

Appropriately enough for a film restoring the old definitions of manhood and womanhood, *Torchy Runs for Mayor* culminates with talk of marriage and babies. Torchy has been elected mayor on a "Make-city-safe-for-babies" platform. At a ceremony following her election, a news photographer says, "Please, your honor, I'd like a picture of you holding this baby. After all, that was your campaign. . . . This baby's named after you—Torchy Blane McGee." Torchy takes the baby into her arms, instantly turning soft and maternal. "Oh, Steve," she blurts, "I don't want to be mayor. I want to get married." Her words go out over the radio. Alarmed, she asks, "Oh, Steve, what did I say?" "Just what you should've said," he replies. "Come on, let's get out of here." And they do. Gahagan is left holding the baby, and the audience is left holding the bag.

Chapter 21

Anything for a Story

Newspaper films have often been blamed for the public's low opinion of the press. "What's the source of those loathsome misconceptions that journalists are hard-drinking, foul-mouthed, dim-witted social misfits concerned only with twisting the truth into scandal and otherwise devoid of conscience, respect for basic human dignity or a healthy fear of God?" asked Chip Rowe in a 1992 article, answering himself: "Hollywood. . . . Tinseltown has tightened the screws on reporters for more than 50 years with hundreds of negative film portrayals. Small wonder," he added, "that opinion polls consistently rate journalists less respected than bankers, lawyers or even members of Congress."[1]

Complaints from journalists that they were "characterized as inebriated or unscrupulous" led the Motion Picture Association in 1947 to conduct a survey of films with the intention of proving that Hollywood wasn't doing the press wrong. The survey found that out of a total of 398 films approved in 1945 by the Production Code Administration—more widely known as the Hays Office—journalists appeared in 77. Of the 81 journalists in the 77 films, 67 were portrayed sympathetically, 5 unsympathetically, and 9 neutrally. The breakdown for 1946 was similar: 70 journalists were portrayed sympathetically, 7 unsympathetically, and 40 neutrally.[2]

Despite these reassuring numbers, the film industry continued to provoke journalistic anger and distrust. In 1986 the Los Angeles chapter of the Society of Professional Journalists became so concerned about journalism's public image after a cycle of negative films that it established "Operation Watchdog," aimed at "leading creative people in the right direction" when portraying journalists.[3] More recently, *Washington Journalism Review* and *Columbia Jour-*

nalism Review published articles—titled, respectively, "Hacks on Film" and "Where Have All the Heroes Gone?"—denouncing Hollywood for increasingly representing journalists as bastards or boobs or both.[4]

Not that novels or television shows have portrayed journalists any better. After examining 50 contemporary novels with journalist protagonists, Jay Black of the University of South Florida–St. Petersburg concluded: "The image created by this body of literature is that journalism is largely an amoral enterprise. . . . Occasionally in the fiction, the journalist of principle, motivated by virtue and a sense of duty, appears. . . . Far more typical is the portrait of the journalist as having more than a touch of sleaze."[5]

Although newspaper reporters are second only to police officers in how often they appear as characters on prime-time television, they rarely play the hero. A mere 24 percent of the reporters are shown favorably, according to one study. Most are depicted as unethical, sloppy, insensitive, and foolish.[6] "They diligently avoid letting the facts get in the way of good stories," Gene Goodwin and Ron F. Smith summed up, "and then run back to their newsrooms to tell gleeful editors about their big scoops."[7]

The relationship between fictional portrayals of journalists and the general reader or viewer has been interpreted in one of two ways. First, some journalists and journalism scholars contend that the public derives many of its notions about the press from novels, television shows, and/or films. Writing in the *Bulletin of the American Society of Newspaper Editors*, Walker Lundy, executive editor of the *Tallahassee Democrat*, observed, "Over the years, we've done a decent job of reporting on everyone's business but our own. Most people get their impressions of us from Hollywood."[8] Professor Black made a similar remark about journalism novels. "Millions of readers who are interested in journalism but who have limited first-hand experience with how the profession operates," he said, "have probably formed distorted opinions about the field if their primary exposure is through these books."[9]

The second interpretation argues that popular entertainment doesn't put things into the public mind so much as express what is already there. Thus Christopher Hanson, Washington correspondent for the *Seattle Post-Intelligencer*, wrote in 1996 that "Hollywood is less concerned with the accuracy of a character than with its fidelity to the mood of the times and its box-office potential." To explain the latest round of negative film portrayals of journalists, he quoted John Katzenbach, a former reporter who has had two novels made into films, as saying, "Because of the explosion of tabloid TV, tabloid journalism, and the mob approach to reporting, the journalist is seen as a ghoul. . . . Hollywood always reflects sooner or later the public feelings—all those polls showing that newspaper reporters rank down there with dentists and serial killers."[10]

My own sense is that the act of watching a film is far more complex and contradictory than the journalists who have protested Hollywood's treatment of journalism have ever allowed. They have claimed that newspaper films dictate what the public thinks, or else that the public dictates what newspaper films show. Maybe, though, there is a space between films and their audiences in which the unpredictable can happen. As Judith Mayne pointed out in her 1993 book, *Cinema and Spectatorship*, the narrative codes of films aren't meaningful unless certain positions are taken up by viewers, but we can't assume that viewers will take up these positions, or that if the positions are taken up, that they will be taken up without resistance or personal variations.[11]

Moreover, meaning is partly a matter of historical context, depending on the discourses and interpretive strategies available at different periods.[12] Today journalists and scholars look back on the 1930s as the golden age of newspaper films, a time when reporters were portrayed as truth seekers—"gruff and hard-bitten yet unwilling to yield to cynicism, intolerant of bullies and crooks and always ready to fight for the right."[13] In a *New York Times* article headlined "Stop the Presses! Movies Blast Media, Viewers Cheer," Glenn Garelik lamented that this image has faded away. "The wisecracking of earlier reporters," he said, "has become arrogance, and reporters who had been shown as the working-class enemies of pretension are now seen as pretentious themselves."[14]

Newspaper films were more numerous in the late twenties and early thirties than ever before or since. But only nostalgia has made the fast-talking, alcohol-fueled reporters in such films as *Big News* (1929), *The Front Page* (1931), and *Hi, Nellie!* (1934) seem "fun-loving, blue-collar, salt-of-the-earth types."[15] Sixty years or so ago, when the films were originally released, journalists weren't flattered by them. In fact, one film-trade paper commented that the "average Horace Greeley resented the manner in which newspaper life was Hollywood handled."[16]

And what the average Horace Greeley resented most were the doubts the films raised about newspaper ethics. Newspapers were already under fire from other quarters. Throughout the twenties, progressives had been attacking the press for its growing commercialism, while conservatives had been attacking it for its growing sensationalism.[17] Everything wrong with the press was symbolized to both groups by the tabloid.

The first tabloid, the *New York Daily News*, appeared on newsstands on the morning of June 25, 1919, two days before the signing of the Treaty of Versailles officially ended World War I. The *News* looked streamlined and jazzy compared to the traditional eight-column newspaper, and was packed with photographs, scareheads, and short, easy-to-read stories on sensational subjects. In 1924 its circulation hit 750,000, the largest circulation for any newspaper in the nation, and climbed to 1.32 million in 1929.[18] Imitators sprang up—the *New York Mirror*, the *New York Graphic*—and also found readers. Attempting to explain the tabloid phenomenon, Silas Bent, perhaps the foremost press critic of the era, wrote, "Ours is a restless populace handcuffed to a mechanical monotony and ever atiptoe for another thrill. In a channel swimmer, a bathing beauty, a tennis player, a pugilist, a motion picture star, it may find vicarious escape from the commonplace of machinery; and the newspaper undertakes profitably to provide the escape."[19]

Torchy Blane worked in her films for a tabloid, or at least a tabloid-style paper. By the late twenties most of the press had been, as Bent put it, "tarred with the stick of the tabloid, tarred with its pictures, its format, its headlines, its sensationalism, its rowdyism, its meddlesomeness."[20] That this was so became particularly obvious with the coverage of the kidnapping of the Lindbergh baby in 1932. Even the older, established papers devoted pages to the story day after day and ballyhooed their own lame attempts to help locate the baby and his kidnappers.[21] Before all the noise died down *Literary Digest* would be prompted to ask, "Has the Press Hampered the Search for the Lindbergh Baby?"[22]

Embarrassing questions were still being asked about the press when the Torchy films began to reach the screen a few years later. The American Society of Newspaper Editors responded by passing the following resolution at its annual convention in 1938:

> We call upon all editors to recognize a growing criticism, to face it fairly, to set their houses in order, to be governed by good taste,

> by a sense of justice, by a complete devotion to the public interest, and to toil unceasingly to educate our readers to such a sense of the value of a free press in America that the citizens of this republic shall become willing co-operators, fellow warriors, in a never-ceasing fight for the maintenance of democratic institutions.[23]

Of course, these stirring words did about as much actual good for newspaper ethics as did one racy blonde with a press pass and a smart mouth.

Torchy Blane, the Unethical Blonde

Torchy faces a wide variety of ethical dilemmas over the course of her nine films. Well, maybe she doesn't exactly face them. It is more like she plows right through them without ever realizing that they are ethical dilemmas at all.

Gene Goodwin and Ron F. Smith, authors of *Groping for Ethics in Journalism*, use the term "foraging for news" to describe ethically questionable methods of newsgathering.[24] Torchy doesn't hesitate to forage for news—to lie, cheat, steal, eavesdrop, impersonate, and break and enter. If forced to justify her actions, she may cite the public's right to know. "Listen, big boy," she says to her city editor in *Torchy Gets Her Man*, "they're not going to muzzle me. I'm a newspaperwoman with a set of old-fashioned morals and ethics that tell me I have an obligation to my readers."

Torchy is a utilitarian as well as a newspaperwoman, though she doesn't know it. Utilitarianism, propounded in the nineteenth century by British philosophers Jeremy Bentham and John Stuart Mill, has been roughly defined as "promoting the greatest good for the greatest number." Under this principle, it may be considered ethical to harm one person for the benefit of the many. Thus an investigative story may hurt the subject of the investigation, but if crime and corruption are exposed, the general welfare advanced, then the story is justifiable.[25]

Utilitarianism is an ethical view well rooted in American society.[26] It is also a view that, taken to extremes, "presents difficulties."[27] And some supposedly responsible journalists have taken it to extremes, arguing that the importance of a story can justify the use of deception in obtaining the story. "It's the small crime versus the greater good," said Don Hewitt, executive producer of *60 Minutes*, a TV newsmagazine known for its undercover reporting. "If you catch someone violating 'thou shall not steal' by your [violation of] 'thou shall not lie,' that's a pretty good trade-off."[28]

The Torchy films sometimes point up the inconsistent way in which the press approaches ethics—lying to get at the truth, breaking laws to trap lawbreakers, and so on. When, in *Torchy Blane in Chinatown*, Torchy is found snooping around outside Sen. Baldwin's house, he asks detectives McBride and Gahagan, "Who is she, a burglar you know?" "No," replies Gahagan, "she's a newspaperwoman." To which McBride wryly adds, "Well, it's practically the same thing."

Such digs notwithstanding, the films usually display no more ethical sense than Torchy herself, who hardly gives ethics a second thought. In *Fly-Away Baby*, she breaks into a hotel room to search for missing jewels. In *Torchy Blane, the Adventurous Blonde*, she steals McBride's badge and uses it to impersonate a police officer. In *Blondes at Work*, she sneaks looks at Gahagan's secret diary. In *Torchy Blane in Chinatown*, she poses as the widow of a murder victim to gain entrance to his funeral. In *Torchy Runs for Mayor*, she wiretaps the mayor's office. There is more and even worse, but the films treat it all matter-of-factly, even showing a certain admiration for Torchy's cunning and coolness.

This routine acceptance of sensational newsgathering techniques reflects the journalism of the era. The thirties were the heyday for undercover newspaper reporting, "perhaps," as Goodwin and Smith noted, "because most cities had two or more papers battling for dwindling Depression dollars."[29] Undercover reports figured prominently in the collections of the best news stories of the year that journalism historian Frank Luther Mott had begun to publish. The 1934 collection, for example, included an exposé of the Drake estate swindlers by a *Milwaukee Journal* reporter posing as a prospective investor and a story by an *Omaha World-Herald* reporter who dressed up as a tramp to spend a night in a shelter for homeless men.[30]

If the Torchy films ever seemed exercised over any ethical issue, it was the growing dominance of business in journalism. Progressives had been warning about the social menace of an increasingly commercial press since at least 1920, when Upton Sinclair raged,

"The Brass Check is found . . . in your pay envelope each week . . . the price of your shame—you who take the fair body of truth and sell it in the market-place, who betray the virgin hopes of mankind into the loathsome brothel of Big Business."[31] The 1929 stock market crash and the Depression only heightened suspicions that businessmen couldn't be trusted to protect the public interest. Around the time Torchy was debuting, in 1937, Leo C. Rosten continued the attack on commercialization in his book, *The Washington Correspondents*. "Newspapers," he wrote, "get the reporters they deserve, and the public gets what the publishers make possible."[32]

In the Torchy films, reporters are portrayed as charming rogues and the city editor as a frantic, overworked drudge, but publishers are—with the exception of old Col. Higgam in *Fly-Away Baby* and Hogarth Ward in *Torchy Runs for Mayor*—little more than colostomy bags. Higgam, who opposes Torchy's joining other reporters in an around-the-world air race, represents the journalistic conscience. "As publisher of the *Herald*," he says, "I've always insisted that people want to read news. At best, this idea of yours is merely a publicity stunt."

By the next film in the series, *Torchy Blane, the Adventurous Blonde*, moral leadership has shifted away from the publisher's office. Mortimer Gray, the publisher of the *Globe*, a rival paper, is revealed as a murderer. When Torchy exposes him, he only adds to his disgrace by attempting suicide.

Professor Black, in his study of recent journalism novels, remarked that the "occasional journalists of principle . . . usually are seen in conflict with their own managements."[33] He never explores the implications of this or whether film portrayals are similar. Had he looked at films, he might have discovered that Torchy has her share of collisions with newsroom authorities. The most frequent and extensive of such conflicts occur in *Torchy Runs for Mayor*, the eighth film in the series and the last with Glenda Farrell.

As the film opens, Torchy is in the midst of a crusade against the evil Dr. Dolan. "City Controlled by Dr. Dolan / Mayor Takes Orders," shouts the headline over one of her stories, while others declare, "Dolan Machine Orders Shakeup" and "Boss Dolan Protects Underworld." Torchy uses questionable methods to gather these stories, from wiretapping the mayor's office to breaking into Dolan's house and stealing a "little red book" in which he records his payoffs. McBride criticizes her underhandedness, saying,

"There's some things that even a newspaper reporter can't get away with."

But *Torchy Runs for Mayor* saves its sharpest criticism for publishers. William Allen White, an editor and publisher himself, once complained, "Too often the publisher . . . is a rich man seeking power and prestige. He has the country club complex . . . and the unconscious arrogance of conscious wealth. Therefore, it is hard to get a modern American newspaper to go the distance necessary to print all the news about many topics."[34] The film supports White's description. In a move designed to silence Torchy, Dolan organizes an advertising boycott of her paper. This spooks the publisher, no longer Col. Higgam, but a Mr. Skinner, sporting the slicked-back hair and pencil-thin moustache of the shyster lawyers, lounge lizards, and other moral bankrupts of thirties films. "Call her off, call her off quick," Skinner orders the city editor, and adds, "Reserve space for a two-column editorial. We're going to have to retract what we've printed as gracefully as we can."

Flashing anger and defiance, Torchy offers her latest exposé of Dolan to the opposition dailies. One publisher says, "No paper would dare print a story like this. I certainly wouldn't." Another says, "You think I want to get shot?" Still another says, "OK, I'll buy it, but I can't print it now." Torchy rips the story out of his hands.

She finally does get it printed—in a little weekly paper, the *South End Blotter*, run by Hogarth Ward. From our first glimpse of Ward, we know he is different from all the other publishers we have seen. Instead of a business suit, he wears a long leather apron, and instead of sitting behind a desk, he stands at the typecase. His pose and attire suggest an older, heroic kind of journalism. And, indeed, when Torchy pitches her story to him, she invokes the name of one of the great editor-publishers of the nineteenth century. "Opportunity is staring you in the face," she says. "I'm holding it here in my hand. The power of the press, Mr. Ward. . . . Listen, if Horace Greeley was standing there in your shoes, if the institutions that he loved were being threatened by corruption, if there were cries for a deliverer, would he speak of limitations? Oh, he would not. He'd start setting type as if his life depended on it."

Torchy might have been referring in the above speech to more than local gangsterism, or at least contemporary audiences might have interpreted her as referring to more—for example, to the darkening international scene. By now, fascists had overrun a big chunk of the world—Ethiopia, China, Czechoslovakia, Austria, Spain—and were making menacing gestures toward the rest. The same month *Torchy Runs for Mayor* was released, May 1939, the Nazi press in Berlin charged the abuse of Germans in Poland.[35] Four months later, the German high command would announce that the conquest of Poland was complete.

As a general European war approached, Americans debated what role, if any, they should play in the conflict. In his 1939 book, *Not Peace But a Sword*, journalist Vincent Sheean predicted that "it will be very hard for us in the New World to look at the inevitable struggle with indifference, going busily about our immediate individual affairs. . . . Interest and emotion alike will propel us into action, and in all probability we shall save [the Old World] again as we did in 1918."[36] Perhaps Gahagan's malapropism in the following exchange, set in the office of the *Blotter*, was humorous to audiences of the time partly because it was politically pertinent.

> **Torchy:** I can depend on you? You won't let me down?
> **Ward:** Oh, I won't. I've been to jail six times for printing the truth, and I'm willing to go a seventh for a girl with. . . .
> **Gahagan:** International fortitude.

Of course, the main focus of *Torchy Runs for Mayor* wasn't America's future role on the world stage. If the film appeared to be about anything in particular, it was the timidity and irresponsibility of the commercial press. For Hollywood to have ever criticized the press for low standards may seem hypocritical, since Hollywood itself has put entertainment and escape above art, and profits above all. But what seems like simple hypocrisy was actually ideological complexity.

By attacking the influence of advertisers and the big-money interests on the press, the film disguised its own origins in finance capitalism and acquired a populist aura it didn't deserve. Wall Street investment houses became involved early on in the affairs of Hollywood. The Morgan and Rockefeller banking groups, for example, largely financed the conversion to sound. When film studios went into receivership during the Depression, these bankers took over management of the distressed companies.[37]

Torchy Runs for Mayor, then, was conservative while seeming progressive. On the narrative level, it combined elements of the gangster film, the newspaper film, and the social exposé, three popular genres closely identified with Warner Brothers in the first half of the 1930s.[38] But on the ideological level, its critique of newspaper ethics functioned less as exposé and more as mystification, a way to conceal the fact that the various branches of the culture industry—newspapers, radio, film, etc.—were "similar in structure or at least fit into each other, ordering themselves into a system almost without a gap."[39]

Well-meaning people often talk about how wonderful the mass media might be. They talk about First Amendment freedoms and the press living up to its social responsibilities. They talk about film as *the* modern art. They talk about making television less commercial and more educational. I would like to believe it. I would like to believe that the media were capable of serving democracy rather than themselves and "blind, opaque authority."[40] I would like to end with an optimistic anecdote about the media being dedicated to promoting truth and beauty, but I don't think I know one.

Chapter 22

In Black and White

Writing in the *Journal of Negro Education* in 1944, L.D. Reddick noted that there were nineteen basic stereotypes of blacks in America, all of which "supplement each other, though they are sometimes mutually contradictory." The stereotypes identified by Reddick were:[1]

1. The savage African
2. The happy slave
3. The devoted servant
4. The corrupt politician
5. The irresponsible citizen
6. The petty thief
7. The social delinquent
8. The vicious criminal
9. The sexual superman
10. The superior athlete
11. The unhappy non-white
12. The naturalborn cook
13. The naturalborn musician
14. The perfect entertainer
15. The superstitious churchgoer
16. The chicken and watermelon eater
17. The razor and knife "toter"
18. The uninhibited expressionist
19. The mental inferior

Film reflected these stereotypes and reinforced them in viewers, generation after generation. In fact, Reddick asserted that "no religious or racial minority is so consistently slandered [by Hollywood] as the Negro."[2]

The handful of blacks who eventually achieved some measure of film fame resented the demeaning roles they were forced to play, but were still glad for the work, particularly during the Depression.[3] Hattie McDaniel, who won an Oscar for her portrayal of "Mammy" in 1939's *Gone with the Wind*, the first ever awarded to a black, said, "The only choice permitted us is either to be servants for $7 a week or portray them for $700 a week."[4]

Most blacks on Hollywood sound stages were extras or bit players. Three appear as Redcaps in *Smart Blonde*, the first Torchy Blane film. Police Lt. Steve McBride traces Dolly Ireland, a singer at the Million Club and a murder suspect, to Union Station. "Any of you boys remember carrying a black patent leather bag for a lady?" he asks. "Had the initials D.I. on it." "Nope," says the Redcap on the right, but the Redcap in the middle, played by Fred "Snowflake" Toones, drawls, "Yeaaah, sur, I's remmmburrr seeeing a black bag. I's puts the ladeee on the Twilight Flyer." "Thanks, George," the lieutenant says and slips him a coin. "Thank you, sur!" "Snowflake" replies with exaggerated gratitude.

This scene conforms to how blacks, and the black man in particular, had traditionally been portrayed. "He is the clown," Reddick pointed out, "but seldom a magnificent clown; a buffoon; a butt of jokes, not the projector of them, except against himself."[5] That the creators of Torchy could only envision blacks in racist terms raises doubts about their view of other underprivileged groups, including women. Recent critics have contended that Torchy was a progressive figure who "represented her sex well in the 'B' detective films of the 1930s."[6] And yet a film series that would exploit the stereotype of the slow-talking, head-scratching "coon" for laughs seems unlikely to have been far advanced in any of its social attitudes.

The racism inherent in the brief scene with the Redcaps is glaringly obvious today. What isn't so obvious is the racism implied by the total absence of blacks from seven of the eight remaining Torchy films. Thomas Cripps, a historian of blacks in Hollywood, once asserted, "Those [1930s] movies that spoke to an urban sensibility"—gangster movies, prison yarns, newspaper pictures—"tamed the facts of the Depression with a cleverness, flippancy, and social optimism free enough of the old racial language to allow greater freedom for blacks. In no sense revolutionary. . . , the urban vista merely tolerated greater racial variety and imposed no Southern party line on ideas."[7] The Torchy films, though, don't bear Cripps out. Despite their urban milieu, the films contain only one other black character besides the Redcaps: a female prison inmate who attacks Torchy with a pair of shears in *Torchy Plays with Dynamite*, the last entry in the series. There isn't even a black stereotype in the rest of the films—not a black cook or black doorkeeper or black taxi driver; not a black shoeshine boy or black musician or black maid. Torchy inhabits a white world, even a white-on-white world.

In 1947, a full decade after Torchy was introduced, Ralph Ellison would use invisibility as a metaphor for black oppression in his novel, *Invisible Man*. "I am an invisible man," he wrote. "No, I am not a spook like those who haunted Edgar Allan Poe; nor am I one of your Hollywood-movie ectoplasms. . . . I am invisible, understand, simply because people refuse to see me."[8] The Torchy films refused to see blacks—excluded them, obliterated them, rendered them invisible. What was even worse, perhaps, was that no one seems to have missed them until now.

Chapter 23

Flameout

The ninth and last film in the Torchy Blane series was produced under one title, *Torchy—Dead or Alive*, and released under another, *Torchy Plays with Dynamite*.[1] Warner Brothers recommended that exhibitors publicize the film with a stunt based on the new, catchier title: "Snipe signs around excavations or on steam shovels. Attract your ready-made audience with sheets reading 'Danger! These men are playing with dynamite! See how "Torchy Plays with Dynamite" at the Strand.' "[2] But though the change in title was chiefly a publicity move, it was also symbolic of the numerous identity switches within the film itself.

For starters, Glenda Farrell and Barton MacLane were replaced in the lead roles for the second time in the series.[3] Jane Wyman became Torchy, and Allen Jenkins became her boyfriend, detective Lt. Steve McBride. Wyman had had a small part as Dixie, a hatcheck girl, in *Smart Blonde*, the first Torchy film. Looking back as a star on her film work in the late thirties, she would recall: "[I was earning] $68 a week after taxes and scared each time my contract came up for renewal that I'd be dropped. I didn't blame anybody but myself for my slow progress. I thank Bryan Foy, who was in charge of the B-unit [at Warners], for keeping me busy."[4] *Torchy Plays with Dynamite*, in the words of one of her biographers, "seemed to be a promotion of sorts."[5]

Jenkins built a long and successful screen career—he appeared in more than 175 films—around his being typecast as a likable roughneck. He affected a side-of-the-mouth, Brooklynese accent in his portrayals of bumbling gangsters, thick-headed cops, and delightfully irresponsible newspapermen. His last film was Billy Wilder's 1974 remake of *The Front Page*. He had acted in the original stage version many years before.[6]

The teaming of Wyman and Jenkins drew mixed reviews. *Variety* claimed, "Pair work smoothly together," but the *Hollywood Reporter* said, "It is impossible at any time to believe that a pretty and smart young girl like Jane Wyman could possibly be in love with a broken down detective who looks like Jenkins."[7] Meanwhile, the *New York Post* observed, "Little Jane Wyman performs as though she had closely followed Glenda Farrell's actions and mannerisms," a criticism since repeated by film historians.[8] In 1972 Elizabeth Dalton wrote that Wyman "evidently had watched Glenda Farrell very carefully. She mimics Glenda's style right down to the fingertips. She even manages to capture the tilt of Glenda's head and the way she charges out of a room—but still, that extra something is missing."[9]

Torchy Plays with Dynamite, whether it means to or not, comments on the precarious nature of modern identity. The film opens with Wyman being stopped by a motorcycle cop for speeding as she returns to her newspaper office from covering a bank robbery, the latest in a series committed by Denver Eddie and his gang. Although she protests that she is Torchy Blane, star reporter and fiancée of Lt. McBride, the cop takes her to court because she doesn't have her driver's license with her. She is thus present when "Jackie" McGuire, Eddie's moll, is sentenced to jail for shoplifiting. With the plot now introduced, McBride shows up and identifies Wyman as Torchy, and the judge releases her forthwith. The scene, with its legal setting, helps establish Wyman's legitimacy vis-à-vis the audience, accustomed to seeing Farrell in the title role.

Dalton called *Torchy Plays with Dynamite* the "silliest" of the Torchy films, noting that it features "all sorts of mistaken identity routines."[10] But far from being silly, these "routines" raise questions, quite possibly fortuitous, about how identity is constructed in the age of mechanical reproduction, when individuality has dribbled away to mass conformity and the looks of various social types have been stylized and marketed.

No sooner is Wyman confirmed in the role of Torchy, for example, than she goes undercover as a jail inmate. Her impersonation consists mostly of wearing a drab prison gown and speaking in a coarse voice, but is enough to convince Jackie, who invites Torchy to break out and go with her to San Francisco, where she will contact Eddie. After arranging the "jailbreak," McBride and his comical sidekick, Gahagan, follow.

From this point on, identity confusion reigns. McBride and Gahagan are tailed by a clueless San Francisco dick, who thinks they are a couple of gangsters. They keep their true identities secret because they don't want the local police to horn in on Eddie's capture and collect the $5,000 reward. When the Frisco detective finally confronts them, they pose as a professional wrestler and his manager. On the other hand, when they meet Jackie, they pose as gangsters nicknamed "Steve the Flathead" and "Harry the Horse" to win her confidence.

It is significant that Jenkins's McBride is first mistaken for and then impersonates a gangster. As the review in *Variety* remarked, Jenkins was "usually seen in gangster roles,"[11] having appeared in previous films as henchman to James Cagney, Humphrey Bogart, and Edward G. Robinson, among other screen heavies.[12] *Torchy Plays with Dynamite* puts an ironic spin on that fact.

A "recurrent aspect of popular culture," film theorist Dana Polan once said, "is its self-reflexive dimension—its pointed commentary on, and even pastiche or parody of, its own status as cultural item."[13] Probably because it was the last film in the series, *Torchy Plays with Dynamite* was also the most self-parodying, full of complicated "in" jokes, such as having an actor known for gangster roles play a detective playing a gangster. Jane Feur, an expert on the Hollywood musical, found the same tendency toward self-irony in senescent film genres. "After an early period in which the conventions themselves seem fresh and noteworthy," she wrote, "genres have to keep giving us something new without sacrificing the appeal those conventions held in the first place. . . . The overall pattern seems to develop from early un-selfconscious conveyance of cultural mythology to a twilight period of reflection and even self-criticism."[14]

But if the Torchy series was ending, so was something else. Americans were emerging from a worldwide depression into a world war that would finish off the primacy of the individual, leaving megacorporations in charge. All the identity switches in *Torchy Plays with Dynamite*, all the instability and confusion, may well reflect the incoherence of modern society—the lights, the noise, the cartoon people. There is just brain-splatter where thoughts should be.

Chapter 24

The Ghost in the Machine

Torchy Blane herself isn't important, just a stereotypical brash blonde in a series of low-budget films. What Torchy represents, however, *is* important, and what she represents is ideology in motley, patriarchy in drag, oppression disguised as humor. She demonstrates the amazing (appalling?) ability of popular culture to ideologize and mystify even while it entertains. "The might of industrial society," Theodor W. Adorno and his frequent coauthor, Max Horkheimer, once wrote, "is lodged in men's minds"—that is, popular culture is like a bullet to the brain.[1] *Blam!*

In the Torchy films, things often mean the exact opposite of what they seem to mean. At first Torchy seems the equal of any man, but ultimately requires a man to rescue her from physical danger. At first Lt. Steve McBride, her fiancé, seems a kind of Keystone cop, but ultimately justifies the repressive state apparatus—police, courts, prisons—by battling the powerful criminal element to a standstill. At first detective work seems to be of higher priority to Torchy and McBride than getting to their own wedding, but ultimately it clears the way for other young couples to find happiness in marriage.

Critics have suggested that such double-facedness creates the possibility for oppositional readings, or what they have called "reading against the grain," during which "one looks," in Dana Polan's words, "for an alternate narrative or series of narratives within a narrative that has previously claimed exclusive representation of a particular situation."[2] The objective is to demystify contradictions that the dominant ideology tries to conceal.

Whether reading—or, in the case of film, viewing—against the grain is actually possible on the mass scale envisioned by radical critics is, I think, open to question. Reception doesn't take place in a vacuum, but in a representational context including advertisements, "promos," Hollywood gossip, film reviews, and parallel cultural productions (TV programs, novelizations, video games, theme-park rides, etc.). This context foregrounds preferred meanings. As V.N. Volosinov, the Russian semiologist, observed in the late 1920s, "The ruling class strives to impart a supraclass, eternal character to the ideological sign, to extinguish or drive inward the struggle between social value judgments which occur in it, to make the sign uniaccentual."[3]

Volosinov believed that the "*inner dialectic quality* of the sign comes out fully in the open only in times of social crisis or revolutionary changes."[4] In our own time, the coordination of preferred meanings across the mass media has become more achievable as media ownership has become more concentrated. Turner Broadcasting System and Time Warner, for example, merged in 1996, creating the largest media conglomerate in the world. Among its $6.3 billion in holdings are cable TV channels (TBS, TNT, TCM, HBO, Cartoon Network), news programming (CNN, CNN International, Headline News), film studios (New Line Cinema, Castle Rock Entertainment, Warner Brothers, Hanna-Barbera Cartoons), music labels (Warner, Elektra, Atlantic), and magazines (*Time*, *People*, *Sports Illustrated*, *Fortune*, *Entertainment Weekly*).[5] Thus many seemingly diverse and autonomous media outlets are, in fact, interlocking and mutually reinforcing. Adorno and Horkheimer were referring to just this sort of integration when they said, "All are free to dance and enjoy themselves. . . . But freedom to choose an ideology . . . everywhere proves to be freedom to choose what is always the same."[6]

Even before the merger, Turner Broadcasting System owned the Warner film library as the result of a previous megadeal. *Torchy Blane in Panama*, *Torchy Gets Her Man*, *Torchy Blane in Chinatown*, *Torchy Runs for Mayo*r, and *Torchy Plays with Dynamite* had all been transferred to videotape—I know because I viewed them on loan—and could show up someday on Turner Classic Movies, a cable channel specializing in films from the 1930s and '40s. If the Torchy films are ever broadcast on cable, they will have come full circle. Begun in the Depression era as a cheap way to fill the bottom half of double bills, the series will have resurfaced in the 1990s as a cheap way to fill TV airtime.

But Torchy will live on even if her films are never widely seen again. She will live on in the girl reporters who dash through popular culture, cracking jokes and solving crimes and falling in love with hard guys. She will live on in the Brenda Starrs and Lois Lanes and Murphy Browns. She is the forever-blonde ghost in the genre machine.

Chapter 25

Cineplexity

Imagine a cineplex where the only films playing were made between 1979 and 1996, and feature a girl reporter among the major characters. In theaters one through three are films set in the world of newspapers: *Absence of Malice* (1981), *The Paper* (1994), and *I Love Trouble* (1994). In theaters four through nine are films set in the world of television news: *The China Syndrome* (1979), *The Electric Horseman* (1979), *Eyewitness* (1981), *Hero* (1992), *To Die For* (1995), and *Up Close and Personal* (1996). As you go from theater to theater, you may be expecting to find that the portrayal of the girl reporter has progressed considerably since Torchy Blane first appeared in the mid-1930s. After all, the sixties and seventies ushered in the sexual revolution and the women's movement, and the eighties and nineties brought the working mom. But you won't find much progress. What you will find is fear, hate, death—and really bad acoustics.

Absence of Malice

Every year for the past few years I have shown my students a videotape of *Absence of Malice*, starring Sally Field as Megan Carter, an overzealous newspaper reporter, and Paul Newman as Michael Gallagher, the innocent man whose life she nearly ruins. When the film came out in 1981, Pauline Kael of *New Yorker* magazine predicted professors eventually would do with it what I have done. "The only thing that's the matter with this material as a movie subject," she said in her review, "is that . . . you could get it all by reading an article; it might easily be an essay-question test in ethics, and, in fact, will probably be used that way in journalism courses."[1]

To Kael, *Absence of Malice* represented "a fairly straightforward querying of journalistic practices." "The whole picture," she wrote, "is in the American-movie tradition of entertaining muckraking."[2] But some members of the press found nothing entertaining about a two-hour-plus film featuring a newspaperwoman who lacks all ethical—or even common—sense. Pulitzer Prize-winning reporter Lucinda Franks, for example, called the film "grotesquely distorted," warning her fellow journalists that it "aims to take away our last bone of glory."[3]

Absence of Malice was so controversial that it merited a front-page article in the Arts & Leisure section of the Sunday *New York Times.* Written by Jonathan Friendly and headlined "A Movie on the Press Stirs a Debate," the article largely sided with those journalists who felt the film misrepresented the reality of newspapering. "Just like the stories Megan Carter writes," Friendly asserted, "the film gets only some of the facts and, trying to be true, fails to be entirely truthful."[4]

Four years later, *Absence of Malice* still rankled reviewers' sensibilities. "More than any other film," Desmond Ryan complained in September 1985 in the *Washington Journalism Review,* "it demonstrates the difference between what reporters do on the street and what they are shown doing on the screen."[5] That June, Ron Rosenbaum, film critic for *Mademoiselle* magazine, reiterated that "*Absence of Malice* leaves the impression that what Sally Field did was typical of how reporters casually and routinely smear innocent citizens. What the movie really does is smear innocent reporters."[6]

Interestingly, the critical reputation of *Absence of Malice* has improved a good deal since the mid-1980s. *Natural Born Killers* (1994), *To Die For* (1995), and other recent films have portrayed journalists with such disdain that *Absence of Malice* seems judicious and responsible by comparison. In the March/April 1996 issue of the *Columbia Journalism Review*, Christopher Hanson, Washington correspondent for the *Seattle Post-Intelligencer*, described *Absence of Malice* as "a somber account of how an over-ambitious newswoman . . . is manipulated into falsely reporting that a local businessman is a murder suspect. . . . *Malice*," he added, "conveys a sense of outrage at the way things can really work in the news business."[7]

So which is it? Is *Absence of Malice*, as earlier critics like Franks and Ryan claimed, full of stupid and ugly lies about the press? Or is it, as Hanson said, an accurate reflection of how the press operates, at least on bad days? Actually, it is neither. The film isn't even primarily about journalism, though many scenes are set in the busy modern newsroom of the *Miami Standard.* Journalism is only a kind of overlay on the film's real targets—feminism and single working women.

That critics have treated *Absence of Malice* exclusively as a journalism film has allowed its gynephobia to circulate unchallenged. The crucial point about Sally Field's character, Megan Carter, isn't that she is an incompetent reporter, but that she is an incompetent *female* reporter. Her femaleness—what it means, where it belongs, how it expresses or doesn't express itself—is the central issue in the film.

Viewers may mistake Megan at first for a female role model. In the opening scene, we see her stop by the headquarters of a federal strike force investigating the disappearance (and presumed murder) of union leader Joey Diaz. With her man-tailored suit, staccato speech, and cynical air, she seems simply an updated, brown-haired version of dear old Torchy Blane. But she isn't. It soon becomes glaringly obvious that she lacks Torchy's intelligence and reporting skill. When the chief of the strike force leaves a file out on his desk for her to find, she uses it just as he planned—to write a bogus story fingering Paul Newman's character, Michael Gallagher, as a suspect in the Diaz case. And so it goes throughout the film. She outsmarts herself far more often than she outsmarts anyone else.

Megan isn't merely dull-witted, she is also unladylike. She swears like a man, drinks like a man, initiates sex like a man. It is for these chronic violations of traditional gender boundaries, rather than for journalistic improprieties, that the film ultimately punishes her. When she argues with Gallagher about the use of anonymous news sources, he suddenly shifts the conversation to the topic of her marital status.

Gallagher: How old are you?
Megan: 34.
Gallagher: How come you're not married?
Megan: Well, maybe I am.
Gallagher: How come you don't wear a ring?
Megan: Haven't you ever heard of liberation?
Gallagher: Most of them are ugly.

Reporter Steve Banks (Robert Armstrong) trades wisecracks with Vera (Cupid Ainsworth), an advice-to-the-lovelorn columnist, in *Big News* (1929). Vera, whom Steve calls "Big Girl" and "Tubby," serves to confirm traditional prejudices that the career woman is a kind of freak.

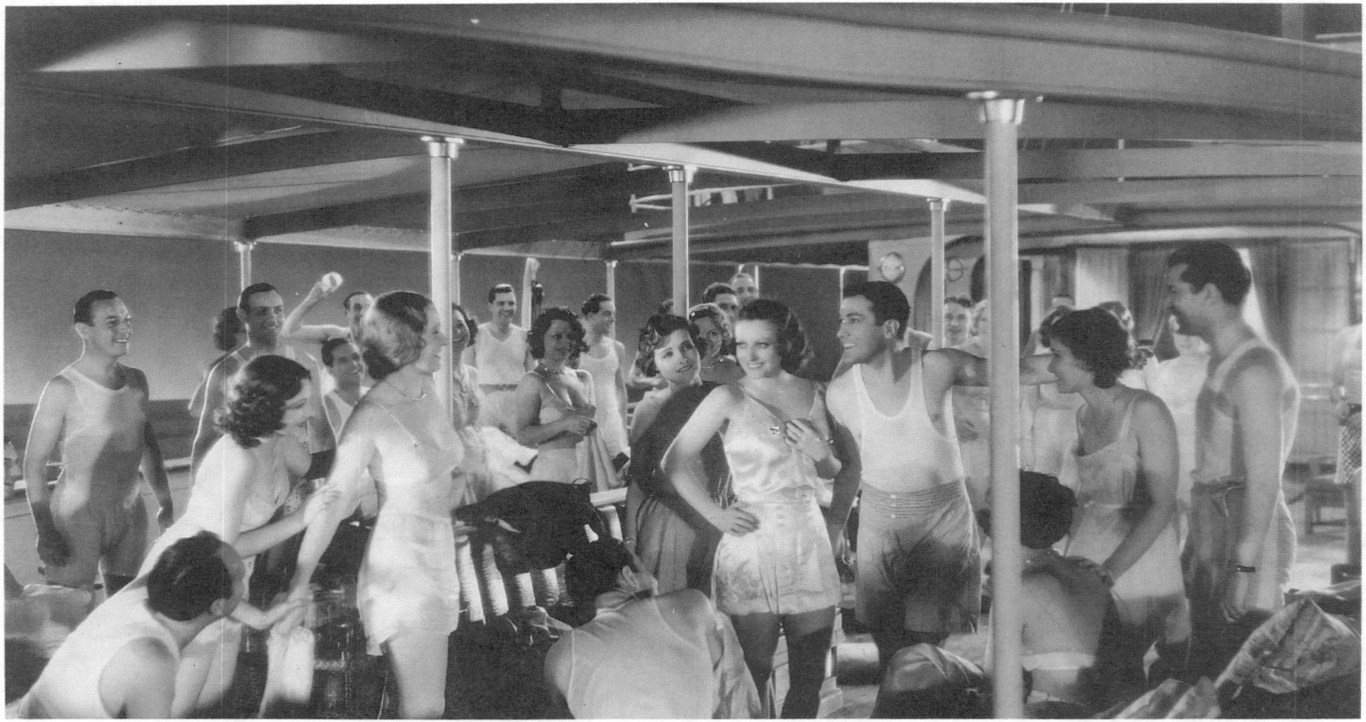

Socialite Bonnie Jordan (Joan Crawford, center) and her rich friends strip for a midnight swim in *Dance, Fools, Dance* (1931). When her father's fortune is wiped out in the stock market crash, Bonnie goes to work as a reporter. Although the film contains allusions to the St. Valentine's Day Massacre and other contemporary events, it is chiefly interested in exploiting Crawford's sex appeal.

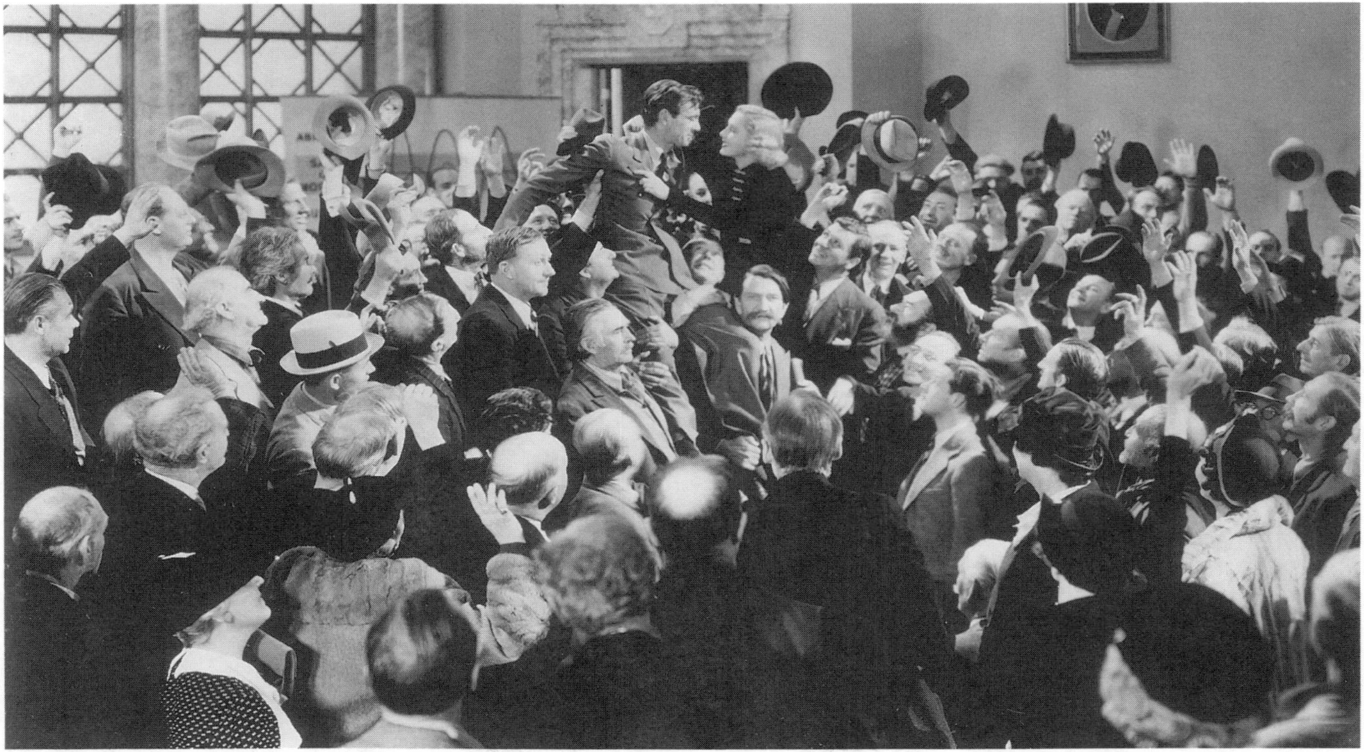

Eccentric millionaire Longfellow Deeds (Gary Cooper) and smart-aleck reporter Babe Bennett (Jean Arthur) are congratulated by supporters after their courtroom victory over greed and fuddy-duddyism in Frank Capra's *Mr. Deeds Goes to Town* (1936).

Although handcuffed, reporter Hildy Johnson (Rosalind Russell) and editor Walter Burns (Cary Grant) still have the upper hand in any battle of wits with the sheriff (Gene Lockhart) in *His Girl Friday*, the 1940 remake of Hecht and MacArthur's *The Front Page*.

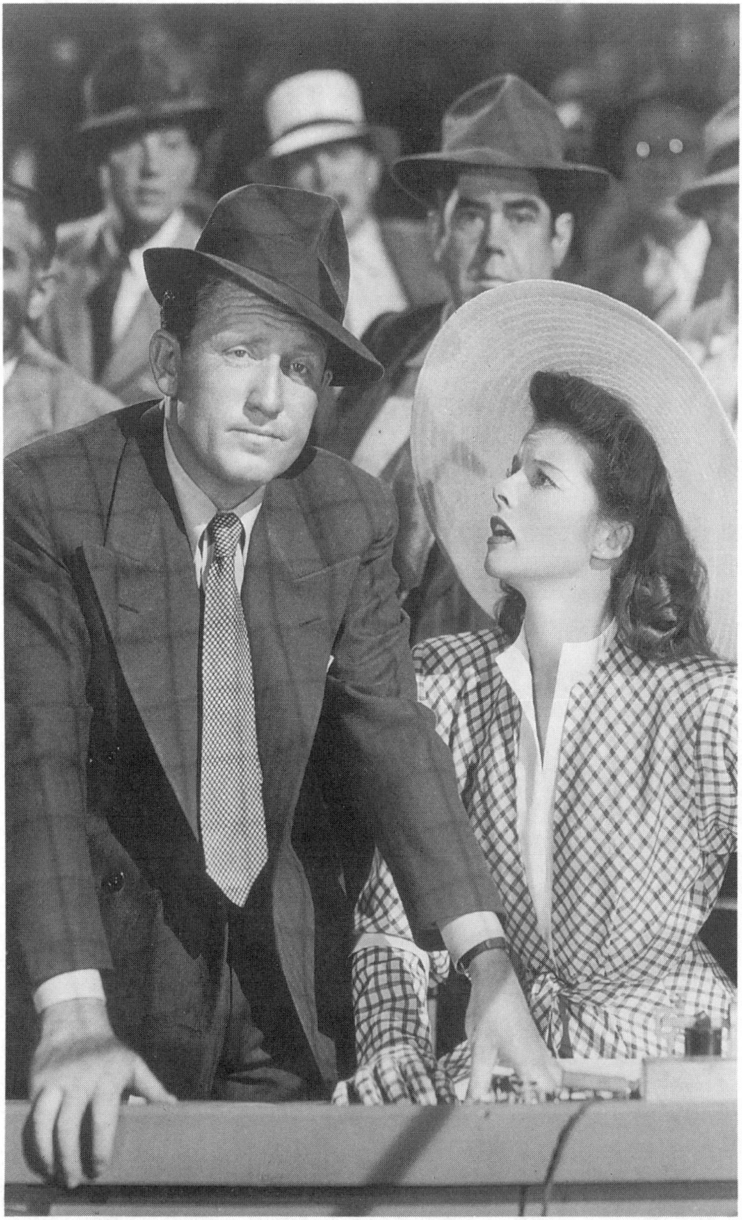

Sportswriter Sam Craig (Spencer Tracy) introduces world-affairs columnist Tess Harding (Katharine Hepburn) to baseball—and love—in *Woman of the Year* (1942).

Glenda Farrell's performance as tough, fast-talking reporter Florence Dempsey in *The Mystery of the Wax Museum* (1933) outshone that of its leading lady, Fay Wray. Florence provided the prototype for Farrell's role in the Torchy Blane series.

Police lieutenant Steve McBride (Barton MacLane) and his reporter girlfriend, Torchy Blane (Glenda Farrell), follow clues to the Million Club in *Smart Blonde* (1937), the first Torchy film. Jane Wyman, who here plays the hat-check girl, would play Torchy in the last film in the series.

Gahagan (Tom Kennedy, left), Lt. McBride's delightfully dim-witted driver, recites a poem of his own creation in *Smart Blonde*.

Torchy and McBride cuddle in the back seat of his police car in *Smart Blonde*. Although contemporary reviewers saw the Torchy films as just routine whodunits, the films were actually more preoccupied with demonstrating the legitimacy and resilience of the traditional heterosexual couple than with solving crimes.

With the help of a professional burglar, Torchy breaks into the cellar of City Hall in *Torchy Runs for Mayor* (1939), the eighth film in the series and the last in which Glenda Farrell appeared. Torchy never hesitates to pursue a story to the limit, even if it involves her in ethically questionable methods of newsgathering.

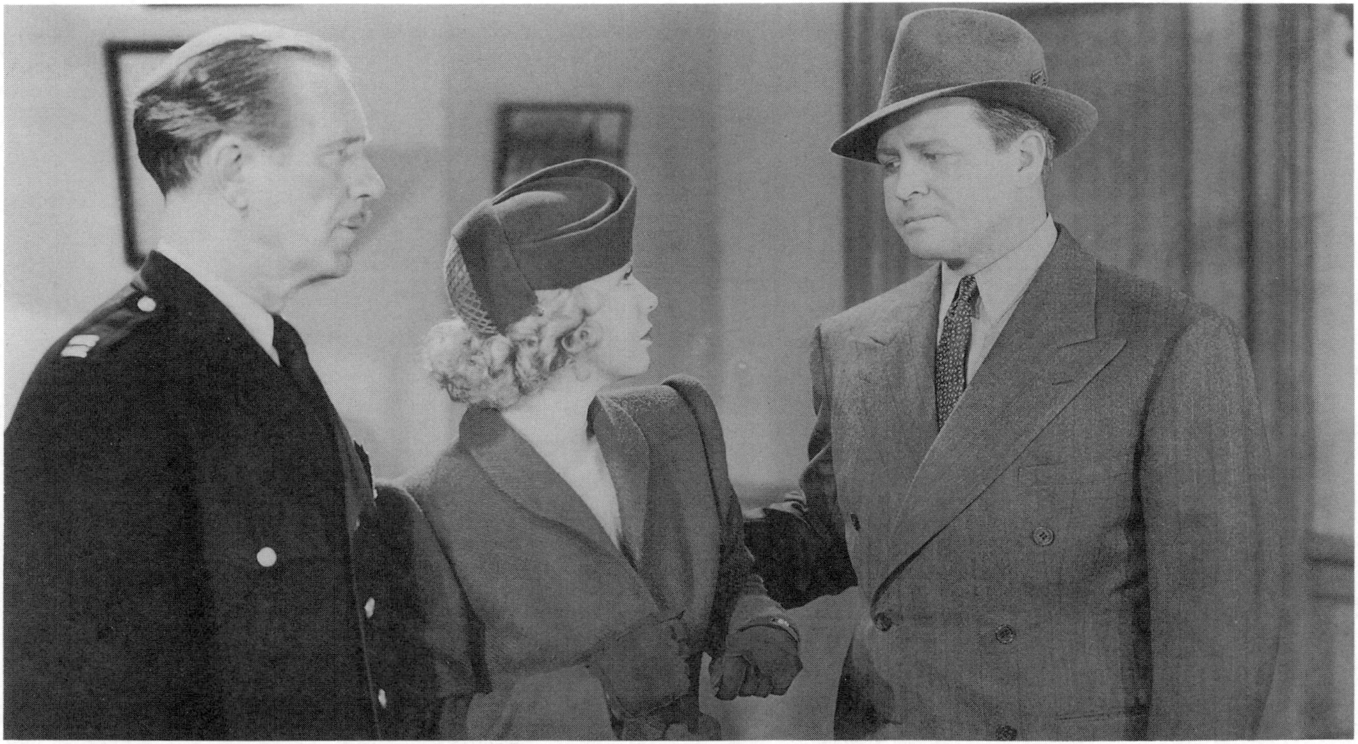

Capt. McTavish (Frank Shannon, left) objected to the unofficial detective partnership formed by Torchy and McBride, not because it didn't produce results, but because it threatened male autonomy.

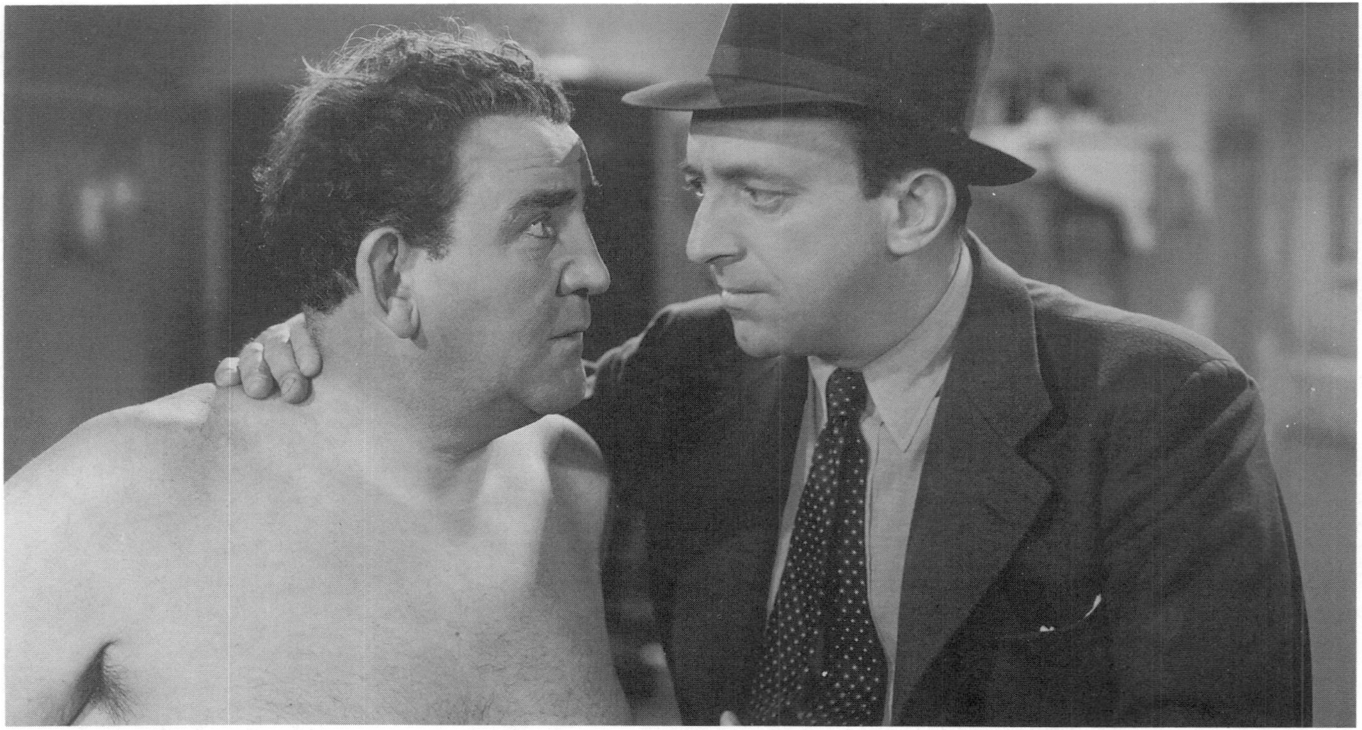

Allen Jenkins (right) took over the role of Lt. McBride from Barton MacLane in *Torchy Plays with Dynamite* (1939), the last Torchy film. Tom Kennedy, who played McBride's poetry-spouting driver Gahagan, was the only actor to appear in all nine films in the series.

Torchy (Jane Wyman with bleached blonde hair and a gun) breaks out of prison as part of an elaborate undercover operation in *Torchy Plays with Dynamite*.

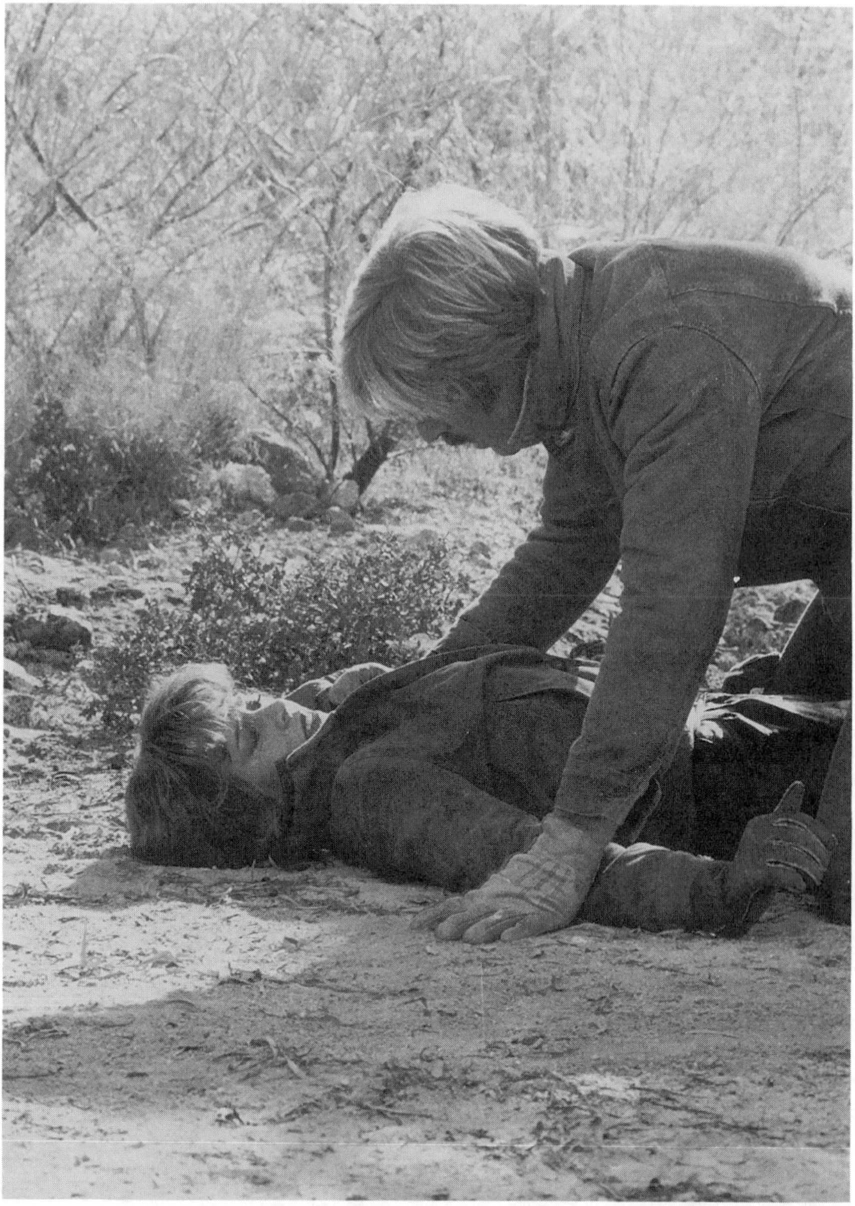

Cowboy Sonny Steele (Robert Redford) tackles TV newswoman Hallie Martin (Jane Fonda) in *The Electric Horseman* (1979). From the 1970s through the 1990s, female reporters in Hollywood films have been punched, slapped, shot, and symbolically raped. What's worse, they have frequently fallen in love with the men who have beaten and humiliated them.

Rich, glamorous TV newscaster Tony Sokolow (Sigourney Weaver) flees a pair of thugs in *Eyewitness* (1981). In a moment, a janitor played by William Hurt will roar to her rescue on his motorcycle. Numerous films over the past 20 years have placed a female professional in the safekeeping of a working-class hero.

Suzanne Stone (Nicole Kidman) does the weather on a local cable station, but schemes obsessively to become the next Diane Sawyer in the 1995 black comedy, *To Die For*.

Romance is an important, though widely underappreciated, element in this film. Kael only mentioned in the *New Yorker* that the film "wants to cook up a bittersweet romance between Megan and Gallagher."[8] Meanwhile, newspaper journalists objected to the romance on ethical grounds. *Times*man Friendly cited a colleague's maxim that "reporters covering the circus must avoid romantic entanglements with the elephants."[9]

The film itself doesn't condemn Megan for sharing her bed with Gallagher. In fact, their romance is presented in an entirely positive light. Until they become romantically involved, she appears shallow, insensitive, ruthless—the liberated woman as a kind of pseudo-man. She even sexually propositions Gallagher after their first date, turning him right off. When they make love, the film suggests, it will be on his terms.

And Gallagher's terms are paleolithic. Although Gallagher is the owner of a liquor wholesale business, a capitalist, Newman plays him as a supermasculine, blue-collar type. He wears jeans and cowboy boots, drinks beer, and takes no shit from anyone—not from the FBI, the Teamsters Union, or the press; not from mobsters, lawyers, or feminists. At a time when the women's movement was forcing open doors to male jobs and popularizing abortion, here was a man who was lean and hard and angry, a righteous figure to put women back in their place. He does this by symbolically raping Megan.

None of the reviewers seems to have recognized as a rape the scene where an explosive Gallagher hurls Megan to the floor, jumps on top of her, and hisses in her ear, but that is essentially what it is, right down to her torn blouse and exposed flesh.[10] Gallagher is wild with grief and rage because of the suicide of Teresa Perrone, his lifelong friend, twitchily played by Melinda Dillon. Unmarried Teresa kills herself—slashing her wrists in the bathtub—when Megan reveals in the paper that Teresa had had an abortion, something she had kept hidden from her devoutly Catholic father. Teresa's grisly fate implies criticism not only of an invasive press, but also of single women, sexual promiscuity, abortion rights, and the general erosion of the middle-class nuclear family.

Significantly, Megan and Gallagher begin their romance after the rape scene. His primal violence batters her into submission, redefines her, caveman-style, as his property. Her new, dependent status is underlined by the dialogue that follows their first night of lovemaking.

Megan: What are you doing? Are you leaving? (Gallagher nods.) What time is it?
Gallagher: 5:30. I got to go.
Megan: Why? What happens at 5:30?
Gallagher: I'll call you.
Megan: I'm free every night but Friday.
Gallagher: How about Friday?
Megan: OK.

Their romance is brief, not because the film doesn't sanction it, but because Megan is too much of a careerist to sustain it. One evening Gallagher arrives at her apartment for dinner. Instead of concentrating on chopping up carrots, she asks suspicious questions about his relationship with the district attorney. "What are you, working?" he says, and stalks out. She has blown her chance to be his wifely supporter—or, in a word, fulfilled.

Megan is eventually fired from the *Standard* for all her screw-ups. The only consolation the film affords her is a certain growth in self-awareness—the self-awareness that she is incompetent and out of her depth. "I know you think what I do for a living is nothing," she tells Gallagher in the closing moments. "But it really isn't nothing. I just did it badly." Journalism is vindicated; it is women who, by their own admission, are the menace.

The Paper

Under the cover of journalistic ethics, *Absence of Malice* punishes Megan for preferring a career to a husband and children. Such camouflage is common in newspaper films of the 1980s and '90s featuring female journalists. If the films were openly hostile to women's rights, they would appear backwards and vicious. So they name another, more politically acceptable target, but still bring down the career woman with a heart shot.

Susan Faludi, in her 1991 book, *Backlash: The Undeclared War against American Women*, documented a culturewide "attempt to retract the handful of small and hard-won victories that the feminist movement did manage to win for women."[11] The counterassault began in earnest in the early 1980s when, for the first time, white men constituted less than 50 percent of the work force; more than 50 percent of women worked; more than 50 percent of married women worked; and more women with children than without children worked.[12] Despite these figures—or, rather, because of them—popular culture preached to women the incompatibility of career and personal happiness. In what Faludi dubbed "the '80s backlash cinema," emancipated women with condominiums of their own "slink wild-eyed between bare walls, paying for their liberty with an empty bed, a barren womb."[13]

The Paper may not be another *Fatal Attraction* (the controversial 1987 film starring Glenn Close as a homicidal single career woman), but it does reflect the backlash thesis: "American women were unhappy because they were too free; liberation had denied them marriage and motherhood."[14] Its principal female characters, managing editor Alicia Clark (Close again) and pregnant former reporter Marty Hackett (Marisa Tomei), are there to be degraded. They demonstrate the foolishness and futility of women trying to compete with men for journalistic power and glory.

Of all the major reviewers, only Richard Corliss of *Time* magazine noted the film's misogyny, which he blamed on co-screenwriter David Koepp, whose previous credits included *Death Becomes Her*.[15] The rest must have taken for granted that career women are haggard, predatory bitches—and positioned audiences to take it for granted as well. Janet Maslin of the *New York Times* even told readers that "Alicia is one of the few characters here who warrant more screen time than they get."[16]

Her time on screen is still enough to establish, among other things, that she is (1) a name-dropper (she drops "Bobby" DeNiro's); (2) an adulteress; (3) a penny pincher at a financially strapped tabloid called the *New York Sun*; (4) a spendthrift when away from it; and (5) an unethical journalist. How unethical? She knowingly prints a false story on the front page—a story that could trigger a race riot—just to keep to deadlines.

Alicia gets punished throughout the film, ostensibly for her ethical lapses, but actually for her unfeminine displays of authority. She is punched in the nose by the city editor, shot in the leg by the city parking commissioner, and, perhaps most injurious of all, put down in public by her publisher (Jason Robards). In what Maslin somehow regarded as "one of the film's livelier scenes," Alicia is so intent on speaking to the publisher at a charity function that she follows him into the men's room.[17] "I would love it," he says, "if you weren't here." She suddenly wakes up to where she is and gasps. An attendant then hands her a towel. The whole scene unfolds like a Freudian nightmare, with the aggressive, elegantly gowned Alicia exposed, amid sinks and urinals, as gender confused.

Initially at least, *The Paper* seems more sympathetic to Marty. A former reporter on the *Sun*, she is now married to Henry Hackett (Michael Keaton), the city editor and the film's hero. They are expecting their first child soon, a fact that scares and depresses her. She is worried that Henry will be too busy at work to help her around the house, and that she will be too busy around the house to go back to work.

It is the classic American conflict between work and family, and the film resolves it in the classic American way—in favor of the man. Henry gets to scoop the competition, in the process saving two black boys from jail and the entire city from a race riot. He also gets to say cool stuff like "Not everything is about money" and "Stop the presses!" Marty, for her part, gets to almost hemorrhage to death when she goes into labor—her punishment, I suppose, for ever doubting the virtues of motherhood.

The Paper is a devious film, hiding its deep conservativism behind a progressive veneer. At one point, Marty, though on maternity leave, hits the street to track down crucial information for what will turn out to be the day's lead story. When she phones the info in, Henry responds—this is the interesting part—in bedroom language. "Oh, honey," he moans, "you're so good, so good. I love you, I love you. . . . I mean you drive me crazy when you're like this." By imbuing woman's work with sexual overtones, the film recuperates the work, tames and trivializes it. The image of an enormously pregnant woman on the job becomes no more threatening to male hegemony than a pinup.

Despite the best disruptive efforts of Alicia and Marty, power is passed on intact from one generation of men to the next in *The Paper*. The older generation is represented by Bernie White (Robert Duvall), the *Sun*'s top editor. Bernie has problems—prostate cancer and a grown daughter who hates him. Thus it is up to Henry to preserve male authority. He punches out Alicia, scores a Pulitzer Prize-type scoop, and becomes a new father, all in 24 hours. Once the baby is born, even Marty recognizes the logic of Henry being boss and disavows her feminism. "All that crap," she says, "I can hardly remember it." The unspoken hope is that viewers won't either.

I Love Trouble

I Love Trouble, a 1994 film starring Nick Nolte and Julia Roberts as rival newspaper reporters, exemplifies what might be called "cineplexity," the quality of fitting perfectly into the artificial environment of the suburban shopping mall. Like the mall, the film is bright, glossy, and hollow. Like the mall, it appeals to the insatiable child in us. Like the mall, it displays brand-name products—in this case, its recognized stars, if not its recognized genre. And, finally, like the mall, the film is full of desperate clutter, distractions that crowd out inner life.

A majority of critics noted that *I Love Trouble* had some of the moves of newspaper films from the thirties and forties, but none of their style or wit. "This film," Christopher Hanson said in *Columbia Journalism Review*, "struggles lamely to draw upon such charming rogue press films of yore as *His Girl Friday* (1940)."[18] Jack Kroll of *Newsweek* similarly invoked the name of director Howard Hawks's classic screwball comedy, a remake of *The Front Page* (1931). "Instead of the crackling repartee of 'His Girl Friday,' " Kroll wrote, "we get stock exchanges, updated now and then by the new sexual frankness, as when Roberts outmachos Nolte. Nolte (referring to a bulldog he's sent to Roberts): 'Does he remind you of me?' Roberts: 'Yeah, I've grown awfully fond of Little Dick.' "[19]

Even *New York Times* critic Caryn James, who described *I Love Trouble* as "loaded with charm," thought its plot somewhat far-fetched and confusing. "To say that the muddled plot involves a chemical company and a secret formula for enhancing milk production," she observed, "is as much as anyone needs to know going in, and probably as much as anyone will remember coming out." She suggested that the story was merely an excuse for superstar columnist Peter Brackett (Nolte) and cub reporter Sabrina Peterson (Roberts) to "race around the country, from Chicago to Wisconsin to Las Vegas, stumbling in and out of danger."[20] It is a suggestion that depoliticizes the film and overlooks the fact that Brackett and Peterson wage, under the guise of journalistic competition, a vicious battle of the sexes.

There are indications early on that Sabrina is destined to lose the battle. Covering a train wreck, she finds a gold wedding ring among the debris scattered on the ground. We see this, interestingly, from Brackett's perspective and through the sparks of acetylane torches—in a kind of shimmering erotic vision. The vision has a twofold effect: it (1) defines Sabrina as primarily a love object even in the midst of a breaking story; and (2) establishes the central importance of marriage.

Objectification recurs throughout the film. In a party scene—again shot from Brackett's perspective—we see Sabrina from behind, dressed in a strapless black sheath emphasizing the lean, elemental lines of her body. The camera cuts to a close-up of her hand caressing her own flank, a seductive gesture that seems to invite others to stroke her. Although the film pretends to take Sabrina seriously as a journalist, it isn't above presenting her as a shoulder, a breast, a thigh, a soft-porn spectacle designed to entice and delight the male gaze.

The plot itself carries her from sexual resistance to sexual submission. She initially fights off the transparent advances of Brackett, a notorious womanizer. "You have zero chance of scoring," she tells him when they first meet, "so move on." But, as in the Torchy Blane series, the murder mystery becomes a vehicle for resolving outstanding gender issues. For their mutual safety and convenience, Brackett and Sabrina agree to form a detective partnership. "If I knew what you knew," he says, "and you knew what I knew, we just might be able to live through this story." The truce in their journalistic rivalry foreshadows an end to the battle of the sexes. In fact, they escape the murderer at one point by hiding in a handy wedding mill in Las Vegas and inadvertently wind up—ha-ha—married.

Most of the joke is on Sabrina. "You know," she remarks, "if anyone told me two weeks ago I'd be married to Peter Brackett. . . ." "Don't worry," he interrupts. "I already checked. We can have it annulled in the morning." "Oh, you did? Good," she says, but clearly doesn't mean it. She has changed because of him, been refeminized. "Tell me something," she is soon pleading, "What is it about me you don't like? I've never had this effect on a man before. . . . I know you think I'm trouble and you curse the day you met me. But, off the record, I don't feel that way about you, at all."

Sabrina is punished in still other ways for having once resisted Brackett. A Boy Scout troop, for example, stumbles across her as she comes out of a lake where she has been skinny-dipping. "When they said, 'Be prepared,' I bet you didn't expect this," Brackett wisecracks while Sabrina cowers naked behind him. "Only in our dreams," one Scout replies. Brackett then steps away, letting the

Scouts all snap her picture. The scene is reminiscent of managing editor Alicia Clark's ordeal in the men's room in *The Paper*. Both episodes have a sadistic edge; both deliberately subject an ambitious female to public embarrassment; both are played for laughs.

Also like Alicia, Sabrina gets punched in the face. She has been captured by the bad guys, and Brackett shows up at Chess Chemical to rescue her. Bullets fly. The lights go out. In the darkness and confusion, he socks her one. An honest mistake? Not in a film whose idea of humor is to humiliate a pretty woman in front of small boys.

The China Syndrome

The China Syndrome, a film about a possible meltdown at a nuclear power plant in California, opened nationwide on March 16, 1979. Twelve days later, life imitated art when a reactor overheated and threatened to explode at the Three Mile Island nuclear power plant near Harrisburg, Pennsylvania.[21] "Incredible," said Michael Douglas, producer and costar of the film. "I can't put it together. It's disturbingly ironic."[22] Among the ironies was that a scientist in the film claims that a meltdown could "render an area the size of Pennsylvania permanently uninhabitable."

Although *The China Syndrome* was a box-office hit from the start, the Three Mile Island accident stimulated extra business. The film, which cost $6 million to make, grossed about $26 million in its first three weeks.[23] It became the biggest non-holiday film in the history of Columbia Pictures.[24]

Most critics recommended *The China Syndrome* even before the accident. Vincent Canby of the *New York Times* said the film was a "smashingly effective, very stylish suspense melodrama," while David Ansen of *Newsweek* called it "a class-act thriller, a fiendishly efficient example of emotional manipulation."[25] But as entertaining as the film was, the critics felt that it had a serious message. " 'Power' was once the title of the movie," Ansen noted, "and that's its real subject, as the various vested interests—the utility company, the media, the guilty construction company—engage in a struggle for survival without consideration for the survival of the species."[26]

In the film, Jane Fonda plays Kimberly Wells, a soft-news reporter for a Los Angeles TV station who stumbles onto a near-catastrophe while doing a feature story about the Ventana nuclear power plant. Fonda was Hollywood's house radical at the time, married to politicial activist Tom Hayden and highly outspoken herself on many issues. At least partly because of her presence in the cast, *The China Syndrome* is remembered today as a progressive or even quasi-feminist film. Susan Faludi classified it with *Norma Rae*, *Julia*, *9 to 5*, and other films of the 1970s whose heroines "wished to transform not only themselves but the world around them."[27]

Ironically, no woman appeared in the cast of the original screenplay of *The China Syndrome*, written by Mike Gray; rather, three male documentary filmmakers observed the near-accident. Richard Dreyfuss agreed to play one of them, but then dropped out in a dispute over money. "I was thinking for some time of changing that role to a woman," recalled Douglas, who had won an Academy Award as producer of 1975's *One Flew Over the Cuckoo's Nest*. "I walked onto the set of 'Coming Home' and handed Jane Fonda the script, which hadn't been rewritten for her yet."[28]

Fonda liked the idea of turning the filmmaker into a TV reporter. She sent director James Bridges a six-page letter in which she outlined her character, chose the name "Kimberly Wells," and asked to play the role with red hair. Nor was that the last of her editorial contributions. Bridges, who rewrote the film with T.S. Cook, told an interviewer: "Jane was one of the first to edit out any heavy statements that crept into the script. We all agreed the picture should be, first of all, an entertainment, to reach the biggest audience possible. I'd write shrill, preachy things, like a dream one character had of a nuclear holocaust with all the birds dying, and Jane would chop them out."[29]

The finished film was still seen as having a "very large social conscience."[30] In fact, Lee Wilkins of the University of Missouri–Columbia recently included it on a list of films that provide a starting point for thinking about ethics. "Jane Fonda's on-screen portrayal of Brenda Starr," he wrote, "raises some important questions surrounding media coverage of technology and crisis."[31]

Yeah, like what? Can a woman reporter who was hired for her looks and not her investigative abilities find happiness doing hard news? Are there too many commercials on TV? Should a station back off a big story for fear of a lawsuit? Is greed good? The answers to such questions are obvious.

What isn't quite so obvious is the way in which *The China Syn-*

drome denies Kimberly life after work. Some of this is the result of her single-minded pursuit of the big time. As she tells her cameraman, Richard Adams (Douglas), "I'm not ashamed I got a good job, and I've every intention of . . . getting a better one." But some of it, maybe most of it, is the result of the film's inability to conceive of a woman who is involved in her work as being happy and complete. When Kimberly comes home at night, it is to a pet turtle and her mother's voice on the telephone answering machine. She has no boyfriend or, for that matter, close friends of any kind. The film can't illustrate the intensity of her work ethic without simultaneously illustrating the depth of her loneliness.

While Kimberly does grow morally and professionally, her growth occurs under male supervision. Two men compete for the right to shape her. One is station manager Dan Jacovich (Peter Donat), who wants her to continue the trivial features that have helped make the local news a ratings success. The other is Richard—described in reviews as "a 60's radical turned into a 70's skeptic," "a bearded Daniel Ellsberg type"—who pushes her to become more than a TV personality.[32]

Richard wins the struggle, though only after calling her a "piece of talking furniture" to her face and leaving a message on her answering machine that says, "Kimberly, you really are an asshole." Stirred into moral action by his words, she begins a probe of safety conditions at the nuclear power plant. This leads ultimately to a shootout in the control room during which chief engineer Jack Godell (Jack Lemmon) is killed. Godell had been Kimberly's prime news source, and when the utility company tells the press that Godell was emotionally unstable, a drunk, she challenges the lie. "I'm sorry I'm not very objective," she sobs on the air.

Kimberly displays stereotypical female behavior by crying. Her loss of self-control reinforces the myth that women aren't as tough or reliable as men. This is the way the film ends—not with a bang, but a whimper.

The Electric Horseman

Jane Fonda played yet another TV reporter the same year in *The Electric Horseman*. Written by Robert Garland and directed by Sidney Pollack, this film was even more conservative in its sexual politics than *The China Syndrome*. Critics compared it to the romantic comedies of the 1930s and '40s, particularly *The Cowboy and the Lady* and *Mr. Deeds Goes To Town*.[33] But such comparisons obscured what was most contemporary about the film; specifically, the malice with which it attacked the career woman.

While *Variety* predicted that *The Electric Horseman* would be only mildly successful at the box office, the public made it one of the ten most popular films of 1979.[34] How much its popularity had to do with its antifeminist subtext is hard to determine. The film also contained an anti-Big Business theme—or, in Vincent Canby's words, "a kind of appealingly dopey populism"—and Robert Redford in his first major screen role in almost four years.[35]

Redford was Sonny Steele, a former world champion rodeo cowboy, now the photogenic but boozy spokesman for Ranch Breakfast cereal. As his name suggests, Redford's character embodies the tension between nature (sun) and civilization (steel), or between the various qualities and uses of steel—its hardness, elasticity, and strength on the one hand, and its association with the horrors of industrial society on the other.

Sonny's plight has added significance because of the special place the cowboy holds in American imagination. Since at least the dime-novel Westerns of the mid-1800s, the cowboy has represented freedom and virility, as well as a startling capacity for violence. Speaking of the Western hero, film critic Robert Warshow once said: "He resembles the gangster in being lonely and to some degree melancholy. But his melancholy comes from the 'simple' recognition that life is unavoidably serious, not from the disproportions of his own temperament. And his loneliness is organic, not imposed on him by his situation but belonging to him intimately and testifying to his completeness."[36] Thus to see Sonny riding a horse around a high-school football field while dressed in an electrified cowboy suit is to see a classic image of American manhood trapped and distorted by modern life and to know that the frontier has disappeared.

Appropriately enough, with the opening credits, country music star Willie Nelson sings "My Heroes Have Always Been Cowboys." The whole goal of the film is to restore Sonny to the manliness and moral clarity of the old Western heroes. This means that he not only must trade in his light-up suit for blue jeans, but that he also must conquer Fonda's character, Hallie Martin, described in one review as a "cynical TV news chick."[37]

They first meet at Caesar's Palace in Las Vegas, where Ampco, the giant conglomerate that owns Ranch Breakfast cereal, is staging a trade show. At a press conference, Hallie asks Sonny a series of abrasive questions, including, "Do you, in fact, eat Ranch Breakfast cereal for breakfast?" He measures her with his cold, gunfighter eyes and then drawls, "Lady, I don't want to tangle with you." But, of course, he does want to "tangle" with her—in fact, the tangling has already begun.

Also on display at the show is Rising Star, horse-racing's winningest stallion and Ampco's newest corporate symbol. "Horse should be staying in stud," Sonny observes. To which his sidekick Wendell (Nelson) adds, "We all should." Rising Star personifies their own denatured masculinity, a point further underscored when we learn that the horse is being fed a diet of painkillers and steroids, and that the steroids can make him sterile.

Outraged by this mistreatment, Sonny steals Rising Star right off the stage. "I'm going to turn him loose," the horse thief explains. "I'm going to get him back to where he was and what he was. It's in his blood. He knows what to do. He's just half forgot, that's all." Sonny might just as well be talking about himself.

The remainder of the film depicts how Sonny nurses Rising Star—that is, his masculinity—back to health. He must overcome Hallie as much as Ampco and the police. A clever and relentless reporter, she tracks him to his desert hideout. He makes a flying tackle on her and slaps her face, ostensibly for surprising him in the dark, but actually establishing who is boss. "You want information, go to the library," he snarls. "I know what you want. It ain't answers. You just want a story, any story. . . . I don't want to be no story. I just retired from public life."

Hallie is soon transformed from hired observer to Sonny's ally. Pursued by a posse of sheriff's deputies, FBI agents, and corporate henchmen, they take Rising Star to Utah and freedom, and fall for each other along the way. The morning after their first night of lovemaking, she wakes up sounding uncharacteristically domestic. "There's coffee and there's cheese," she announces. "Here, have some cheese." Sex on the range with a cowboy has returned her to woman's natural state, which, at least as the film envisions it, is maternal and servile.

The film ends with Hallie jetting off to Paris to cover the French elections and Sonny walking down the highway with his thumb out.

The fact that she doesn't have to give up her job to marry him lends the film a vaguely feminist aura. On the other hand, *he* doesn't have to give up the cowboy's hypermasculine code of personal honor. He can hitchhike away from contemporary society and its corruptions (including the media), and go in search of "something simple—hard maybe, but quiet and plain." As a woman and a TV reporter, Hallie will never know a comparable authenticity. The most she can do is admire his.

Eyewitness

The original title of *Eyewitness* was *The Janitor*.[38] That is because the hero of the 1981 film is Daryll Deever, a night janitor played by William Hurt. The film's author, Steve Tesich, was once himself a janitor in a New York office building. Also like his hero, Tesich was infatuated with a woman reporter on the local TV news.[39] Deever's crush on Tony Sokolow (Sigourney Weaver) is so consuming that he videotapes her every broadcast. When a murder occurs on his shift and she is sent to cover it, he feigns inside knowledge of the crime in order to meet her.

Deever may sound kind of creepy, but the film presents him as charmingly offbeat—a motorcycle-riding Vietnam vet with a gentle manner. At least Tony must find him charming, for she eventually ends up in his bed. She is yet another woman reporter—others include Megan Carter in *Absence of Malice* and Hallie Martin in *The Electric Horseman*—whose veneer of professionalism conceals a longing to be ravished by a working-class man.

The critics were divided over the plausibility of this love affair between a poor, simple janitor and a rich, famous lady reporter. Vincent Canby of the *New York Times* called it "completely believable," while "Har." of *Variety* said it "never rings true."[40] Believable or not, the love affair, by its very presence in the film, suggests that male economic and domestic authority was undergoing serious change in the real world.

Indeed, the traditional male breadwinner vanished sometime during the 1980s.[41] Millions of blue-collar men were thrown out of work by plant closings, and only 60 percent got new jobs—about half at lower pay. Surveys found that most of them blamed their woes on the feminist drive for economic equality.[42] The man in the

White House did nothing to discourage that view. "Part of the unemployment is not as much recession," Ronald Reagan said in a 1982 speech, "as it is the great increase of people going into the job market, and—ladies, I'm not picking on anyone but—because of the increase in women who are working today."[43]

Hollywood tried to symbolically restore the power working-class men had lost. Susan Faludi identified a number of eighties films—*Someone to Watch Over Me*, *Sea of Love*, *Look Who's Talking*—in which "cops and cabbies command respect from cowering affluent women."[44] She didn't mention *Eyewitness*, but she could have. When Deever, helmeted like a knight, roars to Tony's rescue on his big, black, ball-rattling motorcycle, we experience for a moment the illusion that the traditional macho man is still in charge.

Hero

This 1992 film costars Geena Davis as Gale Gayley, a gorgeous but ghoulish reporter for Channel 4, Chicago. In an early scene, she is interviewing a broker when, without warning, he jumps 60 stories to his death. "Did you get it?" she asks her cameraman and then adds in wonder at her own callousness: "Jesus, did I say that?" "Yeah," the cameraman replies to her first question. "Sports training. Learn to follow the ball."

Despite an occasional pang of conscience, Gale never ceases to be scoop crazy. On a flight home from New York, having just received the Silver Mike award for "excellence in the pursuit of truth," her plane goes down in a storm. She is so insanely addicted to reporting that even as she is being loaded into an ambulance, she tells a Channel 4 news crew sent to cover the crash, "It's my story. I did the research."

As much as *Hero* is a satire on the excesses and stupidities of TV news, it is also a male version of the Cinderella story. A homeless Vietnam vet named John Bubber (Andy Garcia) presents a mud-caked shoe as proof that he is the "Angel of Flight 104"—the man who rescued Gale and 53 other passengers from the burning plane and then modestly disappeared. He has "come forward" now because of the $1 million offered by Channel 4 for an exclusive interview with the mystery hero. Overnight, he goes from sleeping outdoors to sleeping in the fanciest hotel in Chicago—and, if he wants, with Gale.

There is just one problem: Bubber is a fake. The real hero is Bernie LaPlante (Dustin Hoffman), a slippery little thief who displayed uncharacteristic courage when the plane crash-landed in front of his car. No one—not his bartender or his lawyer or his ex-wife—believes him when he says he is the "angel." He simply doesn't fit the popular conception of a hero the way handsome, soft-spoken Bubber does. Watching Bubber being lionized on TV, Bernie can only shake his head and mutter, "It's all bullshit, I swear to God."

And Gale is responsible for most of that bullshit. The inscription on her Silver Mike award turns out to be ironic. Gale doesn't pursue truth; she pursues stories. She is a lot like the other girl reporters we have met thus far—smart, glib, ambitious, and usually wrong.

To Die For

Hollywood's attack on the amoral, socially destructive girl reporter reached something of a crescendo in the 1995 film *To Die For*, written by Buck Henry and directed by Gus Van Sant. In the film, Nicole Kidman plays Suzanne Stone, a femme fatale with Barbie Doll looks and an all-consuming ambition to be the next Diane Sawyer. When her husband, Larry (Matt Dillon), gets in the way of her career goals, she recruits three grungy, hapless teenagers to kill him. "Larry's a nice guy," she explains, "but he just doesn't know a thing about television."

Reviewers praised *To Die For* as a wicked send-up of America's TV-based culture. Janet Maslin, for example, wrote, "There are times when we get exactly the satire we deserve, and this is one of them. 'To Die For' . . . takes aim at tabloid ethics and hits a solid bull's-eye."[45] Actually, the film takes aim at more than tabloid ethics. It takes aim at the career woman as well. If Suzanne is a media-mad monster—"You're not anybody in America," she says, "unless you're on TV"—the ultimate horror is that she puts career ahead of family.

Numerous scenes in the film point up her refusal to bear children. The first is perhaps the most interesting, as it introduces a kind of generational gap in expectations for women. Suzanne and Larry, who recently moved into a fancy new condo, have their parents over to dinner. After the meal, Larry says, "Now, hang on everybody because we got a pretty important announcement . . . to make, and I think congratulations are in order." Larry's Italian-American mother begins to shriek, while his WASP mother-in-law merely looks stunned. "Wait, wait, wait," Suzanne interrupts. "Cut, cut, cut, cut. It's not that."

> **Larry's mom:** You're not pregnant?
> **Suzanne:** No, I'm not pregnant. For God's sake.
> **Larry:** Suzie's got a job.
> **Larry's dad (incredulous)**: What?

A cable TV station has hired Suzanne as its weather girl, a rinky-dink job but one that reinforces her egomaniacal fantasies of someday achieving fame. When, at another family gathering, Larry's mom asks her, "What about the idea of kids?" she replies: "I love kids. I absolutely love them. But a woman in my field with a baby has two strikes against her. Say I'm in New York, and I'm suddenly called to go on some foreign assignment, like a royal wedding or a revolution in South America. You can't run from place to place with your crew following and conduct serious interviews with a big fat stomach. Or say you've already had a baby, and you've got this blubber, these boobs out to here. It's just so gross."

Later, Larry himself approaches Suzanne about having kids: "I sure would like to have a couple of 'em around the house. Whaddya think, Suz?" "I think," she snaps, "if you wanted a babysitter, you should've married Mary Poppins."

Suzanne gets her comeuppance in the end. She finds stardom, but only as an accused murderess, not as a glamorous correspondent for *20/20*. Although she beats the charges on some legalism, Larry's dad contacts acquaintances in the Mafia and has her rubbed out, thus suggesting that ethnic patriarchies are wiser and more responsible than the postmodern society that TV represents. Throughout the closing credits, incidentally, an old Donovan song, "Season of the Witch," plays on the soundtrack. For days afterward, it was still playing in my head.

Up Close and Personal

Up Close and Personal, starring Robert Redford and Michelle Pfeiffer, was an immediate hit with older audiences when released in 1996.[46] The film follows the rise of Tally Atwater (Pfeiffer) from desk assistant at a local TV station to network correspondent. Although supposedly based on the pressurized, drug-clouded career of the late Jessica Savitch, the film reminded critics more of *A Star Is Born*.[47] This is no coincidence: Joan Didion and John Gregory Dunne, the husband-and-wife team who wrote the 1976 Streisand version of that sentimental favorite, also wrote *Up Close and Personal.*

Among the film elements Didion and Dunne recycled is the self-sacrificing, Norman Maine type of male. Tally isn't entirely—or even largely—responsible for her own success. She owes most of it to Warren Justice (Redford), a former network star, now news director at Channel 9 in Miami. As his name suggests, Justice represents integrity, "practically at the Supreme Court level."[48] We are given to understand that it is his unwillingness to compromise his integrity that accounts for his downward mobility in the slam-glam world of TV news.

And yet how admirable is Justice actually? One of his earliest remarks to Tally after she arrives at the station as a community college dropout named Sallyanne, is, "You always wear that much makeup?" He proceeds to refashion her according to the superficial ideals of TV, including bestowing upon her the telegenic name Tally. "It's easier to say," he explains.

Tally is more or less passive throughout his invention of her new persona. "Inez," he asks a makeup artist, "can you do something about the hair?" "I'm not cutting my hair," Tally protests. In the very next shot, though, she has the prescribed shorter cut.

The film half-heartedly camouflages its obsession with Tally's looks. For example, Justice lectures her on the news business, and not only on dress and deportment. "Forget yesterday," he tells her. "Yesterday is history. News happens today." But the overwhelming banality of his journalism instruction indicates that the film is mostly interested in her as an erotic object, a soft-porn queen.

Tally's erotic function is confirmed when their relationship shifts from that of mentor-pupil to that of lovers. Under the guise of helping Tally fulfill her career goals, Justice has created the woman of his fantasies—innocent, compatible, and drop-dead gorgeous. His previous relationships with women have all ended in failure. "I've been married," he says. "Twice. Bad idea." His ex-wives include Joanna Kennelly (Kate Nelligan), a high-powered TV correspondent who once double-crossed him on a story. Tally presents no such threat. She is his property, his protégée, his own golden reflection.

Critics described *Up Close and Personal* as "a satisfying, old-fashioned . . . Hollywood romance," "an alluring throwback to the days when movie-star romance really lighted up the screen." "Its guilty pleasures," Janet Maslin wrote in the *New York Times*, "are ones we all remember and plenty of us miss."[49] What she and the other critics meant, whether they realized it or not, was that they were tired of fighting the contemporary gender wars. *Up Close and Personal* is nostalgic, yes, but for a place that has existed only in men's darkest dreams—a place where a man is a man and a woman is anything he wants her to be.

Final Edition

Not long ago, Brooks Robards wrote that the journalist "represents one of the few film professions where women have almost equal status with men."[50] But, as our little visit to the cineplex has shown, this can't possibly be true. From the late 1970s till today, films that feature female reporters have persecuted these women for displaying courage and initiative. They have been punched, slapped, shot, raped, killed. Worse, they have frequently fallen in love with the very men who have beaten and humiliated them.

Violence against women is portrayed in contemporary journalism films as either amusing or socially beneficial. In fact, critics didn't even bother to mention in their reviews the battering women receive in *Absence of Malice*, *The Paper*, *I Love Trouble*, and the rest. Antifeminist feeling is evidently so ingrained in American culture that people take it for granted that the male lead—especially if he looks like a Robert Redford or a Nick Nolte—has every right to knock some sense into a woman.

I have a file folder full of newspaper clippings about the status of women in society. The headline on one says, "Study: Stereotype persists for women." The headline on another says, "Working moms struggle—study." The headline on still another says, "Women's pay trails men's." I was saving the clippings to use as final proof of women's second-class status, but now I find them strangely useless. The films are proof enough that the world needs shaking.

Notes

Introduction

1. I.C. Jarvie, *Movies and Society* (New York: Basic Books, 1970), p. 204.
2. Clifford Geertz, *After the Fact: Two Countries, Four Decades, One Anthropologist* (Cambridge, Mass.: Harvard University Press, 1995), p. 44.
3. Theodor W. Adorno, "Culture Industry Reconsidered," *New German Critique* 6 (Fall 1975): 15.
4. Ruth Ringel and Noelle Schmidt, "Comic Capers," *Middletown* (NY) *Times Herald-Record*, 16 Dec. 1995, sec. "Neighbors Ulster County," p. 1.

Chapter 1

1. Alex Barris, *Stop the Presses! The Newspaperman in American Films* (South Brunswick, N.J.: A. S. Barnes, 1976), p. 12.
2. Ezra Goodman, "Fourth Estate Gets Better Role in Films," *Editor & Publisher* 20 (10 May 1947): 26.
3. Deac Rossell, "Hollywood and the Newsroom," *American Film* 5 (Oct. 1975): 15.
4. Thomas H. Zynda, "The Hollywood Version: Movie Portrayals of the Press," *Journalism History* 6 (Spring 1979): 23.
5. Sam Fuller, "News That's Fit to Film," *American Film* 5 (Oct. 1975): 20.
6. Chip Rowe, "Hacks on Film," *Washington Journalism Review* (Nov. 1992): 28.

Chapter 2

1. Marjorie Rosen, *Popcorn Venus* (New York: Coward, McCann and Geoghegan, 1973), p. 134.

2. Molly Haskell, *From Reverence to Rape: The Treatment of Women in the Movies*, 2d ed. (Chicago: University of Chicago Press, 1987), pp. 30–31.
3. Nick Roddick, *A New Deal in Entertainment* (London: British Film Institute, 1983), pp. 91–92.
4. Deac Rossell, "The Fourth Estate and the Seventh Art," in *Questioning Media Ethics*, ed. Bernard Rubin (New York: Praeger, 1978), p. 244.
5. Elizabeth Dalton, "Meet Torchy Blane," *Film Fan Monthly* 133–34 (July–Aug. 1972): 37.
6. Quoted in ibid., 39.
7. David Zinman, "Torchy Blane and Glenda Farrell," *Filmograph* 3 (1973): 38–39.
8. William K. Everson, *The Detective in Film* (Secaucus, N.J.: Citadel, 1972), p. 135.
9. Frank S. Nugent, "The Screen" [review of *Smart Blonde*], *New York Times* 9 Jan. 1937, p. 21.
10. Shan., "Smart Blonde," *Variety* 13 Jan. 1937, p. 13.
11. Ron Goulart, *The Dime Detectives* (New York: Mysterious, 1988), p. 151; Dave Lewis, "The Backbone of *Black Mask*," *Clues* (Fall–Winter 1981): 120; Will Murray, "Nebel, Louis Frederick," in *Twentieth-Century Crime and Mystery Writers*, ed. John M. Reilly (New York: St. Martin's, 1980), p. 1105.
12. Frederick Nebel, "Take It and Like It," in *The Hard-Boiled Detective: Stories from Black Mask Magazine, 1920–51*, ed. Herbert Ruhm (New York: Vintage, 1977), p. 90.
13. Ibid., p. 94.
14. Murray, "Nebel," p. 1104.
15. Dalton, "Meet," p. 37.
16. Bernard A. Drew, ed., *Hard-Boiled Dames* (New York: St. Martin's, 1986), p. 177.
17. Quoted in ibid., pp. xv–xvi.
18. Dennis Porter, *The Pursuit of Crime: Art and Ideology in Detective Fiction* (New Haven: Yale University Press, 1981), p. 183.
19. Kathleen Gregory Klein, *The Woman Detective: Gender & Genre* (Urbana: University of Illinois Press, 1988), p. 18.

Chapter 3

1. Don Miller, *"B" Movies* (New York: Curtis, 1973), p. 37.
2. Robin Cross, *The Big Book of B Movies* (New York: St. Martin's, 1981), p. 6.
3. Ibid., p. 7.
4. Charles Flynn and Todd McCarthy, "The Economic Imperative:

Why Was the B Movie Necessary?" in *Kings of the Bs*, eds. Flynn and McCarthy (New York: Dutton, 1975), pp. 15, 17.

5. Douglas Gomery, *The Hollywood Studio System* (New York: St. Martin's, 1986), p. 118.

6. Thomas Schatz, *The Genius of the System* (New York: Pantheon, 1988), p. 216.

7. Ibid.; Cross, *Big Book*, p. 56.

8. Hobe., "Torchy Blane Runs for Mayor," *Variety*, 17 May 1939, p. 14.

9. Miller, *"B" Movies*, p. 37.

10. William Beaudine, who directed *Torchy Gets Her Man* and *Torchy Blane in Chinatown* (both 1938), the sixth and seventh films in the series, was perhaps the quintessential B-movie director. He never went over schedule or over budget, and apparently never cared for the films he was assigned to direct. The story is told of a studio executive who rushed onto the set of one of Beaudine's films and demanded to know when the film would be finished. "You mean," Beaudine said, "there's someone out there *waiting* for this?" Wheeler W. Dixon, *The "B" Directors: A Biographical Directory* (Metuchen, N.J.: Scarecrow, 1985), p. 44.

Chapter 4

1. Denis Arnold, ed. *The New Oxford Companion to Music*, vol. 2 (New York: Oxford University Press, 1983), p. 1835.

2. Elizabeth Dalton, "Meet Torchy Blane," *Film Fan Monthly* 133–34 (July–Aug. 1972): 37–42; David Zinman, "Torchy Blane and Glenda Farrell," *Filmograph* 3 (1973): 38–43.

3. John Berger, *Ways of Seeing* (London: Penguin, 1972), pp. 63–64.

4. Laura Mulvey, *Visual and Other Pleasures* (Bloomington: Indiana University Press, 1989), p. 19.

5. Michele Barrett, "Ideology and the Cultural Production of Gender," in *Feminist Criticism and Social Change*, eds. Judith Newton and Deborah Rosenfelt (New York: Methuen, 1985), p. 80.

6. "The domain of ideology," Russian linguist V.N. Volosinov wrote in the 1920s, "coincides with the domain of signs. They equate with one another. Wherever a sign is present, ideology is present." *Marxism and the Philosophy of Language* (New York: Seminar, 1973), p. 10.

7. For Althusser's tremendous influence on film studies since the 1970s, see Judith Mayne, *Cinema and Spectatorship* (London: Routledge, 1993), pp. 13–20.

8. Louis Althusser, "Ideology and Ideological State Apparatuses (Notes

Toward an Investigation)," in *Lenin and Philosophy and Other Essays* (London: NLB, 1971), pp. 128, 146, 169.

Chapter 5

1. Michael Renov, "Advertising/Photojournalism/Cinema, *Quarterly Review of Film and Video* 11 (1989): 2.

2. There were also Jane Arden and Mississippi. Both were resourceful girl reporters, Jane Arden in a comic strip named after her and Mississippi in a strip named after her detective boyfriend, Red Barry. *Jane Arden* ran from 1928 into the 1950s and was drawn by a succession of artists, including Russell Ross, Frank Ellis, Jack McGuire, and Bob Schoenke. *Red Barry* came from the pen of Will Gould, whose brother, Chester Gould, created Dick Tracy. The strip was deemed too violent by King Features Syndicate and had only a short run (1934–1939). As is the case with most older strips, copies of these two are extremely difficult to locate today, but a few sample panels are reproduced in Maurice Horn, *Women in the Comics* (New York: Chelsea, 1977), pp. 47, 52, 96. The sample from *Red Barry*, incidentally, shows Mississippi pining for a date with Barry even while she receives congratulations in the newsroom for her latest scoop. For all her professional accomplishments, she is presented as feeling lost and unfulfilled without a man.

3. Quoted in ibid., pp. 46–47.

4. Ibid., p. 91.

5. Laura Mulvey, *Visual and Other Pleasures* (Bloomington: Indiana University Press, 1989), p. 19.

6. Pam Cook and Claire Johnston, "The Place of Woman in the Cinema of Raoul Walsh," in *Raoul Walsh*, ed. Phil Hardy (Edinburgh: Edinburgh Film Festival, 1974), p. 94.

7. Mulvey, *Visual*, p. 19.

8. John Berger, *Ways of Seeing* (London: Penguin, 1972), p. 47.

9. Horn, *Women*, p. 92.

10. Frank Godwin, *Connie, A Complete Compilation: 1929–1930* (Westport, Conn.: Hyperion, 1977), p. 77.

11. William H. Chafe, *The Paradox of Change: American Women in the 20th Century* (New York: Oxford University Press, 1991), pp. 5, 51–52.

12. Louis Althusser, "Ideology and Ideological State Apparatuses (Notes Toward an Investigation)," in *Lenin and Philosophy and Other Essays* (London: NLB, 1971), p. 155.

13. See M.M. Bakhtin, *The Dialogic Imagination: Four Essays* (Austin: University of Texas, 1982).

14. Kathleen Gregory Klein, *The Woman Detective: Gender & Genre* (Urbana: University of Illinois, 1988), pp. 55–56.

15. Loren Ghiglione, *The American Journalist: Paradox of the Press* (Washington, D.C.: Library of Congress, 1990), pp. 123–25.

16. Paul Gallico, "Solo Job," in *The Great Women Detectives and Criminals: The Female of the Species*, ed. Ellery Queen (Garden City, N.Y.: Blue Ribbon, 1946), pp. 46–47.

17. Ibid., pp. 47, 49.

18. Ibid., p. 52.

19. Ibid., p. 49.

20. Ibid., p. 64.

Chapter 6

1. Elizabeth Dalton, "Meet Torchy Blane," *Film Fan Monthly* 133–34 (July–Aug. 1972): 37.

2. Press book for *Torchy Blane, The Adventurous Blonde* (1937), Motion Picture, Broadcasting and Recorded Sound Division, Library of Congress, Washington, D.C.

3. Rita Freedman, *Beauty Bound* (Lexington, Mass.: D. C. Heath, 1986), pp. 196–97; Susan Brownmiller, *Femininity* (New York: Linden, 1984), pp. 69–70.

4. Marjorie Rosen, *Popcorn Venus* (New York: Coward, McCann and Geoghegan, 1973), p. 147.

5. Richard Corson, *Fashions in Hair* (London: Peter Owen, 1965), p. 73.

6. Quoted in ibid., p. 494.

7. Susan Ware, *Holding Their Own: American Women in the 1930s* (Boston: Twayne, 1982), p. 179.

8. Quoted in Corson, *Fashions*, pp. 621–22.

9. Jackie Stacey, "Feminine Fascinations: Forms of Identification in Star-Audience Relations," in *Stardom: Industry of Desire*, ed. Christine Gledhill (London: Routledge, 1991), p. 155.

10. Charles Eckert, "The Carole Lombard in Macy's Window," in *Fabrications*, eds. Jane Gaines and Charlotte Herzog (New York: Routledge, 1990), pp. 103–04.

11. Susan Ohmer, "Female Spectatorship and Women's Magazines: Hollywood, *Good Housekeeping*, and World War II," *Velvet Light Trap* 25 (Spring 1990): 63–66.

12. Ware, *Holding*, p. 178.

Chapter 7

1. Richard Dyer, *Stars* (London: British Film Institute, 1972), p. 111.
2. Quoted in Polly Birchard, "'I Want to Be Helpless for a Change!' Says Glenda Farrell," *Movie Classics* 5 (Oct. 1933): 55.
3. Dorothy Spensley, "Hitting the High Spots with Glenda," *Motion Picture* 53 (Mar. 1937): 73.
4. Terrence Costello, "Gay, Gifted and Going Places—That's Glenda!" *Motion Picture* 45 (Mar. 1933): 93.
5. Ibid.; "We Nominate for Stardom: Glenda Farrell," *Motion Picture* 45 (Feb. 1933): 42.
6. "Nominate," p. 42; Spensley, "Hitting," p. 74.
7. Birchard, "I Want," p. 77.
8. Ibid., p. 55.
9. "Nominate," p. 42.
10. Spensley, "Hitting," p. 72.
11. Birchard, "I Want," p. 76.
12. Costello, "Gay," p. 93.
13. Maude Cheatham, "Two Blonde Menaces," *Silver Screen* (Nov. 1936): 28.
14. Spensley, "Hitting," p. 73.
15. Birchard, "I Want," p. 79.
16. Richard M. Huber, *The American Idea of Success* (New York: McGraw-Hill, 1971), p. 6.
17. Cheatham, "Two," p. 28.
18. Spensely, "Hitting," p. 74.

Chapter 8

1. Quoted in David Zinman, "Torchy Blane and Glenda Farrell," *Filmograph* 3 (1973): 40.
2. Dorothy Spensley, "Hitting the High Spots with Glenda," *Motion Picture* 53 (Mar. 1937): 72–73.
3. William K. Everson, *The Detective in Film* (Secaucus, N.J.: Citadel, 1972), p. 135.
4. David J. Skal, *The Monster Show: A Cultural History of Horror* (New York: Norton, 1993), pp. 173–74.
5. Abel, "Wax Museum," *Variety Film Reviews, 1930–1933*, vol. 4 (New York: Garland, 1983), Feb. 21, 1933. Richard Harding Davis, perhaps the foremost American journalist of the late nineteenth and early twentieth centuries, wrote numerous short stories with newspaper backgrounds, including "Gallegher, a Newspaper Story," "The Red Cross Girl,"

"A Derelict," "The Reporter Who Made Himself King," and "The Deserter." Jesse Lynch Williams, a former reporter on the *New York Sun*, was the author of *The Stolen Story and Other Newspaper Stories* (1899) and *The Day-Dreamer* (1906). For more on the literary portrayal of journalists, see Howard Good, *Acquainted with the Night: The Image of Journalists in American Fiction, 1890–1930* (Metuchen, N.J.: Scarecrow, 1986).

6. Mordaunt Hall, "Lionel Atwill and Fay Wray in Gruesome Narrative about a Mad Modeler of Wax Figures," *New York Times Film Reviews, 1932–1938*, vol. 2 (New York: New York Times & Arno, 1970), pp. 909–10.

7. Elizabeth Dalton, "Meet Torchy Blane," *Film Fan Monthly* 133–34 (July–Aug. 1972): 37. See also Elizabeth Dalton, "Women at Work: Warners in the Thirties," *Velvet Light Trap* 6 (n.d.): 15–20.

8. Jordan wrote that Miss Masters "wore blonde hair and much red paint," implying that she was no better than a "painted woman," or prostitute. Elizabeth G. Jordan, "Miss Van Dyke's Best Story," in *Tales of the City Room* (New York: Scribner's, 1898), p. 223.

9. Ibid., p. 229.

10. Quoted in Zinman, "Torchy," p. 39.

Chapter 9

1. Vivian Sobchack, "Genre Film: Myth, Ritual, and Sociodrama," in *Film/Culture*, ed. Sari Thomas (Metuchen, N.J.: Scarecrow Press, 1982), pp. 147–65; Rick Altman, *The American Film Musical* (Bloomington: Indiana University Press, 1989), particularly pp. 330–34; and Thomas Schatz, *Hollywood Genres: Formulas, Filmmaking, and the Studio System* (New York: Random House, 1981).

2. Jeffrey Brown Martin, *Ben Hecht, Hollywood Screenwriter* (Ann Arbor, Mich.: UMI Research Press, 1985), p. 41.

3. For recent examples, see Christopher Hanson, "Where Have All the Heroes Gone?" *Columbia Journalism Review*, Mar./Apr. 1996, pp. 45–47; and Chip Rowe, "Hacks on Film," *Washington Journalism Review*, Nov. 1992, pp. 27–29.

4. Sobchack, "Genre Film," p. 159.

5. United Artists cast O'Brien for the film under the mistaken impression that he, and not Lee Tracy, played the role of Hildy on Broadway.

6. Martin, *Hecht*, p. 54.

7. Jane Gross, "Movies and the Press Are an Enduring Romance," *New York Times*, 2 June 1985, sec. 2, p. 1.

8. Rowe, "Hacks," p. 28; Martin, *Hecht*, p. 45.

9. Brooks Robards, "Newshounds and Sob Sisters: The Journalist Goes

to Hollywood," in *Beyond the Stars: Stock Characters in American Popular Film*, vol. 1, eds. Paul Loukides and Linda K. Fuller (Bowling Green, Ohio: Popular Press, 1990), p. 137.

10. Quoted in Mathew C. Ehrlich, "Thinking Critically about Journalism through Popular Culture," *Journalism Educator* 50 (Winter 1996): 39.

11. The phrase comes from a newspaper novel by Ben Ames Williams, *Splendor* (New York: Dutton, 1927), p. 205. Such novels typically explore the downside of newspaper work. See Howard Good, *Acquainted with the Night: The Image of Journalists in American Fiction, 1890–1930* (Metuchen, N.J.: Scarecrow Press, 1986).

12. Quoted in Ted Curtis Smythe, "The Reporter, 1880–1990: Working Conditions and Their Influence on the News," *Journalism History* 7 (Spring 1980): 5.

13. Samuel Blythe, *The Making of a Newspaper Man* (Philadelphia: Henry Altemus, 1912), pp. 28–30.

14. Edwin Shuman, *Practical Journalism* (New York: Appleton, 1903), p. 148.

15. "Bye-the-Bye," *Journalist* (Jan. 26, 1889): 12.

16. Stanley Frank and Paul Sann, "Paper Dolls," in *More Post Biographies*, ed. John E. Drewery (Athens, Ga.: University of Georgia Press, 1947), p. 208.

17. Kay Mills, *A Place in the News: From the Women's Pages to the Front Page* (New York: Dodd, Mead, 1988), p. 4.

18. Lois Banner, *Women in Modern America: A Brief History* (New York: Harcourt Brace Jovanovich, 1974), p. 36.

19. Stephen Hanson, "La Cava, Gregory," in *The International Dictionary of Films and Filmmakers*, vol. 2 (Chicago: St. James Press, 1984), pp. 310–11.

20. Roger McNiven, "Gregory La Cava," in *American Directors*, vol. 1, ed. Jean Pierre Cousdon with Pierre Sauvage (New York: McGraw-Hill, 1983), p. 198.

21. Jesse Lynch Williams, "The Old Reporter," in *The Stolen Story and Other Newspaper Stories* (New York: Scribner's, 1899; reprint ed., Freeport, N.Y.: Books for Libraries Press, 1969), pp. 217–91.

22. H.L. Mencken, *Newspaper Days* (New York: Knopf, 1941), p. 181.

23. Blythe, *Newspaper Man*, p. 236.

24. Charles J. Rosebault, *When Dana Was the Sun* (New York: Robert M. McBride, 1931; reprint ed., Westport, Conn.: Greenwood Press, 1970), pp. 166–67.

25. Richard Hoyt, *30 for a Harry* (New York: M. Evans, 1981), p. 29.

26. Ernest Becker, *The Denial of Death* (New York: Free Press, 1973), p. 74.

27. Waly., "Big News," *Variety*, Oct. 9, 1929, n.p.

28. See, for example, Deac Rossell, "The Fourth Estate and the Seventh Art," in *Questioning Media Ethics*, ed. Bernard Rubin (New York: Praeger, 1978), p. 259. Lingle was Al Capone's favorite newspaperman. He was shot down in the street a day before IRS investigators were to question him about Capone's income. A detailed account of the killing can be found in John Kobler, *Capone* (New York: Collier, 1971), pp. 294–312.

29. Shan., "Dance, Fools, Dance," *Variety*, March 25, 1931, np.

30. Ibid.

31. Graham Greene, "A Director of Genius: Four Reviews," in *Frank Capra: The Man and His Films*, eds. Richard Glatzer and John Raeburn (Ann Arbor, Mich.: University of Michigan Press, 1975), p. 110.

32. Quoted in Andrew Bergman, "Frank Capra and Screwball Comedy," in ibid., p. 77.

33. Joanne L. Yeck, "Mr. Deeds Goes to Town," in *Magill's Survey of Cinema*, series 2, vol. 4 (Englewood Cliffs, N.J.: Salem, 1981), p. 1613.

34. Greene, "Director," p. 110.

35. Yeck, "Mr. Deeds," p. 1613.

36. Charles Maland, *Frank Capra* (Boston: Twayne, 1980), p. 96.

37. Quoted in ibid., p. 98.

38. Rosalind Russell and Chris Chase, *Life Is a Banquet* (New York: Random House, 1977), p. 89.

39. Ibid., p. 87.

40. Ed Sikov, *Screwball: Hollywood's Madcap Romantic Comedies* (New York: Crown, 1989), p. 168.

41. Quoted in Pauline Kael, *The Citizen Kane Book* (Boston: Little, Brown, 1971), p. 48.

42. Molly Haskell, *From Reverence to Rape: The Treatment of Women in the Movies* (New York: Rinehart and Winston, 1974), p. 134; Sikov, *Screwball*, p. 168.

43. Herb., "His Girl Friday," *Variety*, Jan. 10, 1940, n.p.

44. See chapter 2, "Girl Reporter."

45. Martin, *Hecht*, pp. 94–95.

46. Ibid., pp. 95–96.

47. Manny Farber, "Howard Hawks," in *Focus on Howard Hawks*, ed. Joseph McBride (Englewood Cliffs, N.J.: Prentice-Hall, 1972), p. 29; Robin Wood, *Howard Hawks*, rev. ed. (London: British Film Institute, 1981), p. 73; Leland A. Poague, *Howard Hawks* (Boston: Twayne, 1982), p. 131; and Sikov, *Screwball*, p. 168.

48. Donald C. Willis, *The Films of Howard Hawks* (Metuchen, N.J.: Scarecrow Press, 1975), p. 15.

49. Farber, "Hawks," p. 29.

50. Ibid.

51. Wood, *Hawks*, p. 77.

52. Janet St. Claire, "Woman of the Year," in *Magill's Survey of Cinema*, Second Series, vol. 6 (Englewood Cliffs, N.J.: Salem Press, 1981), p. 2705.

53. Herb., "Woman of the Year," *Variety*, Jan. 14, 1942, n.p.

54. Michele Barrett, "Ideology and the Cultural Production of Gender," in *Feminist Criticism and Social Change*, eds. Judith Newton and Deborah Rosenfelt (New York: Methuen, 1985), p. 80.

Chapter 10

1. Marion Marzolf, *Up from the Footnote: A History of Women Journalists* (New York: Hastings, 1977), p. 50.

2. Ishbel Ross, *Ladies of the Press* (New York: Harper & Brothers, 1936), p. 2.

3. Susan Ware, *Holding Their Own: American Women in the 1930s* (Boston: Twayne, 1982), p. 76.

4. Marjorie Rosen, *Popcorn Venus* (New York: Coward, McCann and Geoghegan, 1973), p. 135.

5. Ware, *Holding*, p. 76.

6. Kay Mills, *A Place in the News: From the Women's Pages to the Front Page* (New York: Dodd, Mead, 1988), p. 41.

7. Ross, *Ladies*, p. 13.

8. Quoted in Mills, *Place*, p. 45.

9. Loren Ghiglione, *The American Journalist: Paradox of the Press* (Washington, D.C.: Library of Congress, 1990), p. 98; Nick Roddick, *A New Deal in Entertainment* (London: British Film Institute, 1983), pp. 91–92; Ware, *Holding*, p. 75.

10. Rosen, *Popcorn*, p. 135. See also Deac Rossell, "The Fourth Estate and the Seventh Art," in *Questioning Media Ethics*, ed. Bernard Rubin (New York: Praeger, 1978), p. 244.

11. William H. Chafe, *The Paradox of Change: American Women in the Twentieth Century* (New York: Oxford University Press, 1991), pp. 100–01.

12. Ibid., p. 71.

13. Ibid., p. 65.

14. Rosen, *Popcorn*, p. 134.

15. Molly Haskell, *From Reverence to Rape: The Treatment of Women in the Movies*, 2d ed. (Chicago: University of Chicago Press, 1987), p. 142.

16. Rosen, *Popcorn*, p. 134.

17. Haskell, *Reverence*, p. 12.

18. Knight-Ridder Newspapers, "Bad News," *Middletown* (NY) *Times Herald Record*, July 27, 1995, p. 40.

19. Ross, *Ladies*, pp. 65–66.

20. Mary Margaret McBride, *A Long Way from Missouri* (New York: G.P. Putnam's Sons, 1959), p. 73.
21. Agness Underwood, *Newspaperwoman* (New York: Harper & Brothers, 1949), p. 151.
22. Mills, *Place*, p. 25.
23. Ross, *Ladies*, p. 262.

Chapter 11

1. Quoted in "What Happens to Old Heavies?" *TV Guide* (Apr. 25, 1961): 29.
2. Ibid.
3. Ibid.
4. James Robert Parish, *Hollywood Character Actors* (New Rochelle, N.Y.: Arlington House, 1978), pp. 353–54.
5. Quoted in Michael R. Pitts, *Famous Movie Detectives* (Metuchen, N.J.: Scarecrow Press, 1979), p. 275.
6. Wear., "Fly-Away Baby," *Variety*, 14 July 1937, p. 21.
7. Parish, *Character Actors*, p. 353.
8. Elizabeth Dalton, "Meet Torchy Blane," *Film Fan Monthly* 133–34 (July–Aug. 1972): 37.
9. Frank S. Nugent, "The Screen" [review of *Smart Blonde*], *New York Times*, 9 Jan. 1937, p. 21.
10. G.M., "The Adventurous Blonde," *Motion Picture Herald*, 11 Sept. 1937, p. 40.
11. Ben Taves, "The B Film: Hollywood's Other Half," in *Grand Design: Hollywood as a Modern Business Enterprise, 1930–39*, ed. Tino Balio (Berkeley, Calif.: University of California Press, 1993), pp. 313–50. Vol. 5 of *History of the American Cinema.*
12. Robin Cross, *The Big Book of B Movies* (New York: St. Martin's Press, 1981), p. 50.
13. And so did Farrell, who won an Emmy as best supporting actress in 1963 for her role in an episode of the medical series *Ben Casey*. She also was a guest star on *Wagon Train*, *Bonanza*, *The Fugitive*, *The Defenders*, and *Dr. Kildare*, among other TV shows. "Glenda Farrell, Film Star, Dies at 66," *New York Times*, 2 May 1971, p. 74.
14. Quoted in "Old Heavies," p. 29.
15. Biographical information on Tom Kennedy was drawn from the press book for *Torchy Blane, the Adventurous Blonde* (1938), Motion Picture, Broadcasting and Recorded Sound Division, Library of Congress, as well as from Michael R. Pitts, *Famous Movie Detectives* (Metuchen, N.J.: Scarecrow Press, 1979), p. 275.

16. Pitt, *Famous Detectives*, p. 275; Dalton, "Meet," 37; Hurl., "Blondes at Work," *Variety*, 16 Mar. 1938, p. 17.

Chapter 12

1. *New York Times*, 1 Jan. 1937, p. 1; 9 Jan. 1937, pp. 1, 2, 19.
2. *NYT*, 9 July 1937, p. 1; 10 July, 1937, p. 10.
3. *NYT*, 13 Dec. 1937, p. 25; 18 Dec. 1937, pp. 1, 6.
4. *NYT*, 16 Mar. 1938, pp. 1, 3–4, 23.
5. *NYT*, 13 Apr. 1938, p. 5; 18 Apr. 1938, pp. 5–6.
6. *NYT*, 15 Nov. 1938, p. 1; 18 Nov. 1938, p. 1.
7. *NYT*, 3 Feb. 1939, pp. 2, 19; 5 Feb. 1939, p. 1.
8. *NYT*, 11 May 1939, pp. 1, 4; 17 May 1939, p. 1.
9. *NYT*, 27 Sept. 1939, pp. 1, 16, 23.

Chapter 13

1. Janet Staiger, *Interpreting Films* (Princeton, N.J.: Princeton University Press, 1992), p. 211.

2. Judith Mayne, *Cinema and Spectatorship* (London: Routledge, 1993), p. 146.

3. Ibid.

4. Patricia Zimmerman, "Soldiers of Fortune: Lucas, Spielberg, Indiana Jones and *Raiders of the Lost Ark*," *Wide Angle* 6 (1984): 34.

5. Deac Rossell, "The Fourth Estate and the Seventh Art," *Questioning Media Ethics*, ed. Bernard Rubin (New York: Praeger, 1978), pp. 247–82.

6. Frank S. Nugent, "The Screen" [review of *Smart Blonde*], *New York Times*, 9 Jan. 1937, p. 21.

7. Shan.,"Smart Blonde," *Variety*, 13 Jan. 1937, p. 13; Wear., "Fly-Away Baby," *Variety*, 14 July 1937, p. 21; Hurl., "Blondes at Work," *Variety*, 16 Mar. 1938, p. 17; "Torchy Blane in Panama," *Variety*, 13 Apr. 1938, p. 15; "Torchy Gets Her Man," *Variety*, 12 Oct. 1938, p. 15; *Variety*, 28 Dec. 1938, p. 13; "Torchy Blane Runs for Mayor," *Variety*, 17 May 1939, p. 14.

8. Wheeler W. Dixon, *The "B" Directors: A Biographical Directory* (Metuchen, N.J.: Scarecrow Press, 1985), p. 3.

9. Brian Taves, "The B Film: Hollywood's Other Half," in *Grand Design: Hollywood as a Modern Business Enterprise, 1930–39*, ed. Tino Balio (Berkeley, Calif.: University of California, Press, 1993), p. 335. Vol. 5 of *History of the American Cinema*.

10. Nugent, "Screen," p. 21.

11. T.M.P., "At the Palace" [review of *Fly-Away Baby*], *New York Times*, 9 July 1937, p. 18.

12. B.R.C., "At the Palace" [review of *Torchy Blane, the Adventurous Blonde*], *New York Times*, 18 Dec. 1937, p. 18.

13. Gay Talese, *The Kingdom and the Power* (New York: Bantam, 1969), pp. 74, 583.

14. B.C., "At the Strand" [review of *Torchy Blane in Panama*], *New York Times*, 18 Apr. 1938, p. 11.

15. B.C., "At the Palace" [review of *Torchy Blane in Chinatown*], *New York Times*, 3 Feb. 1939, p. 13.

16. Nugent, "Screen," p. 21; T.M.P., "At the Palace," p. 18; B.R.C., "At the Palace," p. 18; B.C., "At the Strand," p. 11; B.R.C., "At the Palace [review of *Torchy Gets Her Man*], *New York Times*, 18 Nov. 1938, p. 25; B.C., "At the Palace," p. 13.

17. "Torchy Runs for Mayor," *Daily Variety*, 25 Mar. 1939, p. 3.

18. "WB 'Smart Blonde' Routine Wisecracked Mystery Yarn," *Hollywood Reporter*, 18 Nov. 1936, p. 3.

19. "Third Torchy Tale Upholds Standard," *Hollywood Reporter*, 10 Jan. 1938, p. 2; "Film Previews" [review of *Fly-Away Baby*], *Daily Variety*, 2 June 1937, p. 3; "Film Previews" [review of *Torchy Blane, the Adventurous Blonde*], *Daily Variety*, 2 Sept. 1937, p. 3; Hurl., "Blondes at Work," *Variety*, 16 Mar. 1938, p. 17; Hobe., "Torchy Runs for Mayor," *Variety*, 17 May 1939, p. 14.

20. "Preview" [review of *Blondes at Work*], *Daily Variety*, 11 Jan. 1938, p. 3.

21. "Lane, Kelly Stand Out in Slim Story," *Hollywood Reporter*, 2 May 1938, p. 3.

22. "Blondes at Work, *Variety*, 16 Mar. 1938, p. 17.

23. G.M., "The Adventurous Blonde," *Motion Picture Herald*, 11 Sept. 1937, pp. 40–41.

24. P.C.M., "Torchy Blane in Panama," *Motion Picture Herald*, 30 Apr. 1938, pp. 46–47.

25. G.M., "Torchy Gets Her Man," *Motion Picture Herald*, 15 Oct. 1938, p. 40.

26. P.C.M., Jr., "Torchy Blane in Chinatown," *Motion Picture Herald*, 11 Feb. 1939, p. 41.

27. "Torchy in Chinatown," *Variety*, 28 Dec. 1938, p. 13; "Infantile Whodunit Knocks Series Cold," *Hollywood Reporter*, 24 Dec. 1938, p. 3.

28. P.C.M., Jr., "Torchy Blane in Chinatown," p. 41.

Chapter 14

1. Anne Hollander, *Sex and Suits* (New York: Knopf, 1994), p. 7.

2. For a different—more one-sided and contentious—interpretation of

women's clothes, see Jane Gaines, "Costume and Narrative: How Dress Tells the Woman's Story," in *Fabrications: Costume and the Female Body*, eds. Gaines and Charlotte Herzog (New York: Routledge, 1990), pp. 180–211. "Although all characters, regardless of gender, are conceived as 'costumed' in motion pictures," Gaines wrote, "a woman's dress and demeanor, much more than a man's, indexes psychology; if costume represents interiority, it is she who is turned inside out on the screen."

3. Hollander, *Sex*, p. 151.

4. Ruth P. Rubinstein, *Dress Codes: Meanings and Messages in American Culture* (Boulder, Colo.: Westview Press), p.110.

5. Hollander, *Sex*, p. 44.

6. Rubinstein, *Dress Codes*, p. 109.

7. Hollander, *Sex*, p. 23.

8. Quoted in Alison Lurie, *The Language of Clothes* (New York: Random House, 1981), p. 244.

9. By 1930, James Laver remarked, "The universal cloche was abandoned in favour of an immense variety of hats; the only rule was that they had to be extremely small and poked forward over one eye." Laver, *Costume* (London: Cassell, 1963), p. 121.

10. Rita Freedman, *Beauty Bound* (Lexington, Mass.: Lexington Books, 1986), p. 37.

11. B.C., "At the Strand" [review of *Torchy Blane in Panama*], *New York Times*, 18 Apr. 1938, p. 11. Reviewing the same film, the *Hollywood Reporter* described McBride as a detective "who is about as close to zero in detecting intelligence as the screen has offered." "Lane, Kelly Stand Out in Slim Story," *Hollywood Reporter*, 2 May 1938, p. 3.

12. William K. Everson, *The Detective in Film* (Secaucus, N.J.: Citadel, 1972), p. 135.

13. Hollander, *Sex*, p. 124.

Chapter 15

1. Vey, "Non Sequitur," Washington Post Writers Group, 23 Feb. 1996.

2. Lilla Worthington, letter to Jacob Wilk, 4 Feb. 1936, Box 72, Warner Brothers Contract and Copyright File, Wisconsin Center for Film and Theater Research, Madison, Wis.

3. Elizabeth Dalton, "Meet Torchy Blane," *Film Fan Monthy* 133–34 (July–Aug. 1972): 38.

4. For more on Kilgallen, see Ishbel Ross, *Ladies of the Press* (New York: Harper & Brothers, 1936), pp. 240–45.

5. Collier Young, letters to Jacob Wilk, 8 July 1937 and 27 Aug. 1937,

Box 72, Warner Brothers Contract and Copyright File, Wisconsin Center for Film and Theater Research, Madison, Wis.

6. Collier Young, letter to Morris Ebenstein, 20 July 1937, Box 72, Warner Brothers Contract and Copyright File, Wisconsin Center for Film and Theater Research, Madison, Wis.

7. The agreement between Warner Brothers and Nebel was recorded in Book 399, pp. 41–43, U.S. Copyright Office, Washington, D.C., on 29 June 1938.

8. Mr. Einfeld, office memorandum to Mr. Starr, 1 Oct. 1929, Box 72, Warner Brothers Contract and Copyright File, Wisconsin Center for Film and Theater Research, Madison, Wis.

9. Published in the Mar. 4, 1920, issue of *Snappy Stories*.

10. Johnson & Tannebaum, letter to Warner Brothers, 1 Mar. 1948, Box 72, Warner Brothers Contract and Copyright File, Wisconsin Center for Film and Theater Research, Madison, Wis.

11. Thomas Schatz, *The Genius of the System* (New York: Pantheon, 1988), p. 139.

12. Quoted in Ian Hamilton, *Writers in Hollywood, 1915–1951* (New York: Carroll & Graf, 1990), p. 123.

13. Quoted in Ezra Goodman, "Fourth Estate Gets Better Role in Films," *Editor & Publisher* 20 (10 May 1947): 26.

14. Ibid.

15. Chip Rowe, "Hacks on Film," *Washington Journalism Review* (Nov. 1992): 27.

16. I am lightly paraphrasing film producer Lester Cowan, quoted in Goodman, "Fourth Estate," p. 26.

17. Agreement between Warner Brothers and Larry Williams, 4 Oct. 1937, Box 72, Warner Brothers Contract and Copyright File, Wisconsin Center for Film and Theater Research, Madison, Wis.

18. Agreement between Warner Brothers and John Miljan, 5 Nov. 1938, Box 72, Warner Brothers Contract and Copyright File, Wisconsin Center for Film and Theater Research, Madison, Wis.

19. "Direction, Editing Lift Slim Story," *Hollywood Reporter*, 25 Mar. 1939, p. 4. *Variety* was less effusive. "John Miljan," it said, "makes a few tricks do as the suave menace." "Torchy Runs for Mayor," *Variety*, 17 May 1939, p. 14.

20. Warner Brothers, letter to Tom Kennedy, 13 May 1938, 4 Oct. 1937, Box 72, Warner Brothers Contract and Copyright File, Wisconsin Center for Film and Theater Research, Madison, Wis.

21. Dalton, "Meet," pp. 39–40.

22. Warner Brothers, letter to Barton MacLane, 19 May 1938, and letter to Glenda Farrell, 5 May 1938, Box 72, Warner Brothers Contract and Copyright File, Wisconsin Center for Film and Theater Research, Madison, Wis.

23. Elizabeth Dalton, "Women at Work: Warners in the Thirties," *Velvet Light Trap* 6 (n.d.): 15.

24. Schatz, *Genius*, p. 136.

25. Russell Campbell, "Warner Brothers in the Thirties: Some Tentative Notes," *Velvet Light Trap* 6 (n.d.): 3.

26. *Statistical Abstract of the United States 1941* (Washington, D.C.: U.S. Government Printing Office, 1942), p. 347.

Chapter 16

1. See, for example, Frank S. Nugent, "The Screen" [review of *Smart Blonde*], *New York Times*, 9 Jan. 1937, p. 21; Wear., "Fly-Away Baby," *Variety*, 14 July 1937, p. 21; and "Adventurous Blonde," *Film Daily*, 30 Nov. 1937, p. 4.

2. Andrew Bergman observed that during the Depression era, a "great many films appeared that concerned themselves with corrupt and racy people who lived and worked in the city." He referred to these as "shyster films" and said they were similar to gangster films in that "they also assigned a feckless role to the law." In his estimation, the shyster films were "an extended metaphor for national uncertainty, substituting crooks for economic short-circuits." Bergman, *We're in the Money: Depression America and Its Films* (New York: Harper & Row, 1971), pp. 18, 90.

3. John D'Emilio and Estelle B. Freedman, *Intimate Matters: A History of Sexuality in America* (New York: Harper & Row, 1988), p. 234.

4. Quoted in ibid.

5. Ibid., pp. 188–89, 227, 234.

6. Virginia Wright Wexman, *Creating the Couple: Love, Marriage, and Hollywood Performance* (Princeton, N.J.: Princeton University Press, 1993), p. 13.

7. D'Emilio, *Intimate*, p. 265.

8. William F. Chafe, *The Paradox of Change: American Women in the Twentieth Century* (New York: Oxford University Press, 1991), p. 64.

9. Frederick Lewis Allen, *The Big Change: America Transforms Itself, 1900–1950* (New York: Harper & Row, 1952), p. 136.

10. Chafe, *Paradox*, p. 106.

11. D'Emilio, *Intimate*, p. 242.

12. Elizabeth Kendall, *The Runaway Bride: Hollywood Romantic Comedy of the 1930s* (New York: Alfred A. Knopf, 1990), p. xiv.

13. Ibid., p. 44.

14. Wexman, *Couple*, p. ix.

15. Ibid., p. 13.

16. Drawing on *The Anatomy of Criticism* by Northrop Frye, Stanley

Cavell has described the genre of screwball comedy as "an inheritor of the preoccupations and discoveries of Shakespearean romantic comedy." The relation of screwball comedy to the Torchy Blane films is discussed in chapter 17, "The Kiss." Cavell, *Pursuits of Happiness: The Hollywood Comedy of Remarriage* (Cambridge, Mass.: Harvard University Press, 1981), p. 1.

17. D'Emilio, *Intimate*, p. 266.

18. Quoted in Mark Simpson, *Male Impersonation: Men Performing Masculinity* (New York: Routledge, 1994), p. 103.

Chapter 17

1. See Elizabeth Kendall, *The Runaway Bride: Hollywood Romantic Comedy of the 1930s* (New York: Alfred A. Knopf, 1990).

2. Elizabeth Dalton, "Meet Torchy Blane," *Film Fan Monthly* 133–34 (July–Aug. 1972): 37. In *Torchy Gets Her Man*, the sixth film in the series, Farrell delivers a 400-word speech in 40 seconds. David Zinman, "Torchy Blane and Glenda Farrell," *Filmograph* 3 (1973): 38.

3. Wes D. Gehrig. *Screwball Comedy: A Genre of Madcap Romance* (New York: Greenwood Press, 1986), p. 163.

4. Kendall, *Runaway*, p. 54.

5. Ibid., p. xv.

6. Joan Mellen, *Big Bad Wolves: Masculinity in the American Film* (New York: Pantheon, 1977), p. 312.

7. Quoted in John D'Emilio and Estelle B. Freedman, *Intimate Matters: A History of Sexuality in America* (New York: Harper & Row, 1988), p. 197.

8. Quoted in ibid.

9. Ibid., p. 45.

10. Virginia Wright Wexman, *Creating the Couple: Love, Marriage, and Hollywood Performance* (Princeton, N.J.: Princeton University Press, 1993), p. 18.

11. Quoted in Jacques de Caso and Patricia B. Sanders, *Rodin's Sculpture: A Critical Study of the Spreckels Collection* (Rutland, Vt.: Charles E. Tuttle, 1977), p. 149.

12. Ibid.

13. Ibid., pp.149–50.

Chapter 18

1. Joan Mellen, *Big Bad Wolves: Masculinity in the American Film* (New York: Pantheon, 1977), pp. 15, 311–12.

2. Leslie Fiedler, *A Fiedler Reader* (New York: Stein and Day, 1977), pp. 5–7, 12.

3. John H. Gagnon, "Physical Strength, Once of Significance," in *Men and Masculinity*, eds. Joseph H. Pleck and Jack Sawyer (Englewood Cliffs, N.J.: Prentice-Hall, 1974), pp. 139, 148.

4. Arnold R. Beisser, *The Madness in Sports: Psychosocial Observations on Sports* (New York: Appleton-Century-Crofts, 1967), p. 225.

Chapter 19

1. Elizabeth Dalton, "Meet Torchy Blane," *Film Fan Monthly* 133–34 (July–Aug. 1972): 39.

2. Deac Rossell, "The Fourth Estate and the Seventh Art," in *Questioning Media Ethics*, ed. Bernard Rubin (New York: Praeger, 1978), p. 267.

3. Dalton, "Meet," 39. Lola Lane starred with her sisters, Rosemary and Priscilla Lane, in "Four Daughters," "Four Wives," and "Four Mothers," all for Warner Brothers. While best known for their appearances together, the sisters each had a separate career.

4. "Lola Lane, Acted in 30's and 40's," *New York Times*, 25 June 1981, sec. 4, p. 23.

5. James Robert Parish and William T. Leonard, *Hollywood Players: The Thirties* (New Rochelle, N.Y.: Arlington House, 1976), pp. 326–29.

6. Ibid., p. 330.

7. "Torchy Blane in Panama," *Variety*, 13 April 1938, p. 15.

8. "Lane, Kelly Stand Out in Slim Story," *Hollywood Reporter*, 2 May 1938, p. 3.

9. P.C.M., "Torchy Blane in Panama," *Motion Picture Herald*, 30 Apr. 1938, pp. 46, 48.

10. Dalton, "Meet," 39; Michael R. Pitts, *Famous Movie Detectives* (Metuchen, N.J.: Scarecrow Press, 1979), p. 278.

11. B.C., "At the Strand" [review of *Torchy Blane in Panama*], *New York Times*, 18 Apr. 1938, p. 11.

12. Ibid. Other reviews also mention that McBride seems clueless. *Variety*, for example, called him "a not overbright flat-foot." "Panama," *Variety*, p. 15, p. 3.

13. The phrase was coined by M.M. Bakhtin, *The Dialogic Imagination: Four Essays* (Austin: University of Texas, 1982).

14. Kathleen Gregory Klein, *The Woman Detective: Gender and Genre* (Urbana, Ill.: University of Illinois Press, 1988), p. 124.

Chapter 20

1. Kathleen Gregory Klein, *The Woman Detective: Gender & Genre* (Urbana, Ill.: University of Illinois Press, 1988), pp. 186–87, 197.

2. G.M., "Fly-Away Baby," *Motion Picture Herald*, 12 June 1937, p. 78.

3. "Fly-Away Baby," *Daily Variety*, 2 June 1937, p. 3. Another review in *Variety*, this time of *Torchy Blane in Chinatown*, said, "Torchy speeds up solution of the mystery to secure scoop for her sheet, while [McBride] flounders around long enough to pile up footage for an hour's unfolding." "Torchy in Chinatown," *Variety*, 28 Dec. 1938, p. 13.

4. Joan Mellen, *Big Bad Wolves: Masculinity in the American Film* (New York: Pantheon, 1977), p. 3.

5. T.J. Jackson Lears, *No Place of Grace: Antimodernism and the Transformation of American Culture, 1880–1920* (New York: Pantheon, 1981), p. 48.

6. John H. Gagnon, "Physical Strength, Once of Significance," in *Men and Masculinity*, eds. Joseph H. Pleck and Jack Sawyer (Englewood Cliffs, N.J.: Prentice-Hall, 1974), p. 144. See also Arnold R. Beisser, *The Madness in Sports* (New York: Appleton-Century-Crofts, 1967), p. 225.

7. John D'Emilio and Estelle B. Freedman, *Intimate Matters: A History of Sexuality* (New York: Harper & Row, 1988), pp. 234–35. See also Christopher Lasch, *The New Radicalism in America: The Intellectual as a Social Type* (New York: Knopf, 1965), pp. 13, 62, 64.

8. Drawing on Louis Althusser's famous essay, "Ideology and Ideological State Apparatuses (Notes Toward an Investigation)," Dennis Porter asserted that the particular mission of the detective story "involves the celebration of the repressive state apparatus or at least that important element of it formed by the police." *The Pursuit of Crime: Art and Ideology in Detective Fiction* (New Haven: Yale University Press, 1981), p. 121.

9. "One 'Torchy' Ends Tues., Another Begins Wednes.," *Hollywood Reporter*, 12 Aug. 1938, p. 21.

10. Wheeler W. Dixon, *The "B" Directors: A Biographical Directory* (Metuchen, N.J.: Scarecrow Press, 1985), p. 44.

11. "Infantile Whodunit Knocks Series Cold" [review of *Torchy Blane in Chinatown*], *Hollywood Reporter*, 24 Dec. 1938, p. 3.

12. A remark by Mellen seems relevant here: "Most movies portray men in competition with each other, for women, money, status, and power, with the best man . . . winning. Individual initiative and the pleasure of competition are values approved by our economy, and the male star demonstrates their virtue." *Wolves*, pp. 9–10.

13. Warners' publicity department played up the fact that Farrell had been elected honorary mayor of North Hollywood in 1937, easily defeating Bing Crosby and Lewis Stone.

14. Quoted in David Zinman, "Torchy Blane and Glenda Farrell," *Filmograph* 3 (1973): 42.

15. Michael R. Pitts, *Famous Movie Detectives* (Metuchen, N.J.: Scare-

crow, 1979), p. 279; Elizabeth Dalton, "Meet Torchy Blane," *Film Fan Monthly* 133–34 (July–Aug. 1972): 41.

16. Hobe., "Torchy Runs for Mayor," *Variety*, 12 Oct. 1938, p. 15.

Chapter 21

1. Chip Rowe, "Hacks on Film," *Washington Journalism Review*, Nov. 1992, p. 27.

2. Ezra Goodman, "Fourth Estate Gets Better Role in Film," *Editor and Publisher*, May 10, 1947, p. 26.

3. "SPJ, SDX to Watch Journalist Portrayals," *Editor and Publisher*, Sept. 13, 1986, p. 49. The film cycle included *Absence of Malice*, *Under Fire*, *The Right Stuff*, and *The Mean Season*. For a roundup review of these films, see Ron Rosenbaum, "The Reel Scoop," *Mademoiselle*, June 1985, pp. 66–68.

4. Rowe, "Hacks," pp. 27–28; Christopher Hanson, "Where Have All the Heroes Gone?" *Columbia Journalism Review*, Mar.–Apr.1996, pp. 45–47.

5. Jay Black, "Ethics of the Fictional Journalist: How Novelists Portray Decision-making in the News Business," paper presented to Mass Communication and Society Division, Association for Education in Journalism and Mass Communication National Convention, Atlanta, Ga., Aug. 1994, p. 19.

6. Gerald Stone and John Less, "Portrayal of Journalists on Prime Time Television," *Journalism Quarterly* (Winter 1990): 707.

7. Gene Goodwin and Ron F. Smith, *Groping for Ethics in Journalism*, 3d ed. (Ames: Iowa State University Press, 1994), p. 3.

8. Walker Lundy, "Why Do Readers Mistrust the Press?" *Bulletin of the American Society of Newspaper Editors* (Mar. 1982): 5.

9. Black, "Ethics," p. 2.

10. Hanson, "Where?" pp. 45, 47. Among the films that provoked Hanson were *Bob Roberts* (1992), *Hero* (1992), *Quiz Show* (1994), *Natural Born Killers* (1994), and *To Die For* (1995).

11. Judith Mayne, *Cinema and Spectatorship* (London: Routledge, 1993), p. 25.

12. See Jane Staiger, *Interpreting Films* (Princeton, N.J.: Princeton University Press, 1992), pp. 9, 81, 93, 158.

13. Hanson, "Where?" p. 45. For other paeans to reporters in thirties films, see Nick Roddick, *A New Deal in Entertainment* (London: British Film Institute, 1983), p. 91, and Brooks Robards, "Newshounds and Sob Sisters: The Journalist Goes to Hollywood," in *Beyond the Stars: Stock Characters in American Popular Film*, vol. 1, eds. Paul Loukides and Linda K. Fuller (Bowling Green, Ohio: Popular Press, 1990), p. 137.

14. Quoted in Goodwin and Smith, *Groping*, p. 4.

15. Glenn Garelik, "Stop the Presses! Movies Blast Media, Viewers Cheer," *New York Times*, 31 Jan. 1993, sec. H, pp. 11, 18.

16. Quoted in Goodman, "Fourth Estate," p. 26.

17. Marion Tuttle Marzolf, *Civilizing Voices: American Press Criticism, 1880–1950* (New York: Longman, 1991), p. 76.

18. Edwin Emery and Michael Emery, *The Press and America: An Interpretive History of the Mass Media*, 5th ed. (Englewood Cliffs, N.J., 1984), p. 384. See also Simon Michael Bessie, *Jazz Journalism: The Story of the Tabloid Newspaper* (New York: Dutton, 1938).

19. Silas Bent, *Ballyhoo* (New York: Boni & Liveright, 1927), p. 41.

20. Ibid., p. 196.

21. Marzolf, *Civilizing*, p. 86.

22. "Has the Press Hampered the Search for the Lindbergh Baby?" *Literary Digest* 114 (Apr. 30, 1932): 34–35.

23. Quoted in Marzolf, *Civilizing*, p. 145.

24. Goodwin and Smith, *Groping*, p. 277.

25. Philip Patterson and Lee Wilkins, eds., *Media Ethics: Issues and Cases*, 2nd ed. (Madison, Wis.: Brown & Benchmark, 1994), pp. 9–11; Clifford G. Christians, Mark Fackler, and Kim B. Rotzoll, *Media Ethics: Case & Moral Reasoning*, 4th ed. (New York: Longman, 1995), pp. 14–15.

26. Christians, Fackler, and Rotzoll, *Media Ethics*, p. 14.

27. Patterson and Wilkins, *Media Ethics*, p. 12.

28. Quoted in Goodwin and Smith, *Groping*, pp. 209–10.

29. Ibid., p. 205. Undercover reporting goes back to at least the 1890s, when *New York World* reporter Nellie Bly pretended to be insane to investigate how patients were treated in the Blackwell's Island Insane Asylum.

30. Ibid.

31. Quoted in Christians, Fackler, and Rotzoll, *Media Ethics*, p. 32.

32. Quoted in Marzolf, *Civilizing*, p. 143.

33. Black, "Ethics," n.p.

34. Quoted in Christians, Fackler, and Rotzoll, *Media Ethics*, p. 38.

35. *New York Times*, 11 May 1939, p. 17.

36. Vincent Sheean, *Not Peace But a Sword* (New York: Doubleday, Doran, 1939), p. 40.

37. Tino Balio, "Surviving the Depression," in *Grand Design: Hollywood as a Modern Business Enterprise, 1930–1939*, ed. Balio (Berkeley, Calif.: University of California Press, 1993), pp. 21–22, 25. Vol. 5 of *History of American Cinema*.

38. Andrew Bergman, *We're in the Money: Depression America and Its Films* (New York: Harper & Row, 1971), p. 93; Thomas Schatz, *The Genius of the System* (New York: Pantheon, 1988), p. 141.

39. Theodor W. Adorno, "Culture Industry Reconsidered," *New German Critique* 6 (Fall 1975): 12.
40. Ibid., 17.

Chapter 22

1. Quoted in Richard A. Maynard, "Editor's Introduction: Birth of a Stereotype," in *The Black Man on Film: Racial Stereotyping*, ed. Maynard (Rochelle Park, N.J.: Hayden, 1975), p. vi.
2. L.D. Reddick, "Educational Programs for the Improvement of Race Relations: Motion Pictures," in ibid., p. 16.
3. Gary Null, *Black Hollywood: The Negro in Motion Pictures* (Secaucus, N.J.: Citadel Press, 1975), p. 43.
4. Quoted in ibid., p. 76.
5. Reddick, "Educational," p. 5.
6. Michael R. Pitts, *Famous Movie Detectives* (Metuchen, N.J.: Scarecrow Press, 1979), p. 281. David Zinman similarly commented, "A generation before Women's Lib was born, Torchy Blane was going after fast-breaking, cityside stories, asking no quarter and giving none." "Torchy Blane and Glenda Farrell," *Filmograph* 3 (1973): 38.
7. Thomas Cripps, *Slow Fade to Black: The Negro in American Film, 1900–1942* (New York: Oxford University Press, 1977), pp. 279, 282. See also his *Black Film as Genre* (Bloomington: Indiana University Press, 1978).
8. Ralph Ellison, *Invisible Man* (New York: Vintage Books, 1947), p. 3.

Chapter 23

1. "All the Same," *Hollywood Reporter*, 27 May 1939, p. 4.
2. Press book for *Torchy Plays with Dynamite* (1939), Motion Picture, Broadcasting and Recorded Sound Division, Library of Congress, Washington, D.C.
3. Farrell had been replaced by Lola Lane and MacLane by Paul Kelly in 1938's *Torchy Blane in Panama*. See chapter 19, "Accept No Substitutes."
4. Quoted in James Robert Parish and Don E. Stanke, *The Forties Girls* (Westport, Conn.: Arlington House, 1980), p. 373.
5. Ibid., p. 374.
6. Michael R. Pitts, *Famous Movie Detectives* (Metuchen, N.J.: Scarecrow Press, 1979), p. 280; "Allen Jenkins, Character Actor in More Than

175 Films, Dead," *New York Times*, 22 July 1974, p. 32; and Arthur I. McClure, Alfred E. Twomey, and Ken D. Jones, *More Character People* (Secaucus, N.J.: Citadel Press, 1984), n.p.

7. "Failing Material Stymies Whole Cast," *Hollywood Reporter*,10 Aug. 1939, p. 3.

8. Quoted in Parish and Stanke, *Forties Girls*, p. 374.

9. Elizabeth Dalton, "Meet Torchy Blane, *Film Fan Monthly* 133–34 (July–Aug. 1972): 41. In 1979 Michael R. Pitts similiarly wrote, "A blonde Jane Wyman tried to elicit an exact imitation of Glenda Farrell in *Torchy Blane Plays with Dynamite*." *Famous*, p. 279.

10. Dalton, "Meet," 42.

11. Wear., "Torchy Plays with Dynamite," *Variety*, Sept. 27, 1939, p. 12.

12. "Jenkins Dead," p. 32.

13. Dana Polan, "Brief Encounters: Mass Culture and the Evacuation of Sense," in *Studies in Entertainment*, ed. Tania Modleski (Bloomington: Indiana University Press, 1986), p. 175.

14. Jane Feur, *The Hollywood Musical* (Bloomington: Indiana University Press, 1982), p. 88.

Chapter 24

1. Theodor Adorno and Max Horkheimer, "Enlightenment as Mass Deception," in *Mass Communication and Society*, ed. James Curran (London: Edward Arnold, nd), p. 354.

2. Dana Polan, *Power and Paranoia: History, Narrative, and the American Cinema, 1940–1950* (New York: Columbia University Press, 1986), p. 19.

3. V.N. Volosinov, *Marxism and the Philosophy of Language*, trans. Ladislav Matejka and I.R. Titunik (New York: Seminar Press, 1973), p. 23.

4. Ibid.

5. New York Times News Service, "FTC Clears Media Merger," *Middletown* (NY) *Times Herald Record*, 18 July 1996, p. 53.

6. Adorno and Horkheimer, "Enlightenment," p. 383.

Chapter 25

1. Pauline Kael, "Absence of Malice" *New Yorker*, Jan. 4, 1982, p. 85.

2. Ibid.

3. Lucinda Franks, "Hollywood Update," *Columbia Journalism Re-*

view (Nov.–Dec. 1981): 63. See also Robert Hatch, "Absence of Malice," *Nation*, Jan. 29, 1982, p. 28.

4. Jonathan Friendly, "A Movie on the Press Stirs a Debate," *New York Times*, 15 Nov. 1981, sec. 2, p. 1.

5. Desmond Ryan, "The Hollywood Reporter," *Washington Journalism Review* (Sept. 1985): 46.

6. Ron Rosenbaum, "The Reel Scoop," *Mademoiselle*, June 1985, p. 68.

7. Christopher Hanson, "Where Have All the Heroes Gone?" *Columbia Journalism Review* (Mar.–Apr.1996): 47.

8. Kael, "Absence," p. 84.

9. Friendly, "Movie," p. 26.

10. See, in addition to the reviews already mentioned, Richard Schickel, "Lethal Leaks," *Time*, Nov. 23, 1981, p. 98.

11. Susan Faludi, *Backlash: The Undeclared War against American Women* (New York: Doubleday, 1991), p. xviii.

12. Ibid., p. 67.

13. Ibid., pp. xi, 136.

14. Ibid., p. 113.

15. Richard Corliss, "Take Two Tabloids and Call Me," *Time*, Mar. 21, 1994, p. 71.

16. Janet Maslin, "The Paper," *New York Times*, 18 Mar.1995, sec. C, p. 15.

17. Ibid.

18. Hanson, "Heroes," p. 47.

19. Jack Kroll, "Kiss, Bang, Boom," *Newsweek*, July 4, 1994, p. 72.

20. Caryn James, "I Love Trouble," *New York Times*, 29 June 1994, sec. C, p. 15.

21. *The Concise Columbia Encyclopedia*, 2d ed. (New York: Columbia University Press, 1982), p. 825.

22. Quoted in Aljean Harmetz, "When Nuclear Crisis Imitates a Film," *New York Times*, 4 Apr. 1979, sec. 3, p. 18.

23. "Beyond the China Syndrome," *Newsweek*, Apr. 16, 1979, p. 31.

24. Harmetz, "Nuclear Crisis."

25. Vincent Canby, "Nuclear Plant Is Villain in 'China Syndrome,'" *New York Times*, 16 Mar. 1979, sec. C, p. 16; David Ansen, "Nuclear Politics," *Newsweek*, Mar. 19, 1979, p. 103.

26. Ansen, "Nuclear Politics."

27. Faludi, *Backlash*, pp. 125–26. Fonda starred in *Julia* and *9 to 5*.

28. Quoted in Aljean Harmetz, "Fallout from 'China Syndrome' Has Already Begun," *New York Times*, 11 Mar. 1979, sec. 2, p. 19.

29. Quoted in ibid.

30. Ansen, "Nuclear Politics."

31. Lee Wilkins, "Appendix A: Thinking about Ethics with Film," in *Media Ethics: Issues and Cases*, eds. Philip Patterson and Wilkins (Madison, Wis.: Brown & Benchmark, 1991), p. 266.

32. Canby, "Nuclear Plant"; George F. Will, "A Film about Greed," *Newsweek*, Apr. 2, 1979, p. 96.

33. Jack Kroll, "Fun with Bob and Jane," *Newsweek*, Dec. 17, 1979, p. 112; Vincent Canby, "The Electric Horseman," *New York Times*, 21 Dec. 1979, sec. C, p. 10.

34. Poll., "Electric Horseman," *Variety*, Dec. 5, 1979, p. 22; Timothy W. Johnson, "The Electric Horseman," *Magill Survey of Cinema*, series II, vol. 2 (Englewood Cliffs, N.J.: Salem Press, 1981), p. 704.

35. Canby, "Electric."

36. Robert Warshow, *The Immediate Experience* (New York: Atheneum, 1975), p. 137.

37. Kroll, "Fun."

38. Vincent Canby, "Eyewitness," *New York Times*, 27 Feb. 1981, sec. C, p. 12.

39. Har., "Eyewitness," *Variety*, Feb. 18, 1981, p. 18.

40. Canby, "Eyewitness"; Har., "Eyewitness." See also David Ansen, "Classy Comedy of Menace," *Newsweek*, Mar. 2, 1981, p. 81.

41. Faludi, *Backlash*, p. 67. Significantly, 1980 was the year the U.S. Census stopped defining the head of the household as the husband.

42. Ibid., pp. 65–66.

43. Quoted in ibid., p. 67.

44. Ibid., p. 136.

45. Janet Maslin, "She Trusts in TV's Reedeming Power," *New York Times*, 27 Sept. 1995, sec. C, p. 1.

46. Bernard Weinraub, "'Birdcage' Shows Growth in Older Audience's Power," *New York Times*, 12 Mar. 1996, sec. C, p. 1.

47. David Ansen, "A Lesson in Star Chemistry," *Newsweek*, Mar. 4, 1996, pp. 70–71; Richard Corliss, "Hair Today, Star Tomorrow," *Time*, Mar. 4, 1996, p. 63; Janet Maslin, "At the Top of TV News, A Star Is Made, Not Born," *New York Times*, 1 Mar. 1996, sec. C, p. 1ff. For Savitch's career, see Gwenda Blair, *Almost Golden: Jessica Savitch and the Selling of Television News* (New York: Avon, 1988).

48. Maslin, "At the Top," p. 1.

49. Ansen, "Lesson," p. 71; Maslin, "At the Top ," p. 1.

50. Brooks Robards, "Newshounds and Sob Sisters: The Journalist Goes to Hollywood," *Beyond the Stars: Stock Characters in American Popular Film*, vol. 1, eds. Paul Loukides and Linda K. Fuller (Bowling Green, Ohio: Popular Press, 1990), p. 131.

Filmography of Torchy Blane Series

Smart Blonde

Warner Bros., Jan. 1937, 56 mins.
Directed by Frank McDonald
Story by Frederick Nebel
Screenplay by Kenneth Gamet and Don Ryan

Newspaper reporter Torchy Blane solves the killing of a night-club owner that baffles her detective boyfriend.

Torchy Blane	Glenda Farrell
Steve McBride	Barton MacLane
Dolly Ireland	Winifred Shaw
Fitz Mularkay	Addison Richards
Louie Friel	David Carlyle
Tom Carney	Craig Reynolds
Marcia Friel	Charlotte Wynters
Dixie	Jane Wyman
Tiny Torgensen	Joseph Crehan
Gahagan	Tom Kennedy
Blyfuss	John Sheehan
Chuck Cannon	Max Wagner
City Editor	Joe Cunningham
Desk Sergeant	George Guhl

Fly-Away Baby

Warner Bros., June 1937, 60 mins.
Directed by Frank McDonald

Story by Dorothy Kilgallen
Screenplay by Kenneth Gamet and Don Ryan

Torchy wins an around-the-world air race while solving a series of killings.

Torchy Blane	Glenda Farrell
Steve McBride	Barton MacLane
Lucien "Sonny" Croy	Gordon Olivet
Hughie Sprague	Hugh O'Connell
Ila Sayre	Marcia Ralston
Gahagan	Tom Kennedy
Guy Allister	Joseph King
Maxie	Raymond Hatton
Col. Higgam	Harry Davenport
Desk Sergeant	George Guhl

Torchy Blane, the Adventurous Blonde

Warner Bros., Nov. 1937, 60 mins.
Directed by Frank McDonald
Screenplay by Robertson White and David Diamond

A murder hoax turns into the real thing—and delays Torchy's wedding day.

Torchy Blane	Glenda Farrell
Steve McBride	Barton MacLane
Grace Brown	Anne Nagel
Gahagan	Tom Kennedy
Pete	George E. Stone
Theresa Gray	Natalie Moorhead
Matt	William Hopper
Hugo Brand	Anderson Lawlor
Dud	Charles Foy
Mugsy	Bobby Watson
Mortimer Gray	Charles Wilson
Jenny Hammond	Virginia Brissac
Harvey Hammond	Leland Hodgson
Maxie	Raymond Hatton
Capt. McTavish	Frank Shannon
Desk Sergeant	George Guhl

Blondes at Work

Warner Bros., Feb. 1938, 63 mins.
Directed by Frank McDonald
Screenplay by Albert De Mond

Torchy is tossed in jail for contempt of court and other shenanigans.

Torchy Blane	Glenda Farrell
Steve McBride	Barton MacLane
Gahagan	Tom Kennedy
Louisa Revelle	Rosella Towne
Maitland Greer	Donald Briggs
Regan	John Ridgely
Blanche Revelle	Betty Compson
Parker	Thomas E. Jackson
Capt. McTavish	Frank Shannon
District Attorney	Theodor Von Eltz
Judge Wilson	Charles Richman
Desk Sergeant	George Guhl
Maxie	Joe Cunningham

Torchy Blane in Panama

Warner Bros., May 1938, 58 mins.
Directed by William Clemens
Story by Anthony Coldeway
Screenplay by George Bricker

Torchy pursues a murdering bank robber to Panama and almost gets knocked off herself.

Torchy Blane	Lola Lane
Steve McBride	Paul Kelly
Gahagan	Tom Kennedy
Crafton	Anthony Averill
Bill Canby	Larry Williams
Desk Sergeant	George Guhl
Betty Compson	Kitty
Capt. McTavish	Frank Shannon
Maxie	Joe Cunningham

Sparks	John Ridgely
Ship's Captain	John Harron

Torchy Gets Her Man

Warner Bros., Nov. 1938, 62 mins.
Directed by William Beaudine
Screenplay by Albert De Mond

Torchy, her boyfriend, and a police dog named Blitzen expose a gang of counterfeiters.

Torchy Blane	Glenda Farrell
Steve McBride	Barton MacLane
Gahagan	Tom Kennedy
Gilbert	Willard Robertson
Capt. McTavish	Frank Shannon
Desk Sergeant	George Guhl
Bugs	John Ridgely
Gloomy	Tommy Jackson
Professor	Frank Reicher
Brennan	Herbert Rawlinson
Wilkins	John Harron

Torchy Blane in Chinatown

Warner Bros., Feb. 1939, 59 mins.
Directed by William Beaudine
Story by Murray Leinster and Will Jenkins
Screenplay by George Bricker

Torchy matches wits with blackmailers and an uncooperative police department.

Torchy Blane	Glenda Farrell
Steve McBride	Barton MacLane
Gahagan	Tom Kennedy
Sen. Baldwin	Henry O'Neill
Condon	Patric Knowles
Mansfield	James Stephenson

Janet Baldwin	Janet Shaw
Capt. McTavish	Frank Shannon
Desk Sergeant	George Guhl

Torchy Runs for Mayor

Warner Bros., May 1939, 58 mins.
Directed by Ray McCarey
From an Idea by Irving Rubine
Screenplay by Earl Snell

Torchy sets out to expose municipal corruption and winds up being elected mayor.

Torchy Blane	Glenda Farrell
Steve McBride	Barton MacLane
Gahagan	Tom Kennedy
Dr. Dolan	John Miljan
Capt. McTavish	Frank Shannon
Maxie	Joe Cunningham
Desk Sergeant	George Guhl
O'Brien	Joe Downing
Dibble	John Harron
Hogarth Ward	Irving Bacon
Chuck Ball	John Butler

Torchy Plays with Dynamite

Warner Bros., Aug. 1939, 59 mins.
Directed by Noel Smith
Story by Scott Littleton
Screenplay by Earl Snell

Torchy goes undercover in a prison as part of an elaborate scheme to track down bank robber Denver Eddie.

Torchy Blane	Jane Wyman
Steve McBride	Allen Jenkins
Gahagan	Tom Kennedy
"Jackie" McGuire	Sheila Bromley
Maxie	Joe Cunningham
Denver Eddie	Eddie Marr

Jim Simmons	Edgar Dearing
Capt. McTavish	Frank Shannon
Bugsie	Bruce MacFarlane

Supplemental Filmography

Big News

Pathe, Oct. 1929, 75 mins.
Directed by Gregory La Cava
George S. Brooks's story adapted by Jack Jungmeyer
Dialogue by Frank Reicher

A drunken reporter finds a big story—and sobriety—with the help of his wife, a sob sister on a rival newspaper.

Steve Banks	Robert Armstrong
Marge Banks	Carol Lombard
Reno	Sam Hardy
Patrolman Ryan	Tom Kennedy
Hansel	Louis Payne
O'Neill	Wade Boetler
Editor	Charles Sellon

Dance, Fools, Dance

MGM, Mar. 1931, 75 mins.
Directed by Harry Beaumont
Story and dialogue by Aurania Rouverol
Continuity by Richard Schayer

A socialite becomes a crime reporter after her family's fortune is wiped out in the Crash.

Bonnie	Joan Crawford
Bob	Lester Vail
Bert Scranton	Cliff Edwards
Rodney	William Bakewell

Stanley Jordan	William Holden
Jake Luva	Clark Gable
Wally	Earl Foxe
Parker	Purnell H. Pratt
Selby	Hale Hamilton
Della	Natalie Moorhead
Sylvia	Joan Marsh
Whitey	Russell Hopton

The Mystery of the Wax Museum

Warner Bros., Feb. 1933, 75 mins.
Directed by Michael Curtiz
Story by Charles S. Belden
Screenplay by Don Mullally and Carl Erickson

Brash, fast-talking reporter Florence Dempsey, the prototype for Glenda Farrell's role as Torchy Blane, exposes a mad sculptor who embalms his murder victims in wax.

Ivan Igor	Lionell Atwill
Charlotte Duncan	Fay Wray
Florence Dempsey	Glenda Farrell
Jim	Frank McHugh
Ralph Burton	Allen Vincent
Harold Winton	Gavin Gordon
Joe Worth	Edwin Maxwell
Dr. Rasmussen	Holmes Herbert
Detective	Thomas E. Jackson
Captain of Police	DeWitt Jennings
Hugo	Matthew Betz

Mr. Deeds Goes to Town

Columbia, Apr. 1936, 115 mins.
Directed by Frank Capra
Story by Clarence Buddington Kelland
Screenplay by Robert Riskin

A hard-bitten reporter for a New York tabloid dubs a country bumpkin who inherits a fortune the "Cinderella Man" in a series of cynical front-page stories, but then falls in love with him.

Longfellow Deeds	Gary Cooper
Babe Bennett	Jean Arthur
MacWade	George Bancroft
Cornelius Cobb	Lionel Stander
John Cedar	Douglass Dumbrille
Walter	Raymond Walburn
Judge Walker	H.B. Warner
Mme. Pomponi	Margaret Matzenauer
Bodyguard	Warren Hymer
Theresa	Muriel Evans
Mabel Dawson	Ruth Donnelly
Mal	Spencer Charters

His Girl Friday

Columbia, Jan. 1940, 92 mins.
Directed by Howard Hawks
Screenplay by Charles Lederer

In this screwball-comedy remake of Ben Hecht and Charles MacArthur's The Front Page, *star reporter Hildy Johnson is not only a woman, but also the ex-wife of demonic editor Walter Burns.*

Walter Burns	Cary Grant
Hildy Johnson	Rosalind Russell
Bruce Baldwin	Ralph Bellamy
Earl Williams	John Qualen
Molly Malloy	Helen Mack
Sheriff Hartwell	Gene Lockhart
Mayor	Clarence Kolb
Joe Pettibone	Billy Gilbert
McCue	Roscoe Karns
Sanders	Regis Toomey
Bensinger	Ernest Truex

Woman of the Year

MGM, Jan. 1942, 112 mins.
Directed by George Stevens
Screenplay by Ring Lardner, Jr., and Michael Kanin

An earthy sportswriter and a sophisticated columnist feud, fall in love, feud, get married, feud, and finally reconcile in this first of nine films that Spencer Tracy and Katharine Hepburn would make together.

Sam Craig	Spencer Tracy
Tess Harding	Katharine Hepburn
Ellen Whitcomb	Fay Bainter
Clayton	Reginald Owen
William J. Harding	Minor Watson
"Pinkie" Peters	William Bendix
Flo Peters	Gladys Blake
Gerald Howe	Dan Tobin
Phil Whittaker	Roscoe Karns
Elllis	William Tannen

The China Syndrome

Columbia, Mar. 1979, 122 mins.
Directed by James Bridges
Screenplay by Mike Grey, T.S. Cook, and James Bridges

A televison reporter investigates mysterious rumblings at a nuclear power plant over the objections of station management.

Kimberly Wells	Jane Fonda
Jack Godell	Jack Lemmon
Richard Adams	Michael Douglas
Herman De Young	Scott Brady
Dan Jacovich	Peter Donat
Ted Spindler	Wilford Brimley

The Electric Horseman

Columbia, Dec. 1979, 120 mins.
Directed by Sidney Pollack
Screenplay by Robert Garland

A former rodeo cowboy tames a nosy television reporter while setting a champion racehorse free.

Sonny Steele	Robert Redford
Hallie Martin	Jane Fonda

Wendell	Willie Nelson
Hunt Sears	John Saxon
Charlotta	Valerie Perrine
Gus Atwater	Nicolas Coster
Leroy	Timothy Scott
Danny Miles	Allan Arbus

Absence of Malice

Columbia, Nov. 1981, 116 mins.
Directed by Sidney Pollack
Screenplay by Kurt Leudtke

An eager-beaver reporter is controlled and manipulated by her sources.

Megan Carter	Sally Field
Michael Gallagher	Paul Newman
Teresa Perrone	Melinda Dillon
McAdam	Josef Sommer
Rosen	Bob Balaban
Waddell	Barry Primus
Wells	Wilford Brimley
Malderone	Luther Adler
Quinn	Don Hood

Eyewitness

Twentieth Century-Fox, Feb. 1981, 102 mins.
Directed by Peter Yates
Screenplay by Steve Tesich

A janitor infatuated with a rich and beautiful reporter on the local television news comes to her aid during a murder investigation.

Daryll Deever	William Hurt
Tony Sokolow	Sigourney Weaver
Joseph	Christopher Plummer
Aldo	James Woods
Mrs. Sokolow	Irene Worth
Mr. Deever	Kenneth McMillan
Linda	Pamela Reed

Lt. Jacobs	Steven Hill
Lt. Black	Morgan Freeman

Hero

Columbia, Oct. 1992, 112 mins.
Directed by Stephen Frears
Screenplay by David Webb Peoples

A scoop-crazy television reporter and her ratings-obsessed bosses fall for the lies of a homeless Vietnam veteran claiming to be the rescuer of some 50 plane crash victims.

Bernie LaPlante	Dustin Hoffman
Gale Gayley	Geena Davis
John Bubber	Andy Garcia
Evelyn	Joan Cusak
Donna O'Day	Susie Cusak

The Paper

Universal, Mar. 1994, 112 mins.
Directed by Ron Howard
Screenplay by David Koepp and Stephen Koepp

Twenty-four hours in the hectic life of a big-city tabloid during which its staff faces a host of professional and personal crises.

Henry Hackett	Michael Keaton
Bernie White	Robert Duvall
Alicia Clark	Glenn Close
Martha Hackett	Marisa Tomei
McDougal	Randy Quaid
Graham Keighley	Jason Robards
Marion Sandusky	Jason Alexander
Paul Bladden	Spalding Gray
Susan	Catherine O'Hara
Janet	Lynne Thigpen

I Love Trouble

Touchstone, June 1994, 120 mins.
Directed by Charles Shyer

Screenplay by Nancy Meyers and Charles Shyer

Rival reporters find love when they team up to solve a series of murders.

Peter Brackett	Nick Nolte
Sabrina Peterson	Julia Roberts
Jeannie	Olympia Dukakis
Matt Greenfield	Robert Loggia
Sen. Gayle Robbins	Marsha Mason
Sam Smotherman	Saul Rubinek

To Die For

Columbia, Sept. 1995, 103 mins.
Directed by Gus Van Sant
Screenplay by Buck Henry,
based on the book by Joyce Maynard

A woman's hunger for fame as a television correspondent knows no bounds, not even murder, in this black comedy.

Suzanne Stone	Nicole Kidman
Larry Marretto	Matt Dillon
Jimmy Emmett	Joaquin Phoenix
Russell Hines	Casey Affleck
Janice Marretto	Illeana Douglas
Lydia Mertz	Alison Folland
Mr. Marretto	Dan Hedaya
Mrs. Marretto	Maria Tucci

Up Close and Personal

Touchstone, Mar. 1996, 124 mins.
Directed by Jon Avent
Screenplay by Joan Didion and John Gregory Dunne

A veteran of television journalism remakes a newcomer in his own golden image.

Warren Justice	Robert Redford
Tally Atwater	Michelle Pfeiffer
Marcia McGrath	Stockard Channing

Bucky Terranova	Joe Mantegna
Joanna Kennelly	Kate Nelligan
Ned Jackson	Glenn Plummer

Selected Bibliography

Books and Book Chapters

Adorno, Theodor W., and Max Horkheimer. "Enlightenment as Mass Deception." In *Mass Communication and Society*, ed. James Curran. London: Edward Arnold, n.d., pp. 349–83.

Allen, Frederick Lewis. *The Big Change: America Transforms Itself, 1900–1950*. New York: Harper & Row, 1952.

Althusser, Louis. *Lenin and Philosophy and Other Essays*. London: NLB, 1971.

Altman, Rick. *The American Film Musical*. Bloomington: Indiana University Press, 1989.

Bakhtin, M.M. *The Dialogic Imagination: Four Essays.* Austin: University of Texas, 1982.

Balio, Tino, ed. *Grand Design: Hollywood as a Modern Business Enterprise, 1930–39*. Berkeley, Calif.: University of California Press, 1993. Vol. 5 of *History of the American Cinema*.

Banner, Lois. *Women in Modern America: A Brief History*. New York: Harcourt Brace Jovanovich, 1974.

Barris, Alex. *Stop the Presses! The Newspaperman in American Films*. South Brunswick, N.J.: A. S. Barnes, 1976.

Becker, Ernest. *The Denial of Death*. New York: Free Press, 1973.

Bent, Silas. *Ballyhoo*. New York: Boni & Liveright, 1927.

Berger, John. *Ways of Seeing*. London: Penguin, 1972.

Bergman, Andrew. *We're in the Money: Depression America and Its Films*. New York: Harper & Row, 1971.

Bessie, Simon Michael. *Jazz Journalism: The Story of the Tabloid Newspaper*. New York: Duttton, 1938.

Blythe, Samuel. *The Making of a Newspaper Man.* Philadelphia: Henry Altemus, 1912.

Brownmiller, Susan. *Femininity.* New York: Linden, 1984.

Cavell, Stanley. *Pursuits of Happiness: The Hollywood Comedy of Remarriage.* Cambridge, Mass.: Harvard University Press, 1981.

Chafe, William H. *The Paradox of Change: American Women in the Twentieth Century.* New York: Oxford University Press, 1991.

Christians, Clifford G., Mark Fackler, and Kim B. Rotzoll. *Media Ethics: Case & Moral Reasoning,* 4th ed. New York: Longman, 1995.

Cornillon, Susan Koppelman, ed. *Images of Women in Fiction.* Bowling Green, Ohio: Popular Press, 1972.

Corson, Richard. *Fashions in Hair.* London: Peter Owen, 1965.

Cripps, Thomas. *Black Film as Genre.* Bloomington: Indiana University Press, 1978.

———. *Slow Fade to Black: The Negro in American Film, 1900–1942.* New York: Oxford University Press, 1977.

Cross, Robin. *The Big Book of B Movies.* New York: St. Martin's, 1981.

D'Emilio, John, and Estelle B. Freedman. *Intimate Matters: A History of Sexuality in America.* New York: Harper & Row, 1988.

Dixon, Wheeler W. *The "B" Directors: A Biographical Directory.* Metuchen, N.J.: Scarecrow, 1985.

Drew, Bernard A., ed. *Hard-Boiled Dames.* New York: St. Martin's, 1986.

Dyer, Richard. *Stars.* London: British Film Institute, 1972.

Everson, William K. *The Detective in Film.* Secaucus, N.J.: Citadel, 1972.

Faludi, Susan. *Backlash: The Undeclared War against American Women.* New York: Doubleday, 1991.

Feur, Jane. *The Hollywood Musical.* Bloomington: Indiana University Press, 1982.

Flynn, Charles, and Todd McCarthy, eds. *Kings of the Bs.* New York: Dutton, 1975.

Fowles, Jib. *Starstruck: Celebrity Performers and the American Public.* Washington, D.C.: Smithsonian Institution, 1992.

Francke, Lizzie. *Script Girls: Women Screenwriters in Hollywood.* London: British Film Institute, 1994.

Frank, Stanley, and Paul Sann. "Paper Dolls." In *More Post Biographies,* ed. John E. Drewery. Athens, Ga.: University of Georgia Press, 1947, pp. 206–17.

Freedman, Rita. *Beauty Bound.* Lexington, Mass.: Lexington Books, 1986.

Gaines, Jane, and Charlotte Herzog, eds. *Fabrications: Costume and the Female Body*. New York: Routledge, 1990.

Geertz, Clifford. *After the Fact: Two Countries, Four Decades, One Anthropologist*. Cambridge, Mass.: Harvard University Press, 1995.

Gehrig, Wes D. *Screwball Comedy: A Genre of Madcap Romance*. New York: Greenwood Press, 1986.

Ghiglione, Loren. *The American Journalist: Paradox of the Press*. Washington, D.C.: Library of Congress, 1990.

Glatzer, Richard, and John Raeburn, eds. *Frank Capra: The Man and His Films*. Ann Arbor, Mich.: University of Michigan Press, 1975.

Gledhill, Christine, ed. *Stardom: Industry of Desire*. London: Routledge, 1991.

Godwin, Frank. *Connie, A Complete Compilation: 1929–1930*. Westport, Conn.: Hyperion, 1977.

Gomery, Douglas. *The Hollywood Studio System*. New York: St. Martin's, 1986.

Good, Howard. *Acquainted with the Night: The Image of Journalists in American Fiction, 1890–1930*. Metuchen, N.J.: Scarecrow, 1986.

Goodwin, Gene, and Ron F. Smith. *Groping for Ethics in Journalism*, 3d ed. Ames: Iowa State University Press, 1994.

Goulart, Ron. *The Dime Detectives*. New York: Mysterious Press, 1988.

Hamilton, Ian. *Writers in Hollywood, 1915–1951*. New York: Carroll & Graf, 1990.

Hardy, Phil, ed. *Raoul Walsh*. Edinburgh: Edinburgh Film Festival, 1974.

Haskell, Molly. *From Reverence to Rape: The Treatment of Women in the Movies*, 2d ed. Chicago: University of Chicago Press, 1987.

Higham, Charles. *Warner Brothers*. New York: Scribner's, 1975.

Hollander, Anne. *Sex and Suits*. New York: Knopf, 1994.

Horn, Maurice. *Women in the Comics*. New York: Chelsea, 1977.

Huber, Richard M. *The American Idea of Success*. New York: McGraw-Hill, 1971.

Huf, Linda. *A Portrait of the Artist as a Young Woman: The Writer as Heroine in American Literature*. New York: Ungar, 1983.

Jarvie, I.C. *Movies and Society*. New York: Basic Books, 1970.

Kael, Pauline. *The Citizen Kane Book*. Boston: Little, Brown, 1971.

Kazon, Alfred. *Starting Out in the Thirties*. Boston: Little, Brown, 1965.

Kendall, Elizabeth. *The Runaway Bride: Hollywood Romantic Comedy of the 1930s*. New York: Alfred A. Knopf, 1990.

Klein, Kathleen Gregory. *The Woman Detective: Gender & Genre*. Urbana: University of Illinois Press, 1988.

Kobler, John. *Capone*. New York: Collier, 1971.

Lasch, Christopher. *The New Radicalism in America: The Intellectual as a Social Type*. New York: Knopf, 1965.

Laver, James. *Costume*. London: Cassell, 1963.

Lears, T.J. Jackson. *No Place of Grace: Antimodernism and the Transformation of American Culture, 1880–1920*. New York: Pantheon, 1981.

Lewis, Jon. *The Road to Romance and Ruin: Teen Films and Youth Culture*. New York: Routledge, 1992.

Loukides, Paul, and Linda K. Fuller, eds. *Beyond the Stars: Stock Characters in American Popular Film*. Vol. 1. Bowling Green, Ohio: Popular Press, 1990.

Lurie, Alison. *The Language of Clothes*. New York: Random House, 1981.

McBride, Joseph, ed. *Focus on Howard Hawks*. Englewood Cliffs, N.J.: Prentice-Hall, 1972.

McBride, Mary Margaret. *A Long Way from Missouri*. New York: G. P. Putnam's Sons, 1959.

McClure, Arthur I., Alfred E. Twomey, and Ken D. Jones. *More Character People*. Secaucus, N.J.: Citadel Press, 1984.

Maland, Charles. *Frank Capra*. Boston: Twayne, 1980.

Martin, Jeffrey Brown. *Ben Hecht, Hollywood Screenwriter*. Ann Arbor, Mich.: UMI Research Press, 1985.

Marzolf, Marion Tuttle. *Civilizing Voices: American Press Criticism, 1880–1950*. New York: Longman, 1991.

———. *Up from the Footnote: A History of Women Journalists*. New York: Hastings, 1977.

Maynard, Richard A., ed. *The Black Man on Film: Racial Stereotyping*. Rochelle Park, N.J.: Hayden, 1975.

Mayne, Judith. *Cinema and Spectatorship*. London: Routledge, 1993.

Mellen, Joan. *Big Bad Wolves: Masculinity in the American Film*. New York: Pantheon, 1977.

Mencken, H.L. *Newspaper Days*. New York: Knopf, 1941.

Miller, Don. *"B" Movies*. New York: Curtis, 1973.

Mills, Kay. *A Place in the News: From the Women's Pages to the Front Page*. New York: Dodd, Mead, 1988.

Modleski, Tania, ed. *Studies in Entertainment*. Bloomington: Indiana University Press, 1986.

Mordeen, Ethan. *The Hollywood Studio*. New York: Knopf, 1988.

Mulvey, Laura. *Visual and Other Pleasures*. Bloomington: Indiana University Press, 1989.

Newton, Judith, and Deborah Rosenfelt, eds. *Feminist Criticism and Social Change*. New York: Methuen, 1985.

Null, Gary. *Black Hollywood: The Negro in Motion Pictures*. Secaucus, N.J.: Citadel Press, 1975.

Parish, James Robert. *Hollywood Character Actors*. New Rochelle, N.Y.: Arlington House, 1978.

Parish, James Robert, and William T. Leonard. *Hollywood Players: The Thirties*. New Rochelle, N.Y.: Arlington House, 1976.

Parish, James Robert, and Don E. Stanke. *The Forties Girls*. Westport, Conn.: Arlington House, 1980.

Patterson, Philip, and Lee Wilkins, eds. *Media Ethics: Issues and Cases*, 2d ed. Madison, Wis.: Brown & Benchmark, 1994.

Pitts, Michael R. *Famous Movie Detectives*. Metuchen, N.J.: Scarecrow Press, 1979.

Pleck, Joseph H., and Jack Sawyer. eds. *Men and Masculinity*. Englewood Cliffs, N.J.: Prentice-Hall, 1974.

Poague, Leland A. *Howard Hawks*. Boston: Twayne, 1982.

Polan, Dana. *Power and Paranoia: History, Narrative, and the American Cinema, 1940–1950*. New York: Columbia University Press, 1986.

Porter, Dennis. *The Pursuit of Crime: Art and Ideology in Detective Fiction*. New Haven: Yale University Press, 1981.

Queen, Ellery, ed. *The Great Women Detectives and Criminals: The Female of the Species*. Garden City, N.Y.: Blue Ribbon, 1946.

Reilly, John M., ed. *Twentieth-Century Crime and Mystery Writers*. New York: St. Martin's, 1980.

Roddick, Nick. *A New Deal in Entertainment*. London: British Film Institute, 1983.

Rosebault, Charles J. *When Dana Was the Sun*. New York: Robert M. McBride, 1931; reprint ed., Westport, Conn.: Greenwood Press, 1970.

Rosen, Marjorie. *Popcorn Venus*. New York: Coward, McCann and Geoghegan, 1973.

Ross, Ishbel. *Ladies of the Press*. New York: Harper & Brothers, 1936.

Rossell, Deac. "The Fourth Estate and the Seventh Art." In *Questioning Media Ethics*, ed. Bernard Rubin. New York: Praeger, 1978, pp. 232–82.

Rubinstein, Ruth P. *Dress Codes: Meanings and Messages in American Culture.* Boulder, Colo.: Westview Press, 1995.

Ruhm, Herbert, ed. *The Hard-Boiled Detective: Stories from Black Mask Magazine, 1920–51.* New York: Vintage, 1977.

Russell, Rosalind, and Chris Chase. *Life Is a Banquet.* New York: Random House, 1977.

Schatz, Thomas. *The Genius of the System.* New York: Pantheon, 1988.

———. *Hollywood Genres: Formulas, Filmmaking, and the Studio System.* New York: Random House, 1981.

Sheean, Vincent. *Not Peace But a Sword.* New York: Doubleday, Doran, 1939.

Shuman, Edwin. *Practical Journalism.* New York: Appleton, 1903.

Sikov, Ed. *Screwball: Hollywood's Madcap Romantic Comedies.* New York: Crown, 1989.

Simpson, Mark. *Male Impersonation: Men Performing Masculinity.* New York: Routledge, 1994.

Skal, David J. *The Monster Show: A Cultural History of Horror.* New York: Norton, 1993.

Sobchack, Vivian. "Genre Film: Myth, Ritual, and Sociodrama." In *Film/Culture*, ed. Sari Thomas. Metuchen, N.J.: Scarecrow Press, 1982, pp. 147–65.

Staiger, Jane. *Interpreting Films.* Princeton, N.J.: Princeton University Press, 1992.

Twitchell, James B. *Preposterous Violence: Fables of Aggression in Modern Culture.* New York: Oxford University Press, 1989.

Underwood, Agness. *Newspaperwoman.* New York: Harper & Brothers, 1949.

Volosinov, V.N. *Marxism and the Philosophy of Language.* Trans. Ladislav Matejka and I.R. Titunik. New York: Seminar, 1973.

Ware, Susan. *Holding Their Own: American Women in the 1930s.* Boston: Twayne, 1982.

Warshow, Robert. *The Immediate Experience.* New York: Atheneum, 1975.

Wexman, Virginia Wright. *Creating the Couple: Love, Marriage, and Hollywood Performance.* Princeton, N.J.: Princeton University Press, 1993.

Willis, Donald C. *The Films of Howard Hawks.* Metuchen, N.J.: Scarecrow Press, 1975.

Wood, Robin. *Howard Hawks.* Rev. ed. London: British Film Institute, 1981.

Articles and Papers

Adorno, Theodor W. "Culture Industry Reconsidered." *New German Critique* 6 (Fall 1975): 12–19.

Black, Jay. "Ethics of the Fictional Journalist: How Novelists Portray Decision-making in the News Business." Paper presented to Mass Communication and Society Division, Association for Education in Journalism and Mass Communication National Convention, Atlanta, Ga., Aug. 1994.

Campbell, Russell. "Warner Brothers in the Thirties: Some Tentative Notes." *Velvet Light Trap* 6 (n.d.): 2–4.

Cowie, Elizabeth. "The Popular Film as Progressive Text—'Coma.' " *m/f* 3–4 (1979–80): 59–81.

Dalton, Elizabeth. "Meet Torchy Blane." *Film Fan Monthly* 133–34 (July–Aug. 1972): 37–42.

———. "Women at Work: Warners in the Thirties." *Velvet Light Trap* 6 (n.d.): 15–20.

Ehrlich, Mathew C. "Thinking Critically about Journalism through Popular Culture." *Journalism Educator* 50 (Winter 1996): 35–41.

Fuller, Sam. "News That's Fit to Film." *American Film* 5 (Oct. 1975): 20–24.

Goodman, Ezra. "Fourth Estate Gets Better Role in Films." *Editor & Publisher* 20 (10 May 1947): 26ff.

Gross, Jane. "Movies and the Press Are an Enduring Romance." *New York Times*, 2 June 1985, sec. 2, p. 1ff.

Hanson, Christopher. "Where Have All the Heroes Gone?" *Columbia Journalism Review*, Mar.–Apr. 1996, pp. 45–47.

Ohmer, Susan. "Female Spectatorship and Women's Magazines: Hollywood, *Good Housekeeping*, and World War II." *Velvet Light Trap* 25 (Spring 1990): 53–68.

Renov, Michael. "Advertising/Photojournalism/Cinema." *Quarterly Review of Film and Video* 11 (1989): 1–21.

Rosenbaum, Ron. "The Reel Scoop," *Mademoiselle*, June 1985, pp. 66–68.

Rossell, Deac. "Hollywood and the Newsroom." *American Film* 5 (Oct. 1975): 14–18.

Rowe, Chip. "Hacks on Film." *Washington Journalism Review* (Nov. 1992): 27–29.

Ryan, Desmond. "The Hollywood Reporter." *Washington Journalism Review* (Sept. 1985): 45–47.

Smythe, Ted Curtis. "The Reporter, 1880–1990: Working Conditions and Their Influence on the News." *Journalism History* 7 (Spring 1980): 1–9.

Zimmerman, Patricia. "Soldiers of Fortune: Lucas, Spielberg, Indiana Jones and *Raiders of the Lost Ark*." *Wide Angle* 6 (1984): 34–39.

Zinman, David. "Torchy Blane and Glenda Farrell." *Filmograph* 3 (1973): 38–43.

Zynda, Thomas H. "The Hollywood Version: Movie Portrayals of the Press." *Journalism History* 6 (Spring 1979): 16–32.

Index

About the Author

Howard Good (B.A., Bard College; M.A., University of Iowa; Ph.D., University of Michigan) is a professor of journalism at the State University of New York at New Paltz. He is the author of four previous books, including *The Journalist as Autobiographer* (Scarecrow, 1993) and *Diamonds in the Dark: America, Baseball, and the Movies* (Scarecrow, 1997). His articles have appeared in *Journalism Monographs, Journalism Quarterly, Journalism Educator, American Journalism, Quill*, the *Chronicle of Higher Education, Education Week*, and the *American School Board Journal.* He has contributed scholarly essays to several collections, including *American Literary Journalists, 1945–1995* (Gale Research); *A Sourcebook on American Literary Journalism: Representative Writers in an Emerging Genre* (Greenwood Press); and volumes 3 and 5 of *Beyond the Stars: Studies in Popular American Film* (Popular Press). He is a member of the Board of Education in the Highland (N.Y.) Central School District. His current project, *The Drunken Journalist: The Biography of a Film Stereotype*, will also be published by Scarecrow Press.